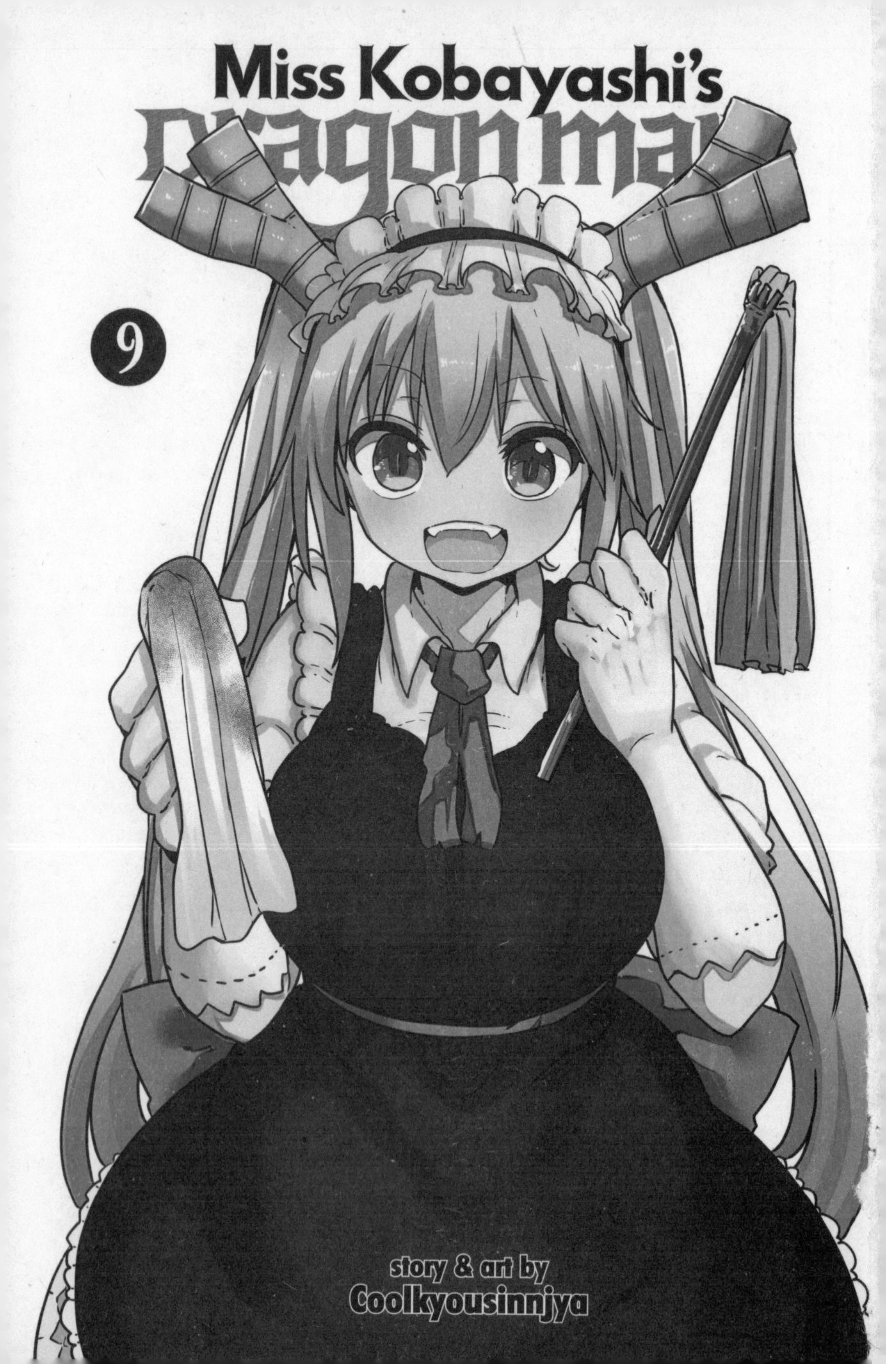
Miss Kobayashi's
9
story & art by
Coolkyousinnjya

Miss Kobayashi's
DRAGON MAID

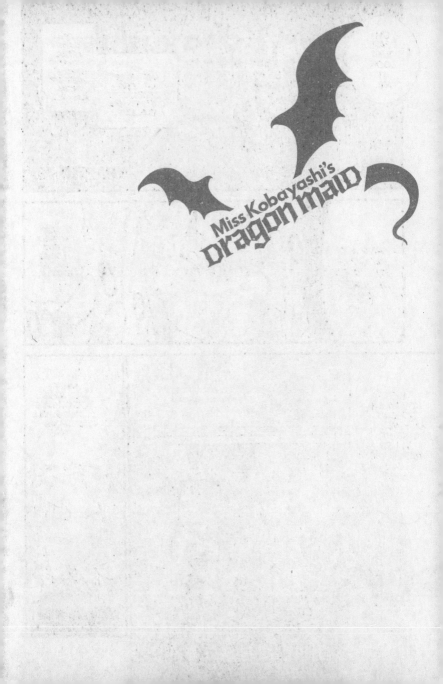

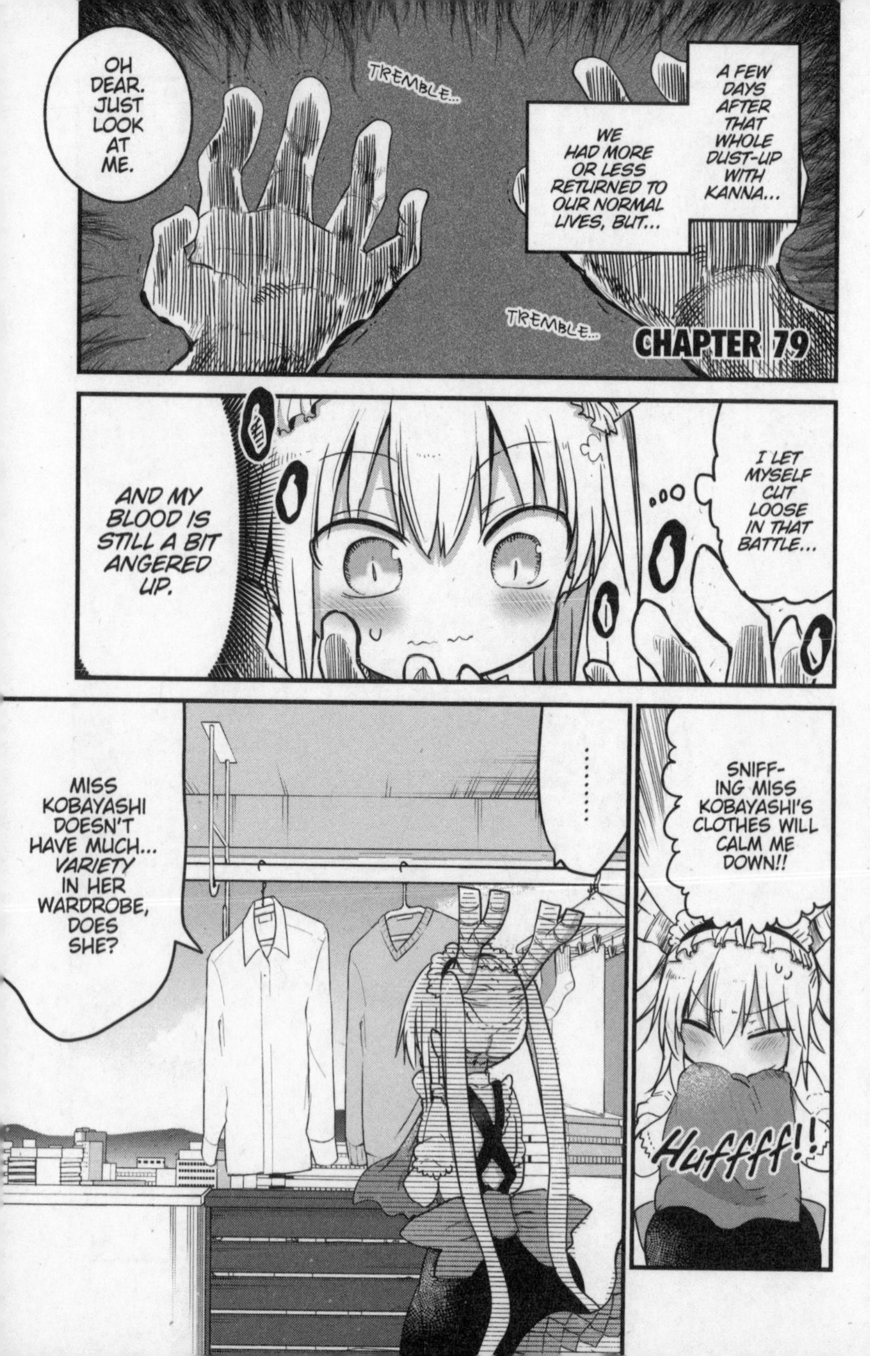
CHAPTER 79
A FEW DAYS AFTER THAT WHOLE DUST-UP WITH KANNA...
WE HAD MORE OR LESS RETURNED TO OUR NORMAL LIVES, BUT...
TREMBLE...
OH DEAR. JUST LOOK AT ME.
TREMBLE...
I LET MYSELF CUT LOOSE IN THAT BATTLE...
AND MY BLOOD IS STILL A BIT ANGERED UP.
SNIFFING MISS KOBAYASHI'S CLOTHES WILL CALM ME DOWN!!
Huffff!!
......
MISS KOBAYASHI DOESN'T HAVE MUCH... VARIETY IN HER WARDROBE, DOES SHE?

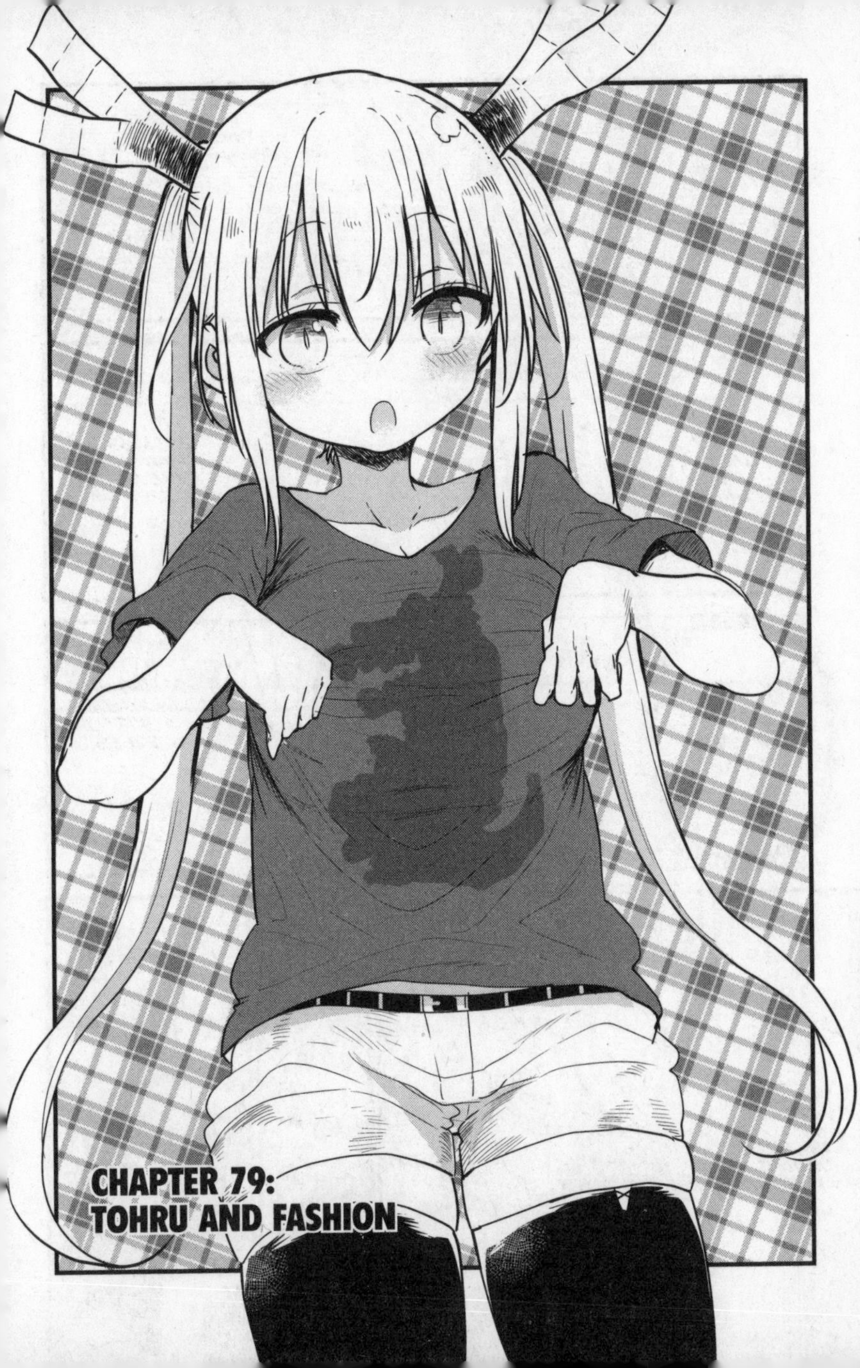
CHAPTER 79:
TOHRU AND FASHION

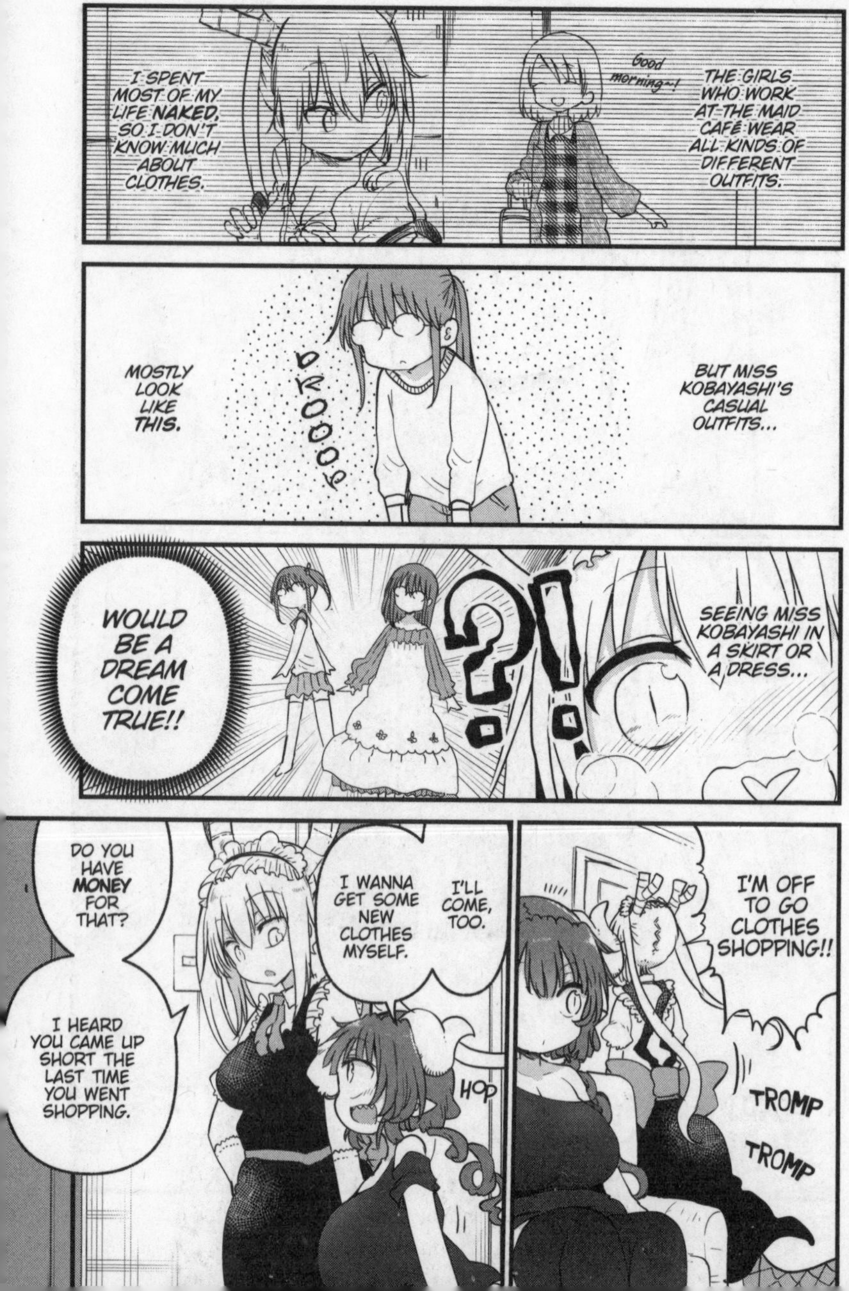
Good morning~!
THE GIRLS WHO WORK AT THE MAID CAFÉ WEAR ALL KINDS OF DIFFERENT OUTFITS.
I SPENT MOST OF MY LIFE NAKED, SO I DON'T KNOW MUCH ABOUT CLOTHES.
BUT MISS KOBAYASHI'S CASUAL OUTFITS...
DROOOOP
MOSTLY LOOK LIKE THIS.
SEEING MISS KOBAYASHI IN A SKIRT OR A DRESS...
?!
WOULD BE A DREAM COME TRUE!!
I'M OFF TO GO CLOTHES SHOPPING!!
TROMP
TROMP
I'LL COME, TOO.
I WANNA GET SOME NEW CLOTHES MYSELF.
HOP
DO YOU HAVE MONEY FOR THAT?
I HEARD YOU CAME UP SHORT THE LAST TIME YOU WENT SHOPPING.

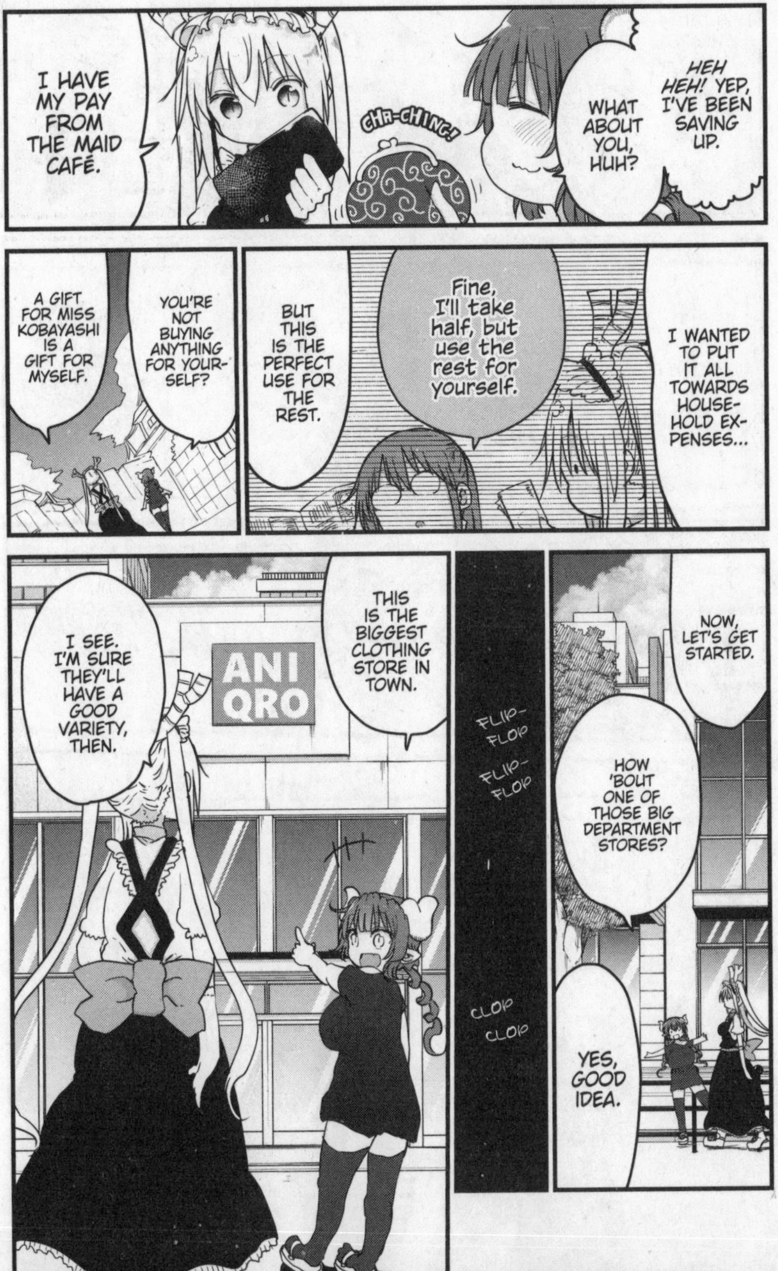
HEH HEH! YEP, I'VE BEEN SAVING UP.
WHAT ABOUT YOU, HUH?
CHA-CHING!
I HAVE MY PAY FROM THE MAID CAFÉ.
I WANTED TO PUT IT ALL TOWARDS HOUSE-HOLD EX-PENSES...
Fine, I'll take half, but use the rest for yourself.
BUT THIS IS THE PERFECT USE FOR THE REST.
YOU'RE NOT BUYING ANYTHING FOR YOUR-SELF?
A GIFT FOR MISS KOBAYASHI IS A GIFT FOR MYSELF.
NOW, LET'S GET STARTED.
HOW 'BOUT ONE OF THOSE BIG DEPARTMENT STORES?
YES, GOOD IDEA.
FLIP-FLOP FLIP-FLOP
CLOP CLOP
THIS IS THE BIGGEST CLOTHING STORE IN TOWN.
ANI QRO
I SEE. I'M SURE THEY'LL HAVE A GOOD VARIETY, THEN.

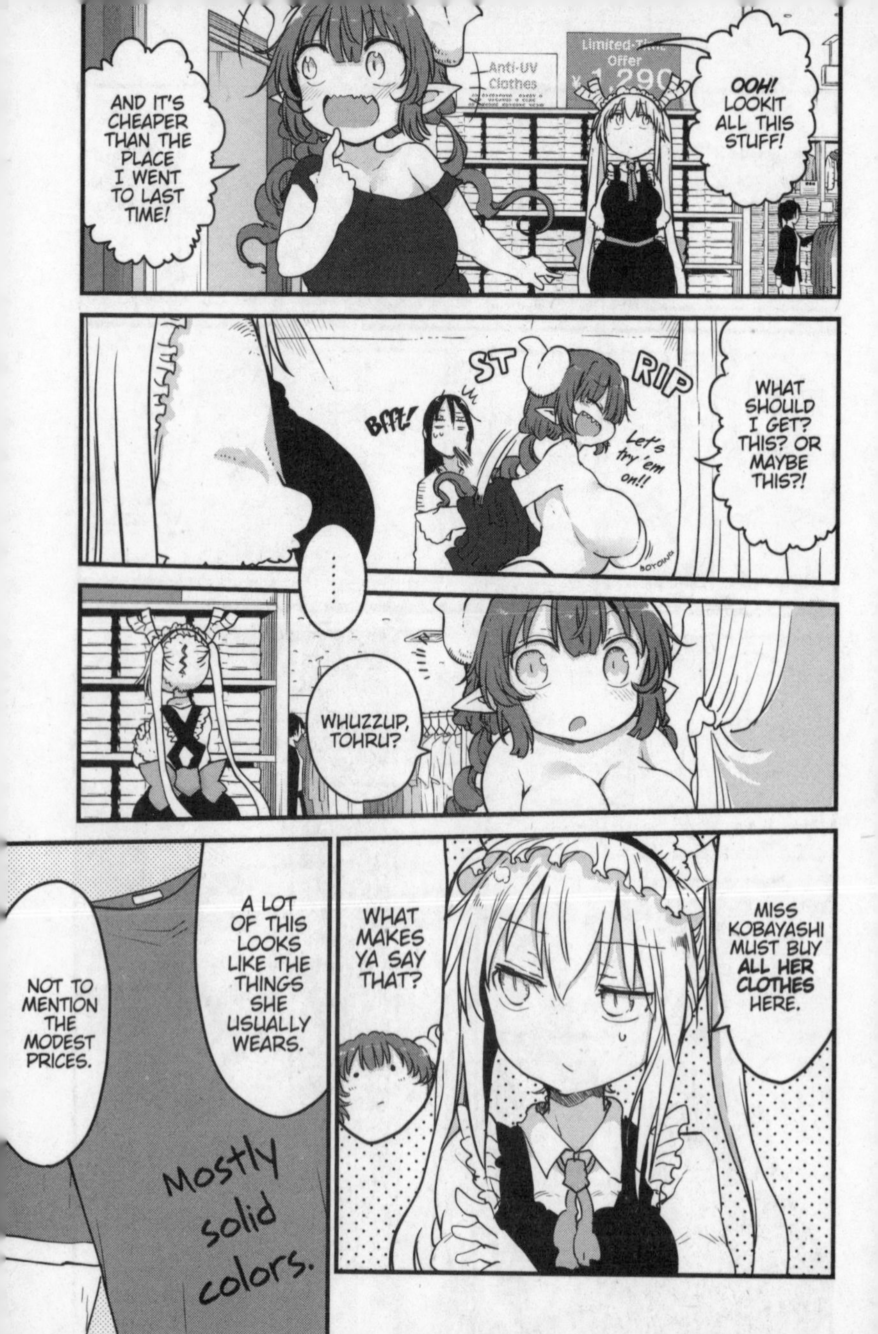
Limited-Time Offer
OOH! LOOKIT ALL THIS STUFF!
Anti-UV Clothes
AND IT'S CHEAPER THAN THE PLACE I WENT TO LAST TIME!
WHAT SHOULD I GET? THIS? OR MAYBE THIS?!
ST RIP
Let's try 'em on!!
Bfft!
BOYOING
......
WHUZZUP, TOHRU?
MISS KOBAYASHI MUST BUY **ALL HER CLOTHES** HERE.
WHAT MAKES YA SAY THAT?
A LOT OF THIS LOOKS LIKE THE THINGS SHE USUALLY WEARS.
NOT TO MENTION THE MODEST PRICES.
Mostly solid colors.

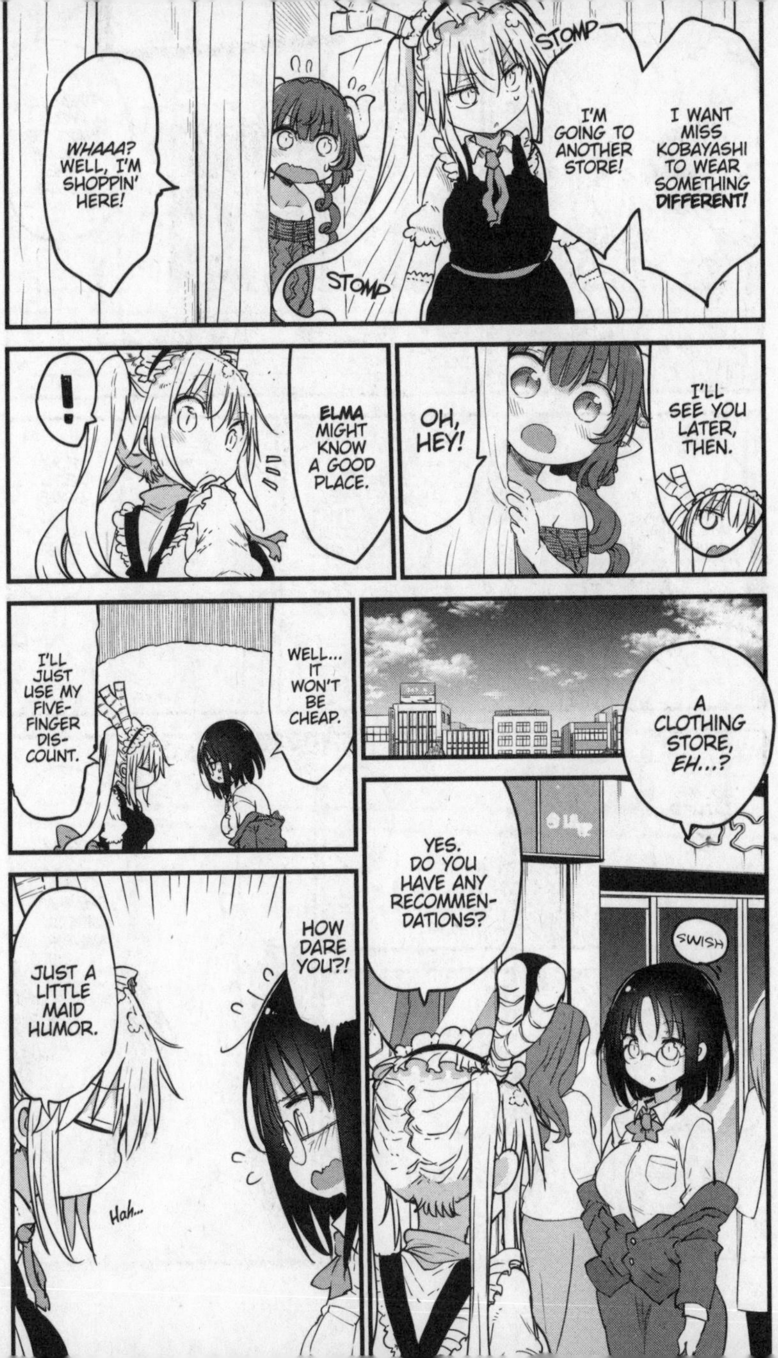
STOMP
I WANT MISS KOBAYASHI TO WEAR SOMETHING DIFFERENT!
I'M GOING TO ANOTHER STORE!
STOMP
WHAAA? WELL, I'M SHOPPIN' HERE!
I'LL SEE YOU LATER, THEN.
OH, HEY!
ELMA MIGHT KNOW A GOOD PLACE.
!
A CLOTHING STORE, EH...?
YES. DO YOU HAVE ANY RECOMMEN-DATIONS?
SWISH
WELL... IT WON'T BE CHEAP.
I'LL JUST USE MY FIVE-FINGER DIS-COUNT.
HOW DARE YOU?!
JUST A LITTLE MAID HUMOR.
Hah...

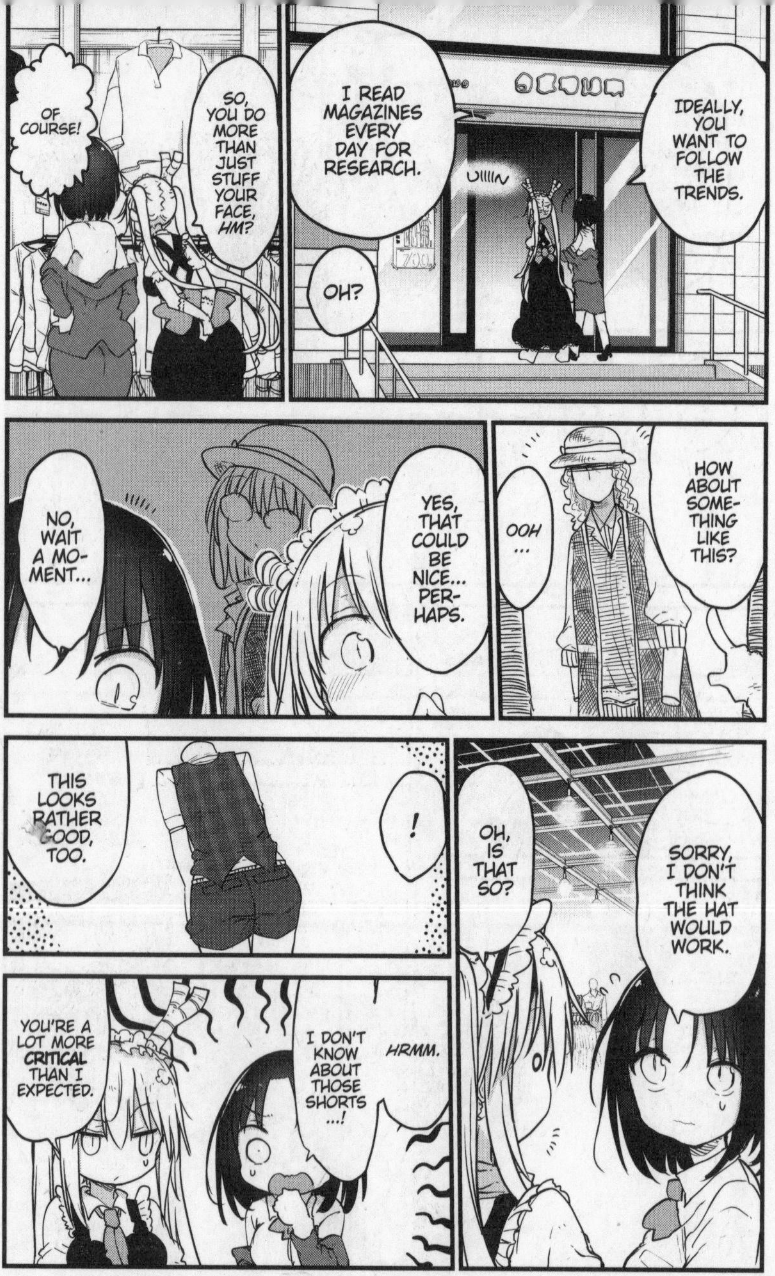
IDEALLY, YOU WANT TO FOLLOW THE TRENDS.
UIIIN
I READ MAGAZINES EVERY DAY FOR RESEARCH.
OH?
SO, YOU DO MORE THAN JUST STUFF YOUR FACE, HM?
OF COURSE!
HOW ABOUT SOMETHING LIKE THIS?
OOH ...
YES, THAT COULD BE NICE... PERHAPS.
NO, WAIT A MOMENT...
SORRY, I DON'T THINK THE HAT WOULD WORK.
OH, IS THAT SO?
!
THIS LOOKS RATHER GOOD, TOO.
HRMM.
I DON'T KNOW ABOUT THOSE SHORTS ...!
YOU'RE A LOT MORE **CRITICAL** THAN I EXPECTED.

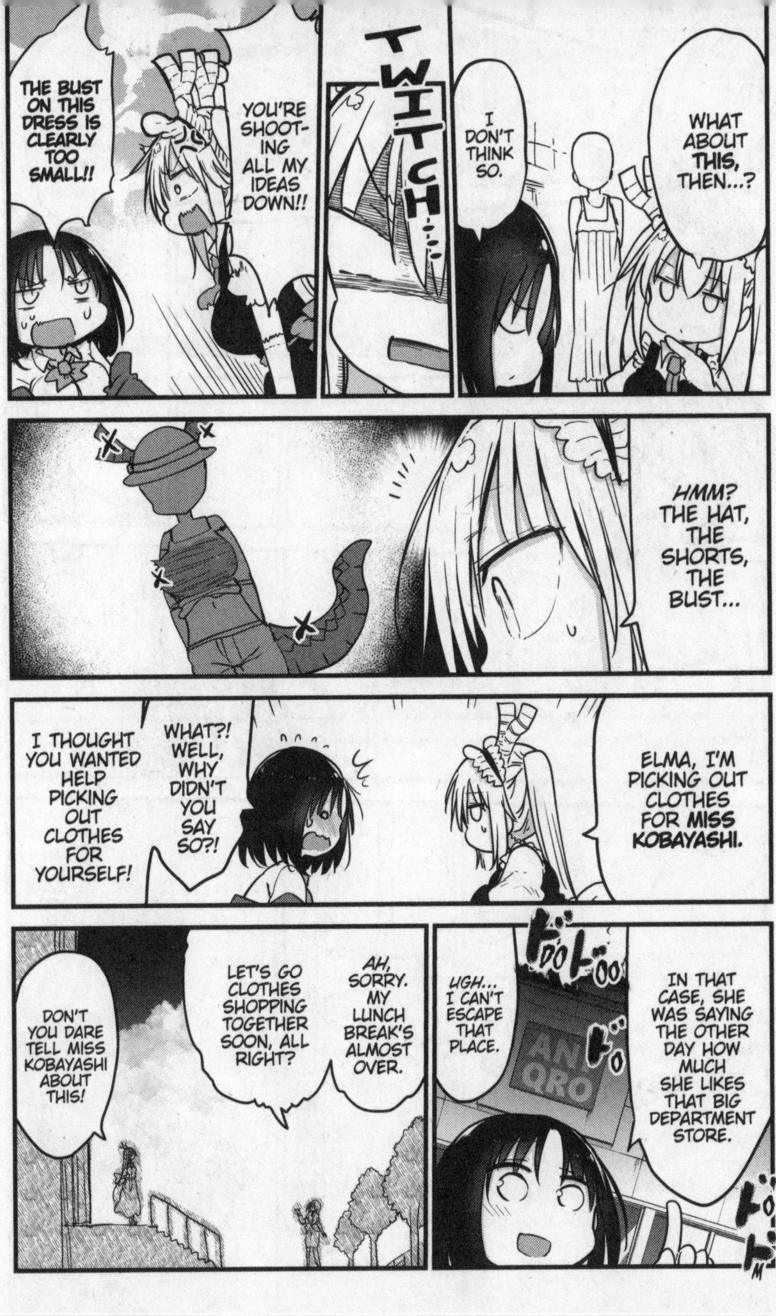
WHAT ABOUT THIS, THEN...?
I DON'T THINK SO.
TWITCH...
YOU'RE SHOOTING ALL MY IDEAS DOWN!!
THE BUST ON THIS DRESS IS CLEARLY TOO SMALL!!
HMM? THE HAT, THE SHORTS, THE BUST...
ELMA, I'M PICKING OUT CLOTHES FOR MISS KOBAYASHI.
WHAT?! WELL, WHY DIDN'T YOU SAY SO?!
I THOUGHT YOU WANTED HELP PICKING OUT CLOTHES FOR YOURSELF!
IN THAT CASE, SHE WAS SAYING THE OTHER DAY HOW MUCH SHE LIKES THAT BIG DEPARTMENT STORE.
UGH... I CAN'T ESCAPE THAT PLACE.
AN
QRO
AH, SORRY. MY LUNCH BREAK'S ALMOST OVER.
LET'S GO CLOTHES SHOPPING TOGETHER SOON, ALL RIGHT?
DON'T YOU DARE TELL MISS KOBAYASHI ABOUT THIS!

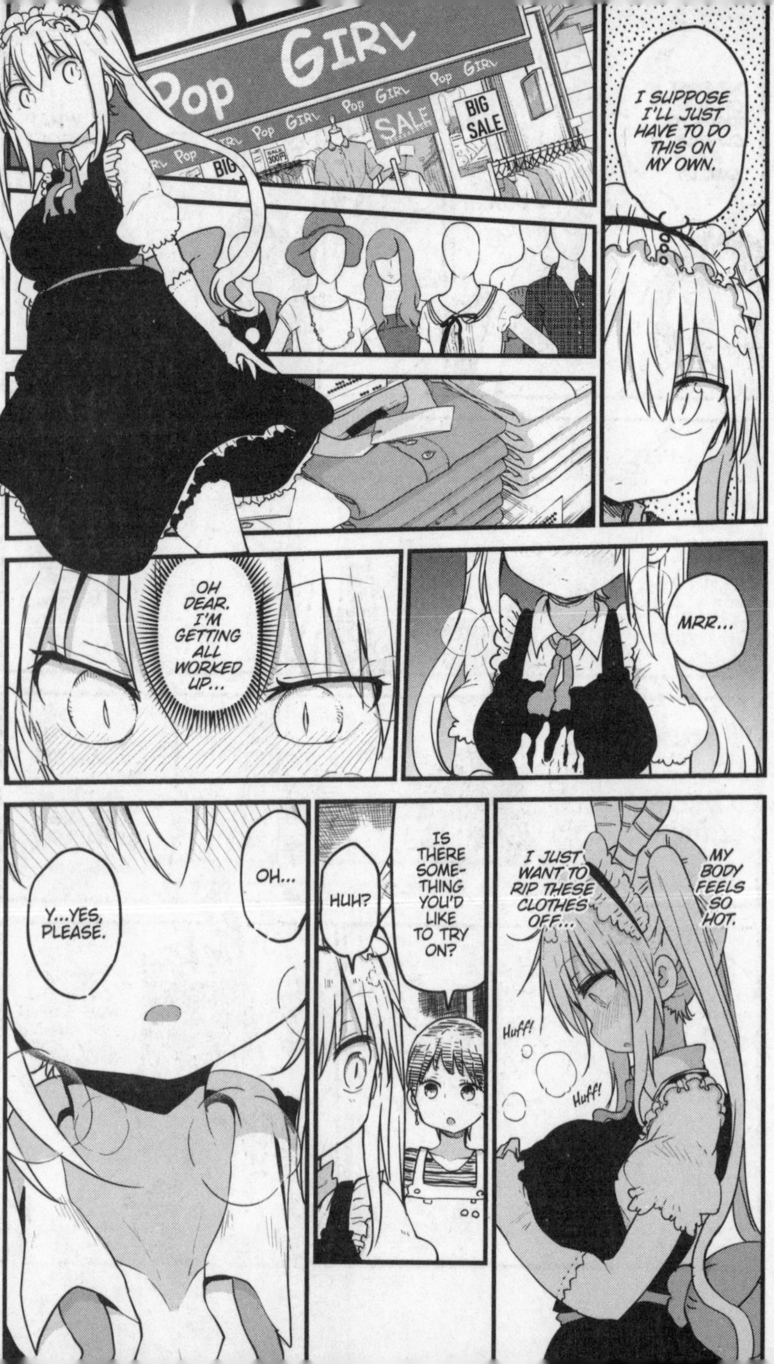
I SUPPOSE I'LL JUST HAVE TO DO THIS ON MY OWN.
Pop GIRL
BIG SALE
SALE
MRR...
OH DEAR. I'M GETTING ALL WORKED UP...
MY BODY FEELS SO HOT.
I JUST WANT TO RIP THESE CLOTHES OFF...
Huff!
Huff!
IS THERE SOMETHING YOU'D LIKE TO TRY ON?
HUH?
OH...
Y...YES, PLEASE.

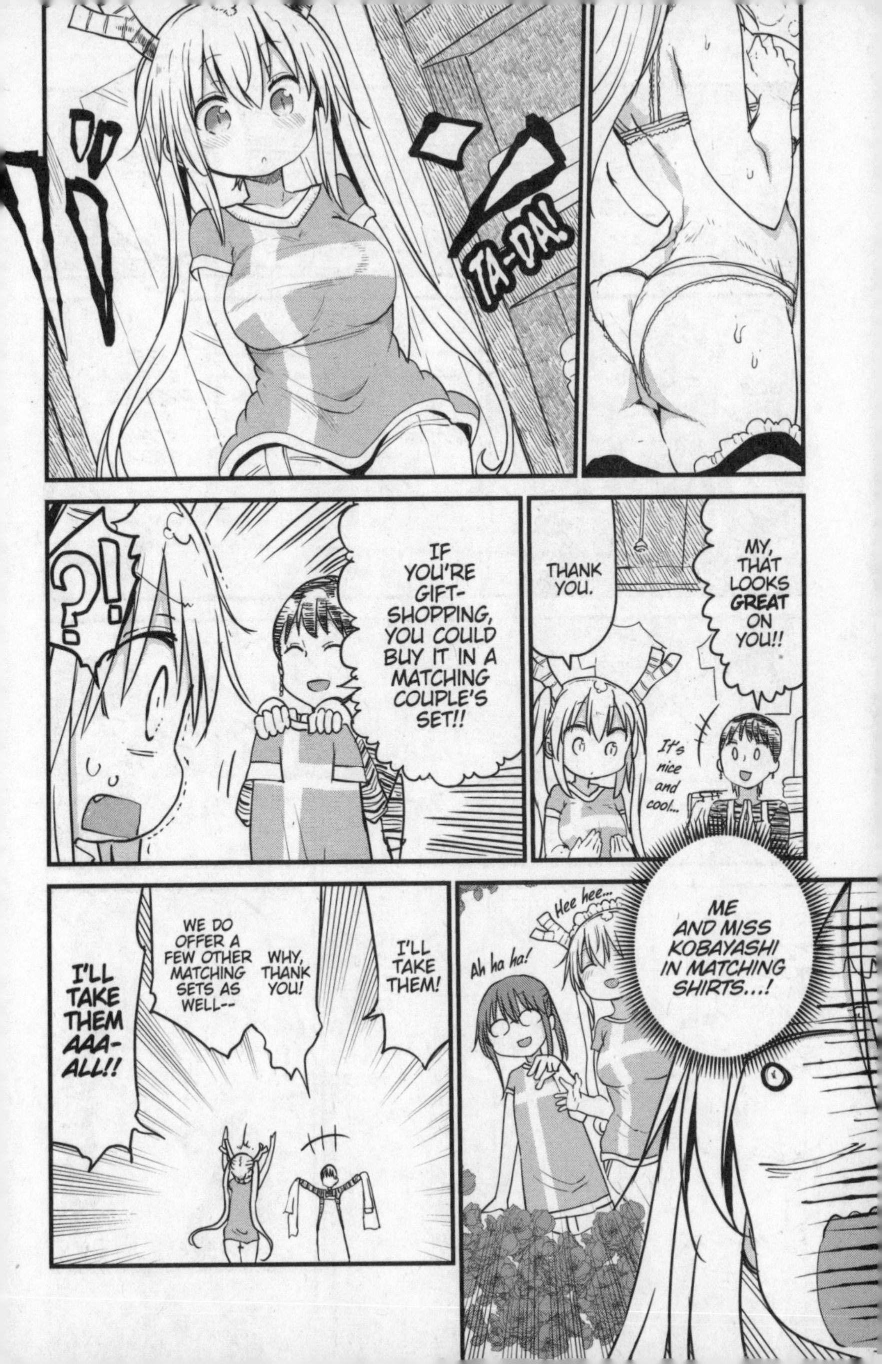
TA-DA!
MY, THAT LOOKS GREAT ON YOU!!
THANK YOU.
It's nice and cool...
IF YOU'RE GIFT-SHOPPING, YOU COULD BUY IT IN A MATCHING COUPLE'S SET!!
?!
ME AND MISS KOBAYASHI IN MATCHING SHIRTS...!
Hee hee...
Ah ha ha!
I'LL TAKE THEM!
WHY, THANK YOU!
WE DO OFFER A FEW OTHER MATCHING SETS AS WELL--
I'LL TAKE THEM AAA-ALL!!

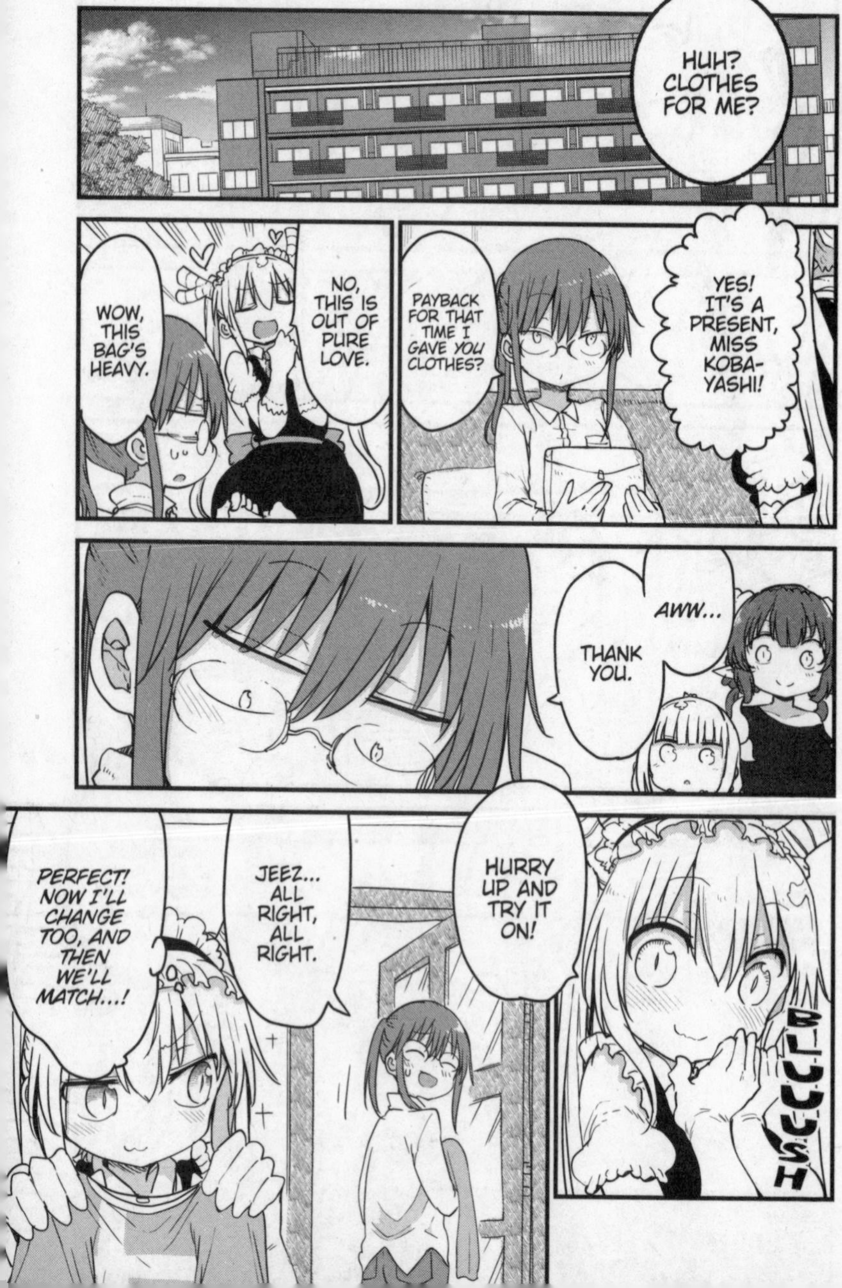
HUH? CLOTHES FOR ME?
YES! IT'S A PRESENT, MISS KOBA-YASHI!
PAYBACK FOR THAT TIME I GAVE *YOU* CLOTHES?
NO, THIS IS OUT OF PURE LOVE.
WOW, THIS BAG'S HEAVY.
AWW...
THANK YOU.
HURRY UP AND TRY IT ON!
BLUUUSH
JEEZ... ALL RIGHT, ALL RIGHT.
PERFECT! NOW I'LL CHANGE TOO, AND THEN WE'LL MATCH...!

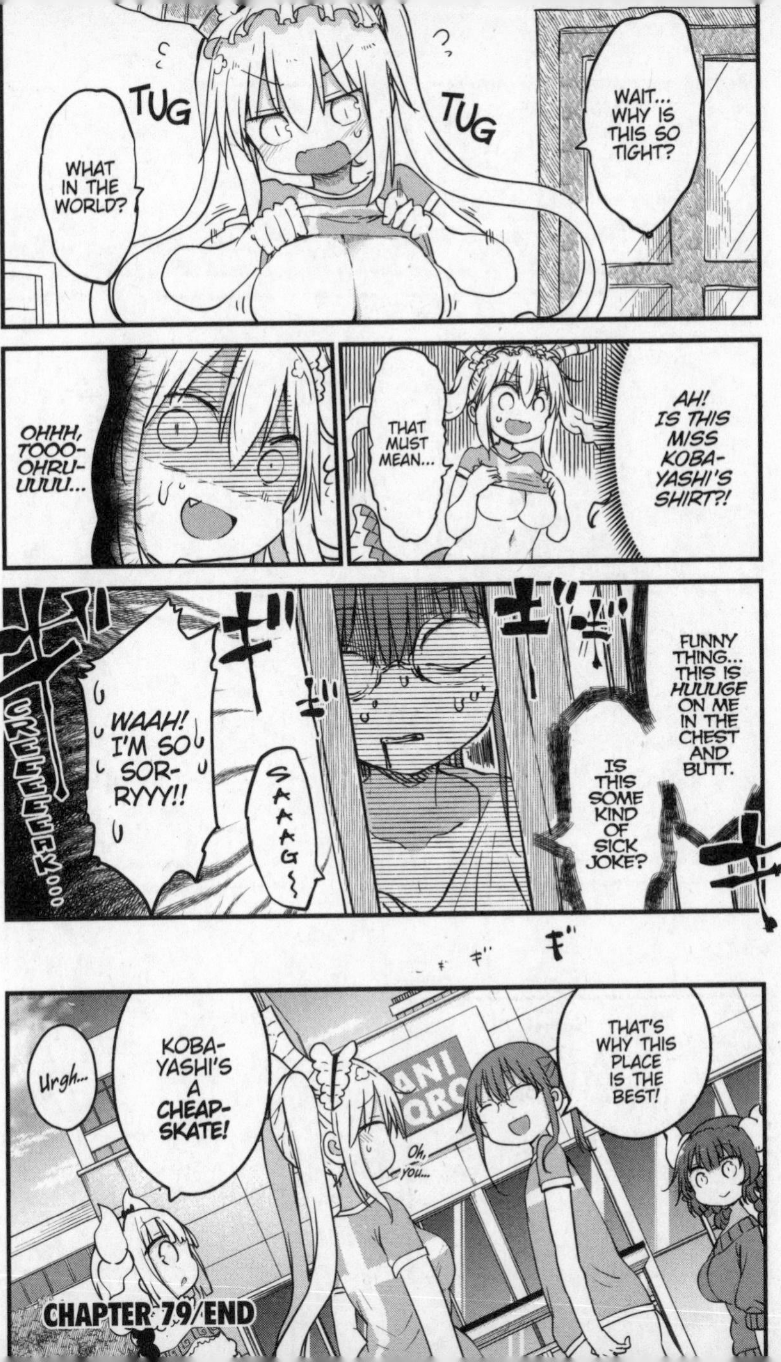
WAIT... WHY IS THIS SO TIGHT?
TUG
TUG
WHAT IN THE WORLD?
AH! IS THIS MISS KOBA-YASHI'S SHIRT?!
THAT MUST MEAN...
OHHH, TOOO-OHRU-UUUU...
FUNNY THING... THIS IS HUUUGE ON ME IN THE CHEST AND BUTT.
IS THIS SOME KIND OF SICK JOKE?
WAAH! I'M SO SOR-RYYY!!
SAAAG~
CREEEEAK...
THAT'S WHY THIS PLACE IS THE BEST!
ANI QRO
Oh, you...
KOBA-YASHI'S A CHEAP-SKATE!
Urgh...
CHAPTER 79/END

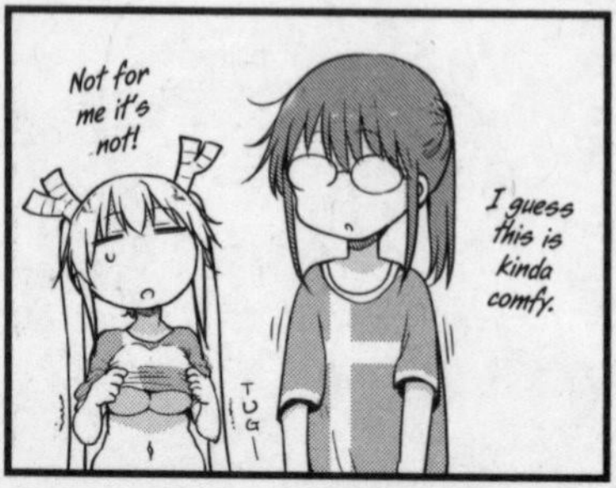
I guess this is kinda comfy.
Not for me it's not!
TUG

Miss Kobayashi's Dragon Maid

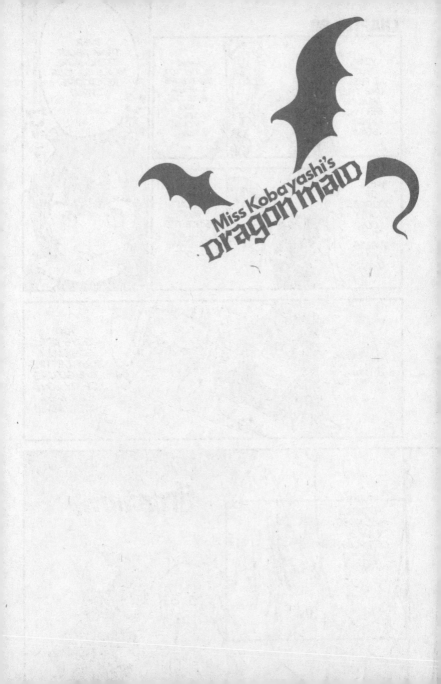

CHAPTER 80

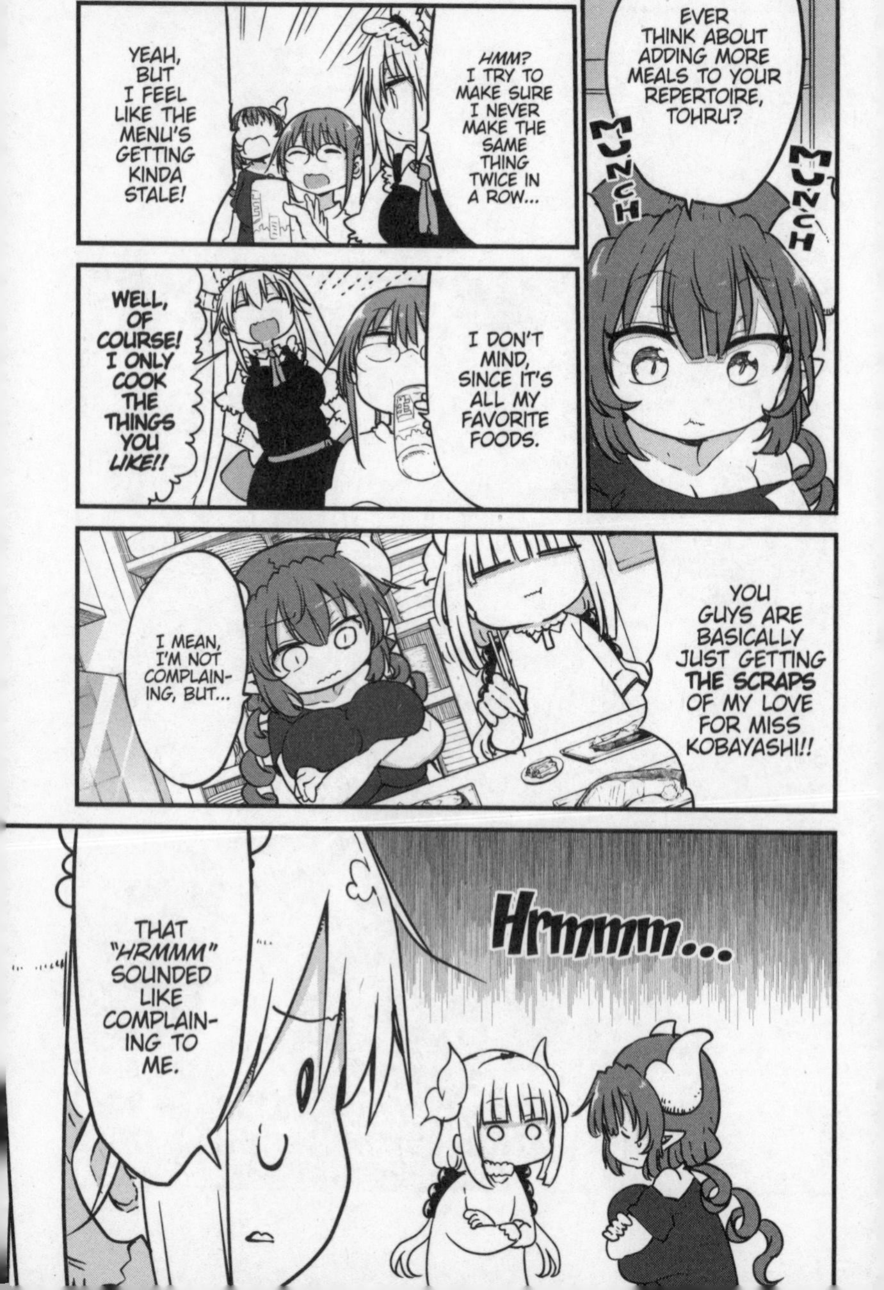
EVER THINK ABOUT ADDING MORE MEALS TO YOUR REPERTOIRE, TOHRU?
MUNCH
MUNCH
HMM? I TRY TO MAKE SURE I NEVER MAKE THE SAME THING TWICE IN A ROW...
YEAH, BUT I FEEL LIKE THE MENU'S GETTING KINDA STALE!
I DON'T MIND, SINCE IT'S ALL MY FAVORITE FOODS.
WELL, OF COURSE! I ONLY COOK THE THINGS YOU LIKE!!
YOU GUYS ARE BASICALLY JUST GETTING THE SCRAPS OF MY LOVE FOR MISS KOBAYASHI!!
I MEAN, I'M NOT COMPLAINING, BUT...
Hrmmmm...
...
THAT "HRMMM" SOUNDED LIKE COMPLAINING TO ME.
...

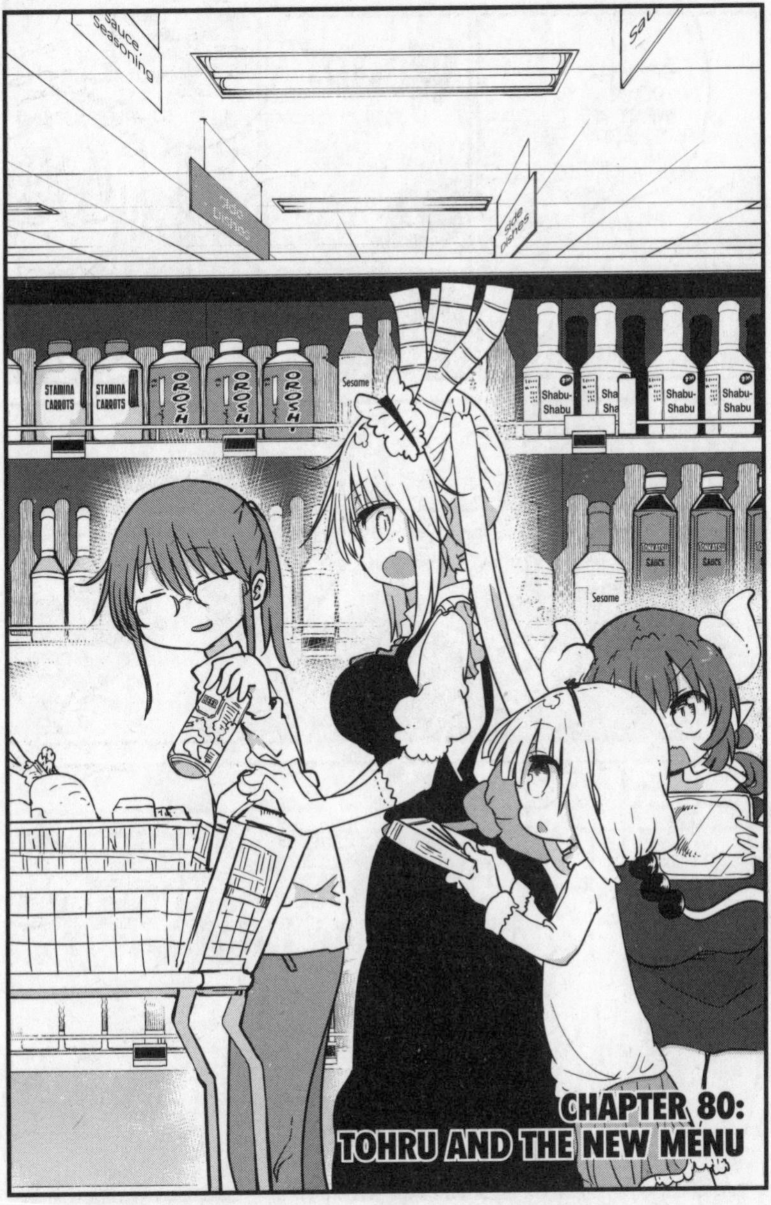
Sauce, Seasoning
side Dishes
STAMINA CARROTS
STAMINA CARROTS
Sesame
Shabu-Shabu
Shabu-Shabu
Shabu-Shabu
TONKATSU SAUCE
TONKATSU SAUCE
Sesame
CHAPTER 80:
TOHRU AND THE NEW MENU

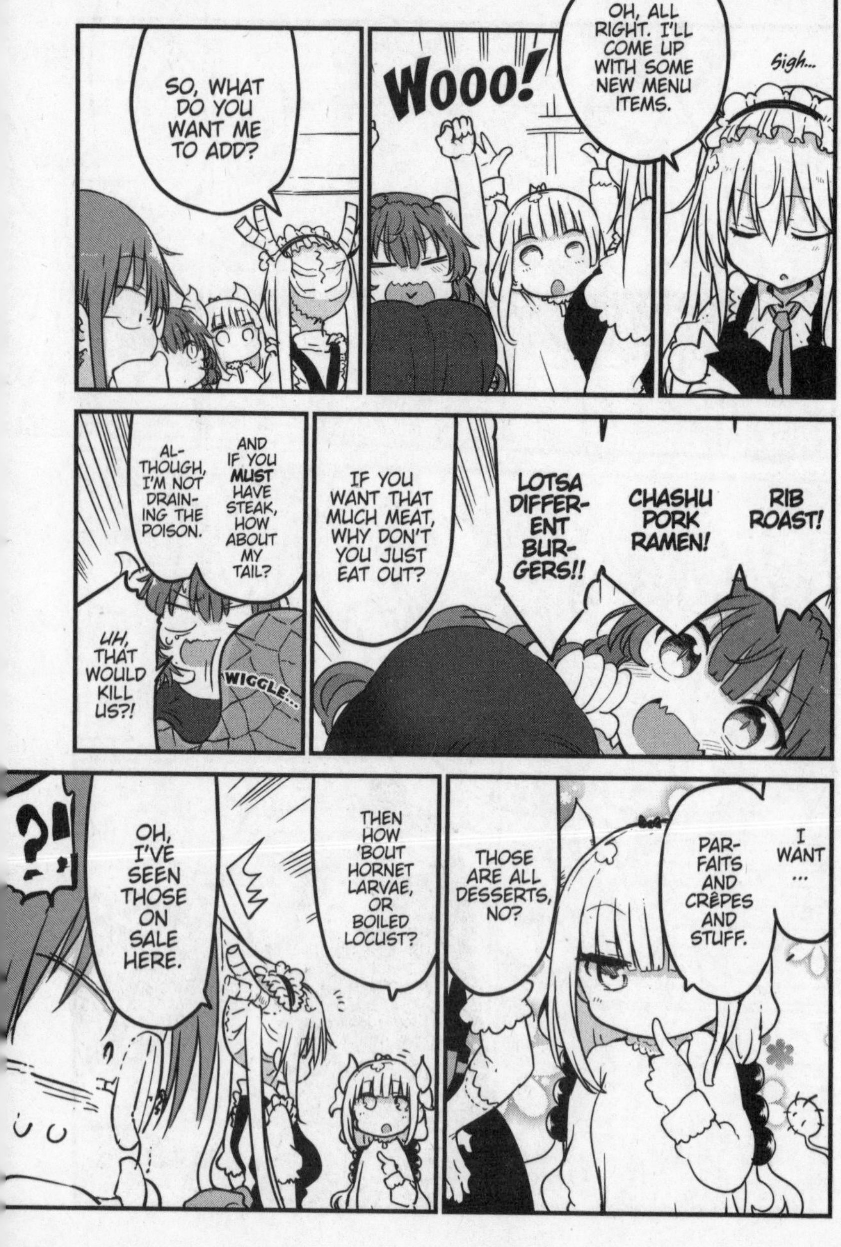
Sigh...
OH, ALL RIGHT. I'LL COME UP WITH SOME NEW MENU ITEMS.
WOOO!
SO, WHAT DO YOU WANT ME TO ADD?
RIB ROAST!
CHASHU PORK RAMEN!
LOTSA DIFFERENT BURGERS!!
IF YOU WANT THAT MUCH MEAT, WHY DON'T YOU JUST EAT OUT?
AND IF YOU **MUST** HAVE STEAK, HOW ABOUT MY TAIL?
ALTHOUGH, I'M NOT DRAINING THE POISON.
WIGGLE...
UH, THAT WOULD KILL US?!
I WANT ...
PARFAITS AND CRÊPES AND STUFF.
THOSE ARE ALL DESSERTS, NO?
THEN HOW 'BOUT HORNET LARVAE, OR BOILED LOCUST?
OH, I'VE SEEN THOSE ON SALE HERE.
?!

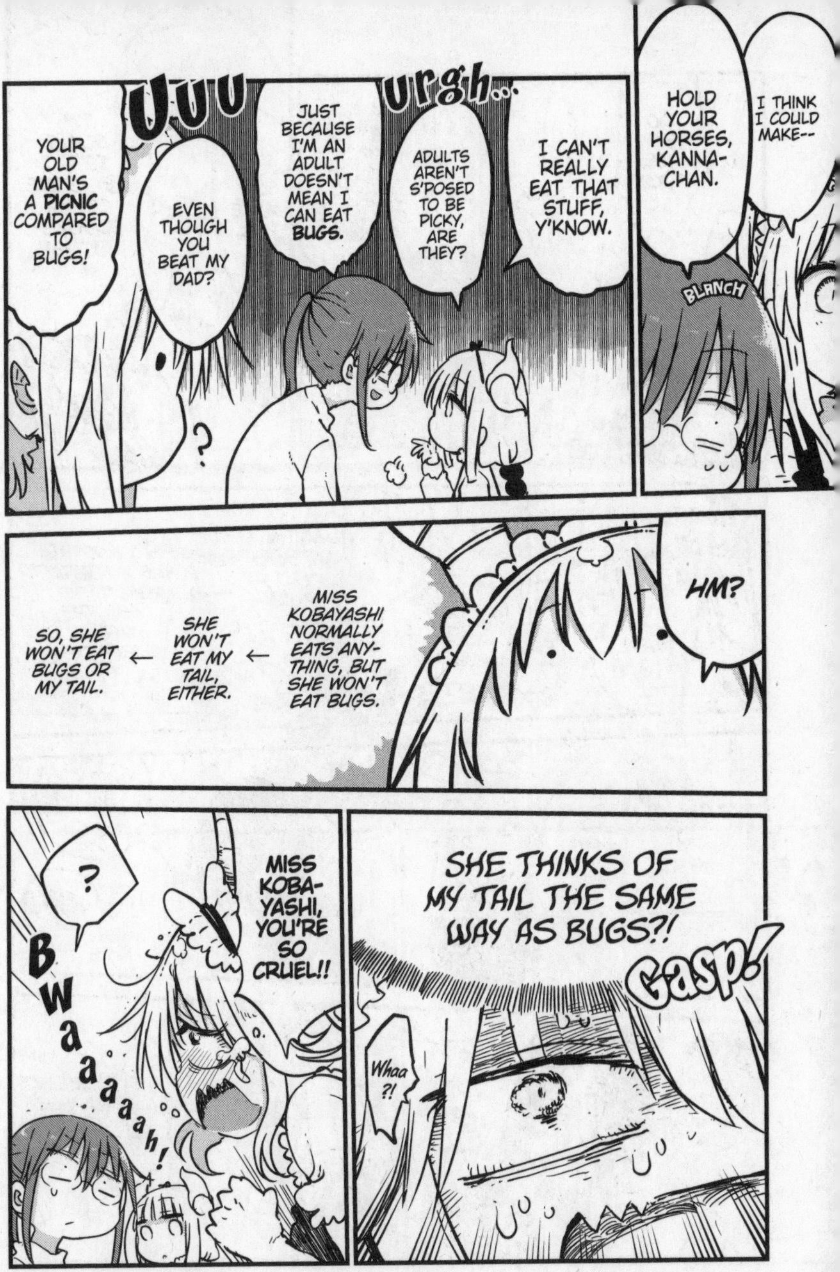
I THINK I COULD MAKE--
HOLD YOUR HORSES, KANNA-CHAN.
BLANCH
I CAN'T REALLY EAT THAT STUFF, Y'KNOW.
ADULTS AREN'T S'POSED TO BE PICKY, ARE THEY?
JUST BECAUSE I'M AN ADULT DOESN'T MEAN I CAN EAT **BUGS.**
Uuuurgh...
EVEN THOUGH YOU BEAT MY DAD?
YOUR OLD MAN'S A **PICNIC** COMPARED TO BUGS!
?
HM?
MISS KOBAYASHI NORMALLY EATS ANYTHING, BUT SHE WON'T EAT BUGS. ←
SHE WON'T EAT MY TAIL, EITHER. ←
SO, SHE WON'T EAT BUGS OR MY TAIL.
Gasp!
SHE THINKS OF MY TAIL THE SAME WAY AS BUGS?!
Whaa?!
MISS KOBAYASHI, YOU'RE SO CRUEL!!
?
Bwaaaaaah!

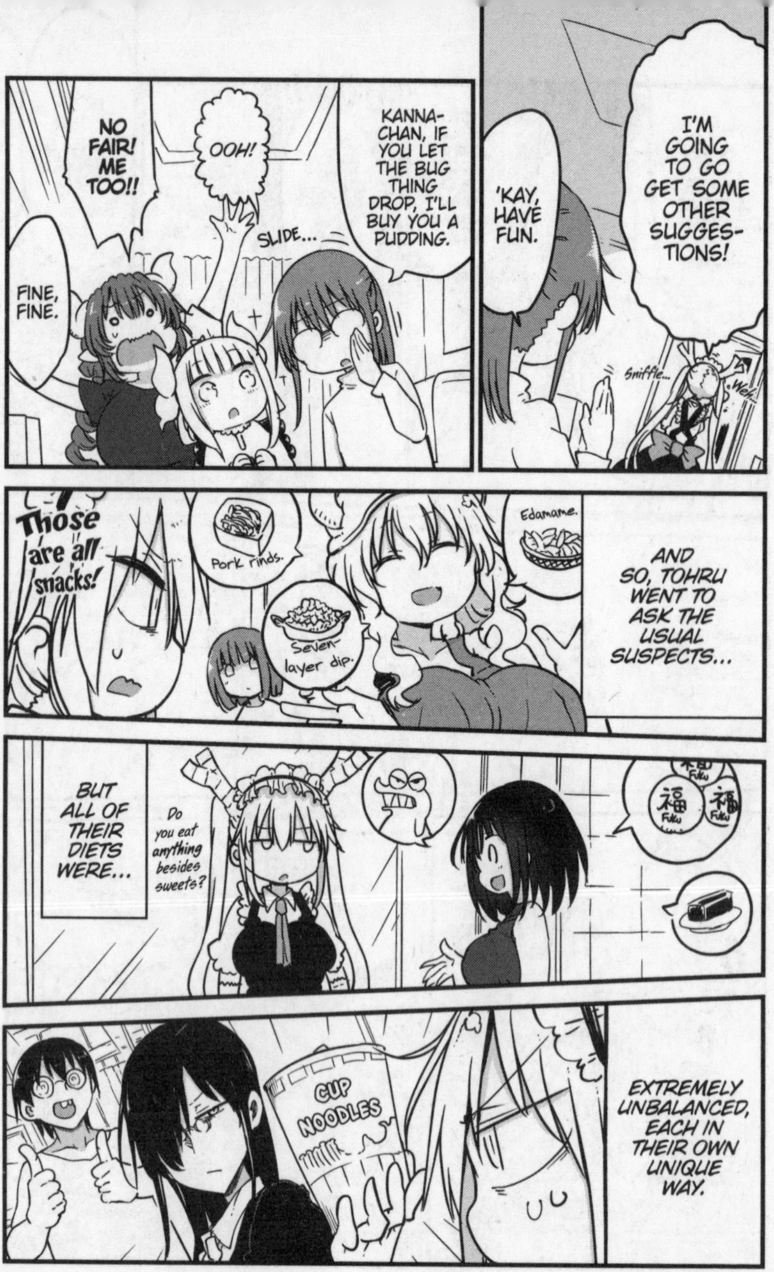
I'M GOING TO GO GET SOME OTHER SUGGES-TIONS!
'KAY, HAVE FUN.
Sniffle...
Weh...
KANNA-CHAN, IF YOU LET THE BUG THING DROP, I'LL BUY YOU A PUDDING.
SLIDE...
OOH!
NO FAIR! ME TOO!!
FINE, FINE.
AND SO, TOHRU WENT TO ASK THE USUAL SUSPECTS...
Edamame.
Pork rinds.
Seven layer dip.
Those are all snacks!
Fuku
福 Fuku
福 Fuku
Do you eat anything besides sweets?
BUT ALL OF THEIR DIETS WERE...
EXTREMELY UNBALANCED, EACH IN THEIR OWN UNIQUE WAY.
CUP NOODLES

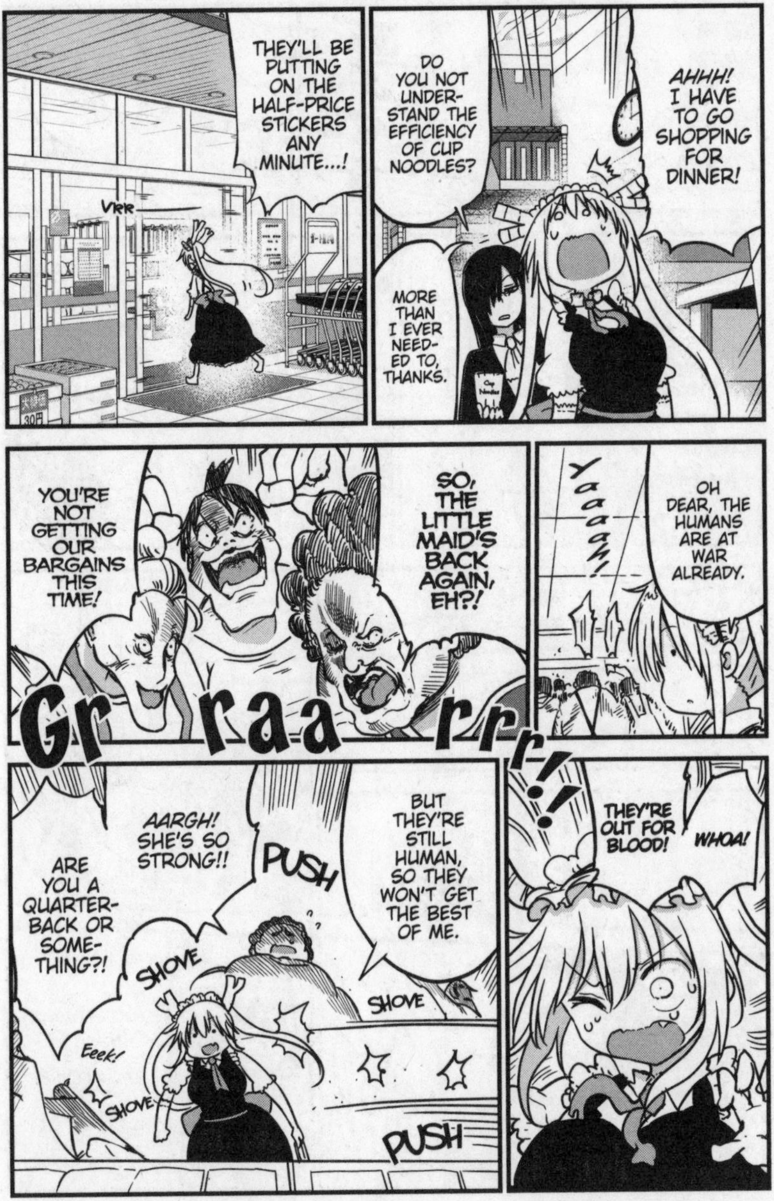
AHHH! I HAVE TO GO SHOPPING FOR DINNER!
DO YOU NOT UNDER-STAND THE EFFICIENCY OF CUP NOODLES?
MORE THAN I EVER NEED-ED TO, THANKS.
THEY'LL BE PUTTING ON THE HALF-PRICE STICKERS ANY MINUTE...!
VRR
Yaaaah!
OH DEAR, THE HUMANS ARE AT WAR ALREADY.
SO, THE LITTLE MAID'S BACK AGAIN, EH?!
YOU'RE NOT GETTING OUR BARGAINS THIS TIME!
Grraaarrr!!
THEY'RE OUT FOR BLOOD!
WHOA!
BUT THEY'RE STILL HUMAN, SO THEY WON'T GET THE BEST OF ME.
PUSH
AARGH! SHE'S SO STRONG!!
ARE YOU A QUARTER-BACK OR SOME-THING?!
SHOVE
SHOVE
Eeek!
SHOVE
PUSH

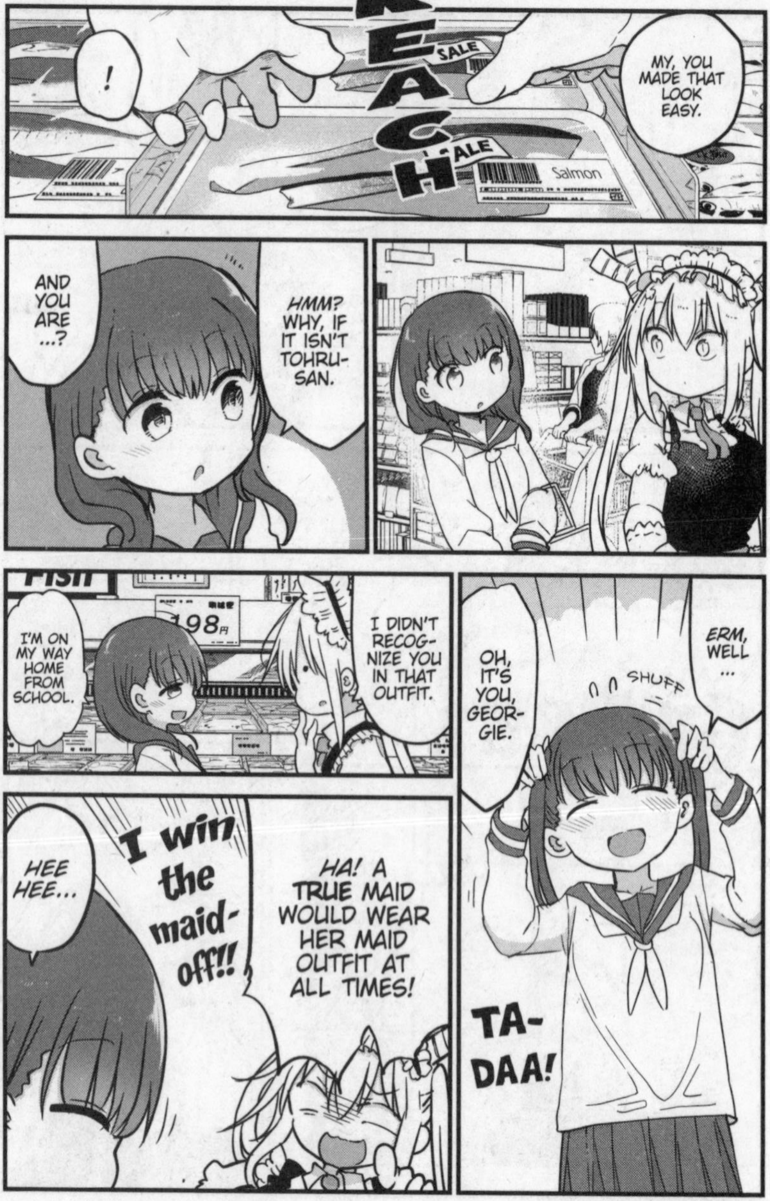
MY, YOU MADE THAT LOOK EASY.
REACH
SALE
SALE
Salmon
!
HMM? WHY, IF IT ISN'T TOHRU-SAN.
AND YOU ARE ...?
ERM, WELL ...
SHUFF
OH, IT'S YOU, GEORGIE.
TA-DAA!
FISH
198円
I DIDN'T RECOGNIZE YOU IN THAT OUTFIT.
I'M ON MY WAY HOME FROM SCHOOL.
HA! A TRUE MAID WOULD WEAR HER MAID OUTFIT AT ALL TIMES!
I win the maid-off!!
HEE HEE...

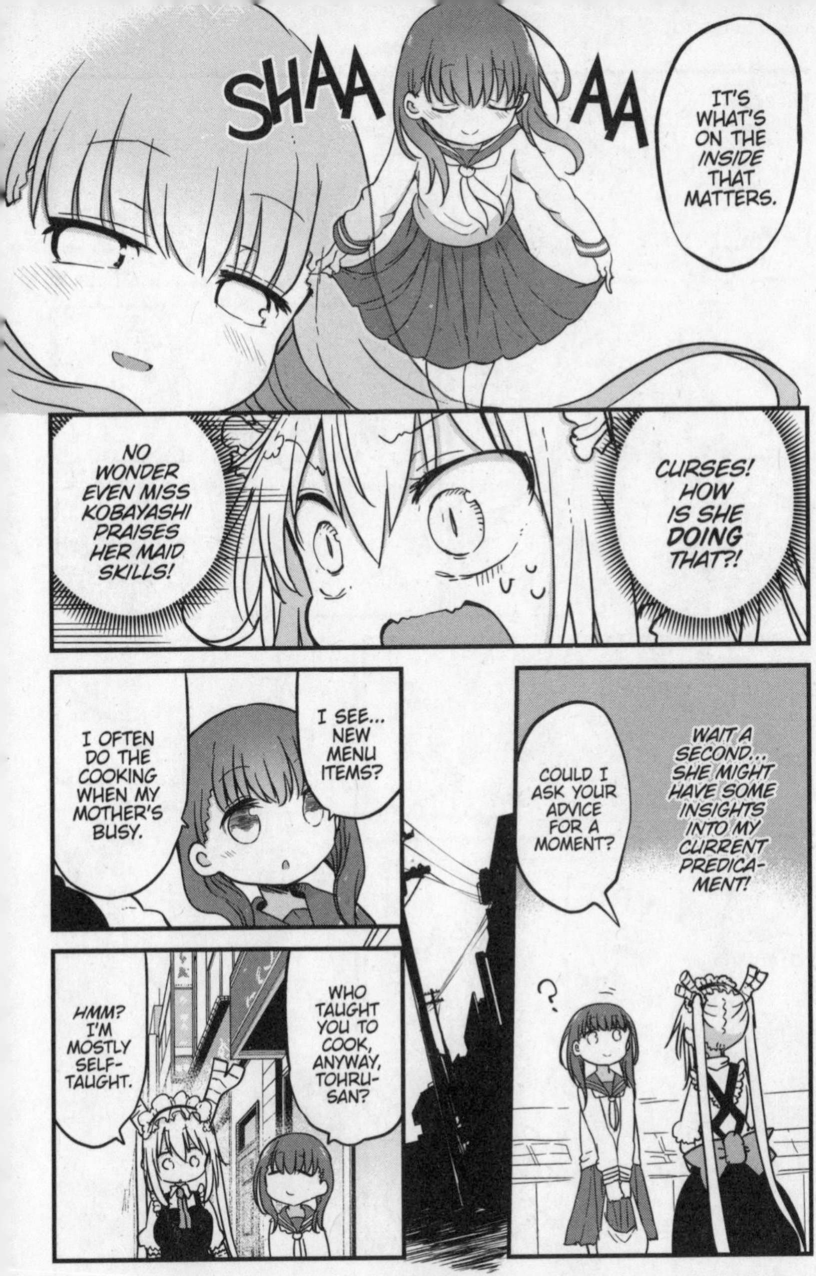
SHAAAA
IT'S WHAT'S ON THE *INSIDE* THAT MATTERS.
CURSES! HOW IS SHE **DOING** THAT?!
NO WONDER EVEN MISS KOBAYASHI PRAISES HER MAID SKILLS!
WAIT A SECOND... SHE MIGHT HAVE SOME INSIGHTS INTO MY CURRENT PREDICAMENT!
COULD I ASK YOUR ADVICE FOR A MOMENT?
?
I SEE... NEW MENU ITEMS?
I OFTEN DO THE COOKING WHEN MY MOTHER'S BUSY.
WHO TAUGHT YOU TO COOK, ANYWAY, TOHRU-SAN?
HMM? I'M MOSTLY SELF-TAUGHT.

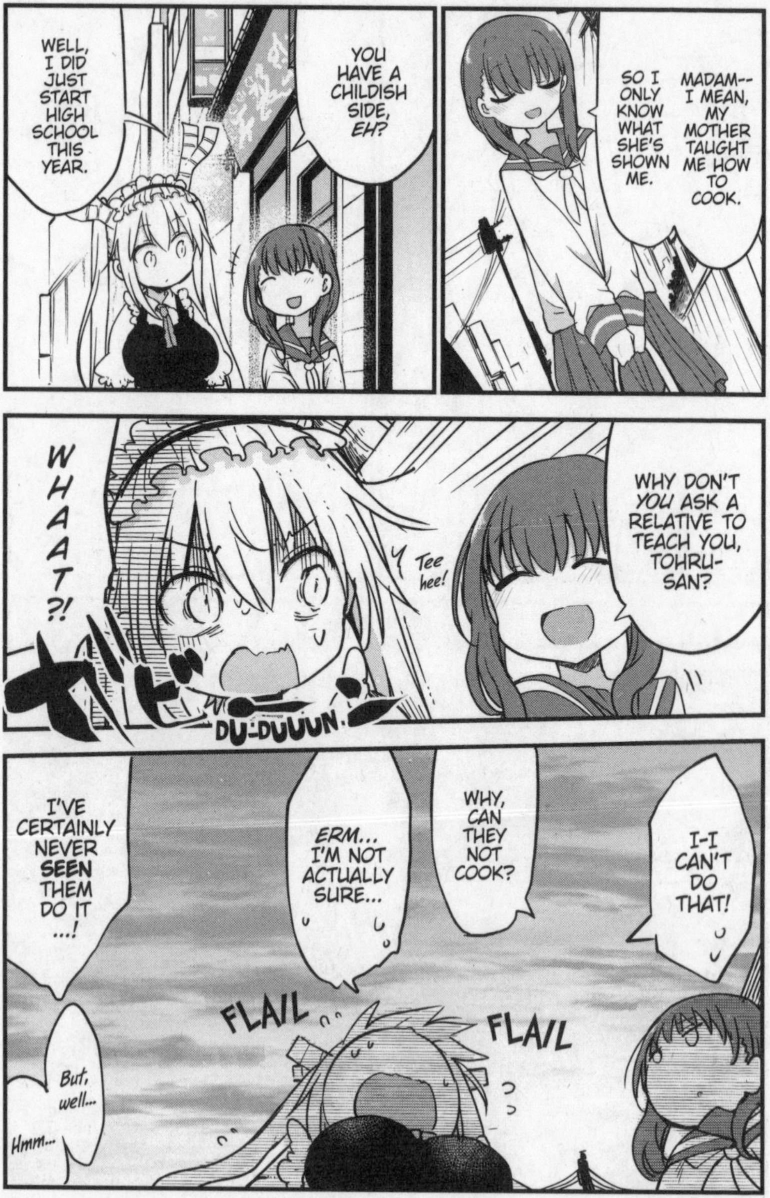
MADAM-- I MEAN, MY MOTHER TAUGHT ME HOW TO COOK.
SO I ONLY KNOW WHAT SHE'S SHOWN ME.
YOU HAVE A CHILDISH SIDE, *EH?*
WELL, I DID JUST START HIGH SCHOOL THIS YEAR.
WHY DON'T *YOU* ASK A RELATIVE TO TEACH YOU, TOHRU-SAN?
Tee hee!
WHAAAT?!
DU-DUUUN
I-I CAN'T DO THAT!
WHY, CAN THEY NOT COOK?
ERM... I'M NOT ACTUALLY SURE...
I'VE CERTAINLY NEVER **SEEN** THEM DO IT ...!
FLAIL
FLAIL
But, well...
Hmm...

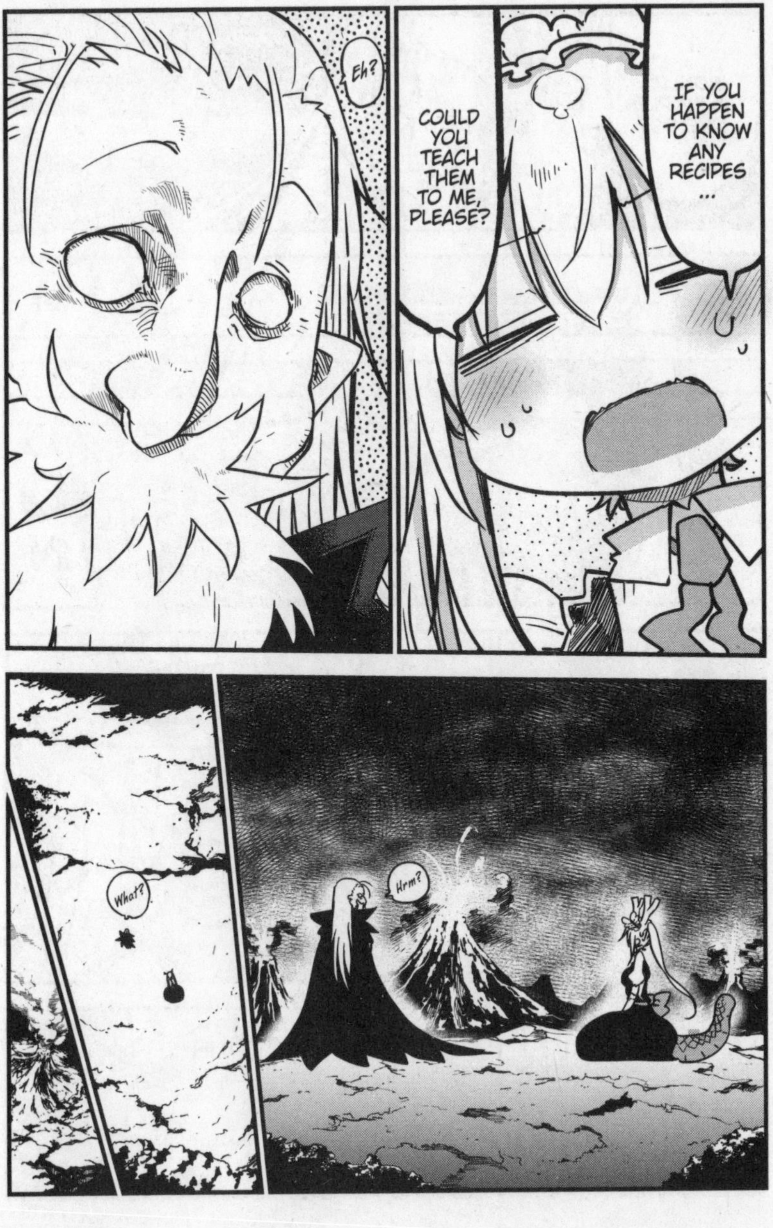
IF YOU HAPPEN TO KNOW ANY RECIPES ...
COULD YOU TEACH THEM TO ME, PLEASE?
Eh?
Hrm?
What?

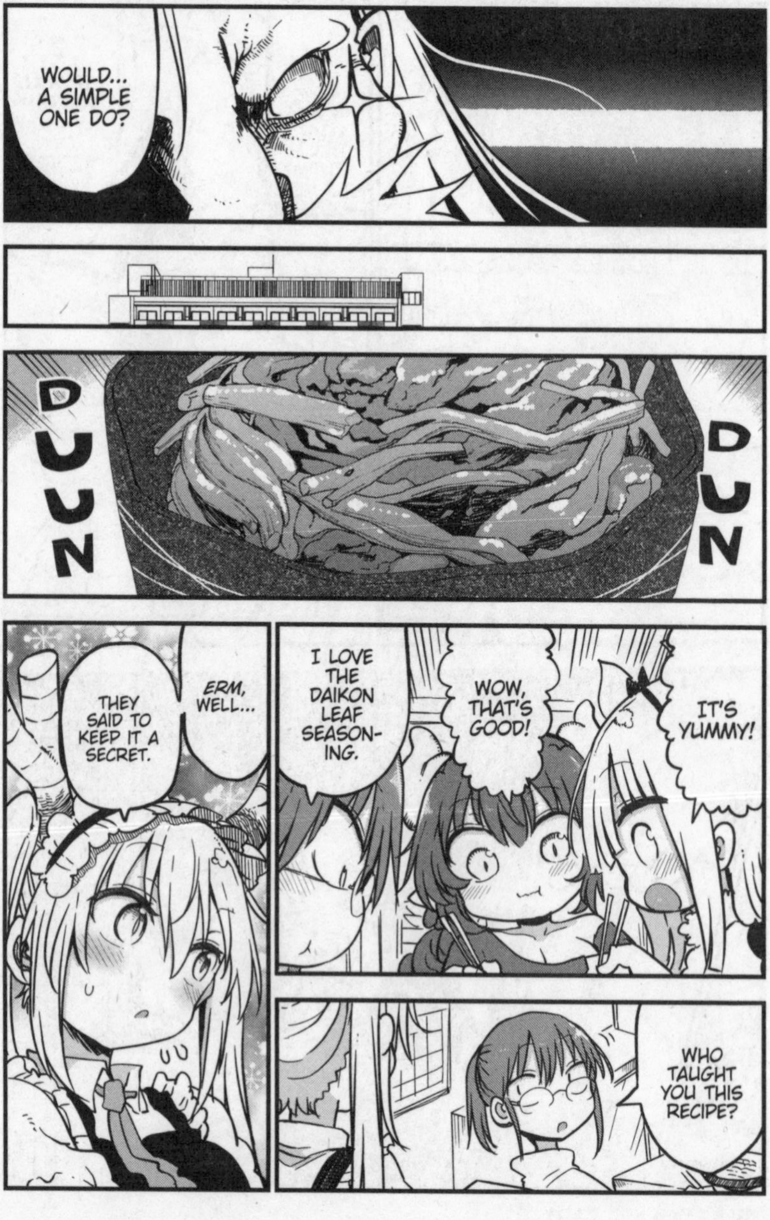
WOULD... A SIMPLE ONE DO?
DUN
DUUN
IT'S YUMMY!
WOW, THAT'S GOOD!
I LOVE THE DAIKON LEAF SEASON-ING.
WHO TAUGHT YOU THIS RECIPE?
ERM, WELL...
THEY SAID TO KEEP IT A SECRET.

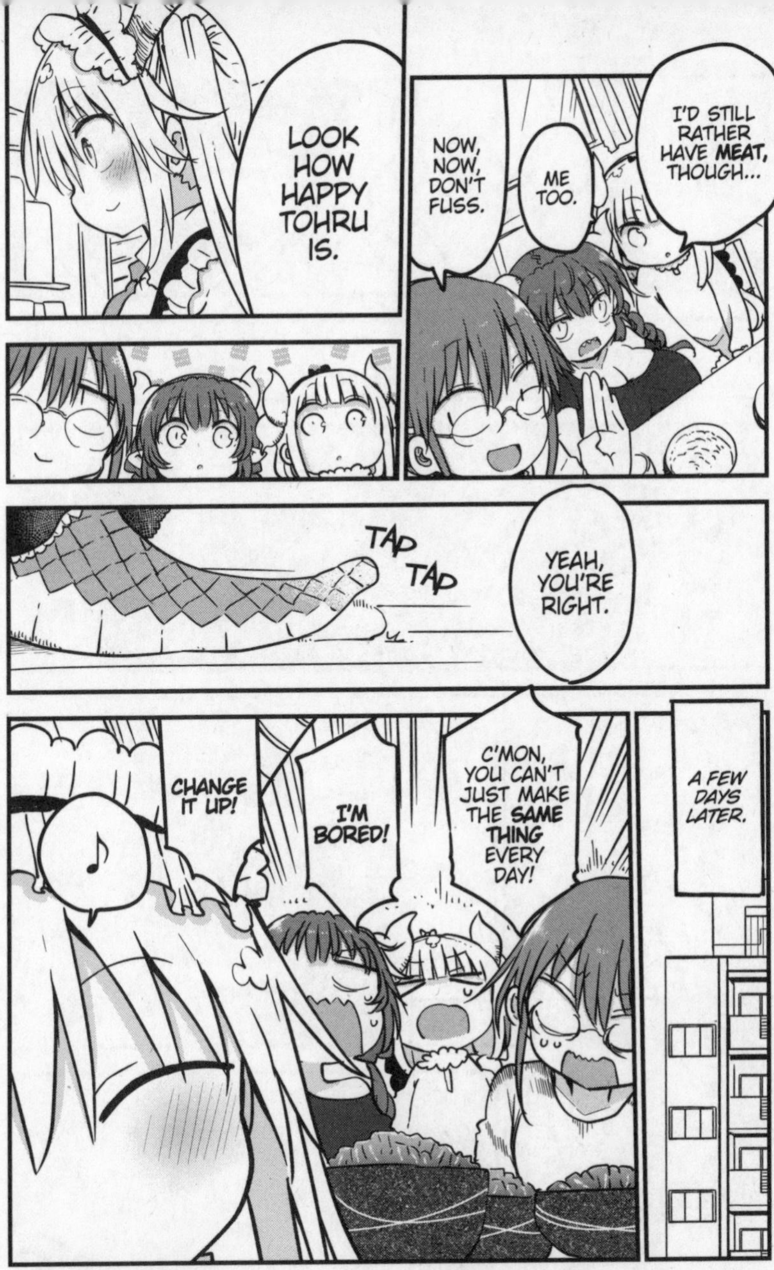
I'D STILL RATHER HAVE MEAT, THOUGH...
ME TOO.
NOW, NOW, DON'T FUSS.
LOOK HOW HAPPY TOHRU IS.
YEAH, YOU'RE RIGHT.
TAP TAP
A FEW DAYS LATER.
C'MON, YOU CAN'T JUST MAKE THE SAME THING EVERY DAY!
I'M BORED!
CHANGE IT UP!
♪

CHAPTER 80/END

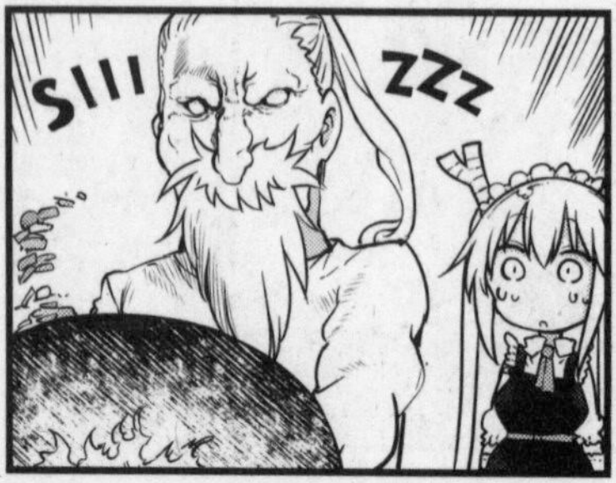
SIII
ZZZ

Miss Kobayashi's Dragon Maid

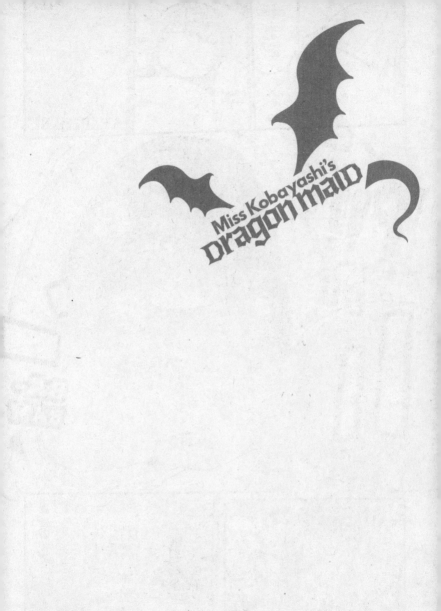

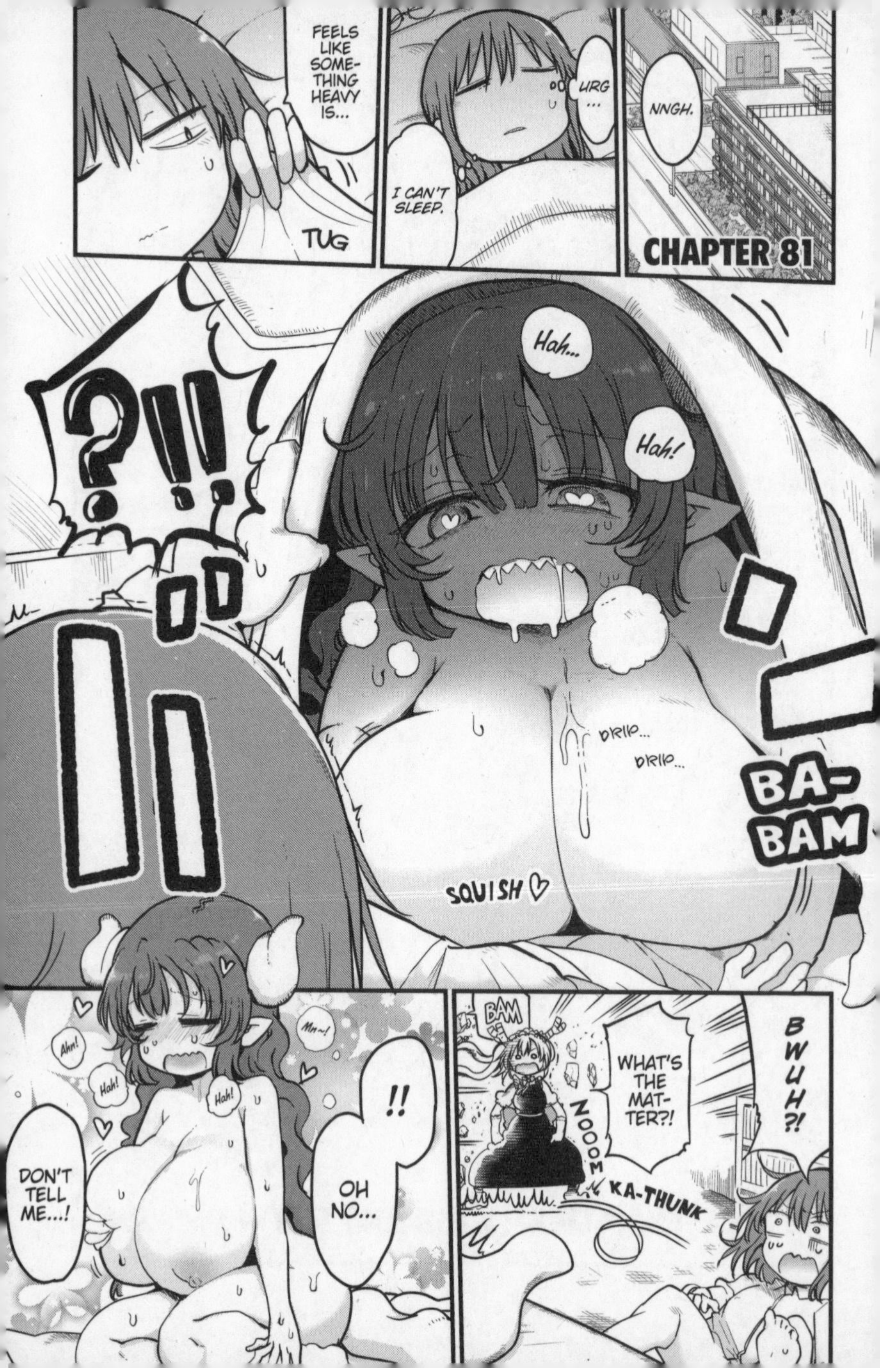
NNGH.
CHAPTER 81
URG ...
I CAN'T SLEEP.
FEELS LIKE SOME-THING HEAVY IS...
TUG
Hah...
Hah!
BA-BAM
DRIP...
DRIP...
SQUISH ♡
?!!
BWUH?!
BAM
WHAT'S THE MAT-TER?!
ZOOOOM
KA-THUNK
Mn~!
!!
OH NO...
Ahn!
Hah!
Hah!
DON'T TELL ME...!

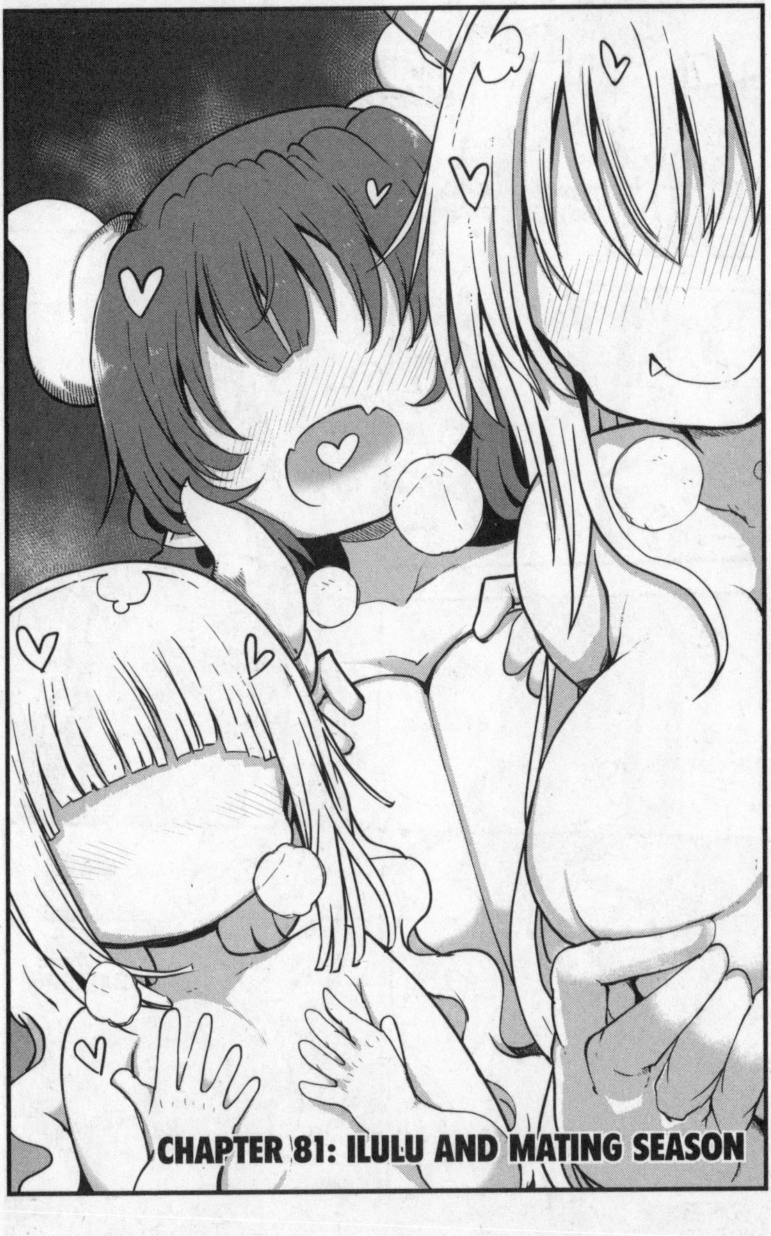
CHAPTER 81: ILULU AND MATING SEASON

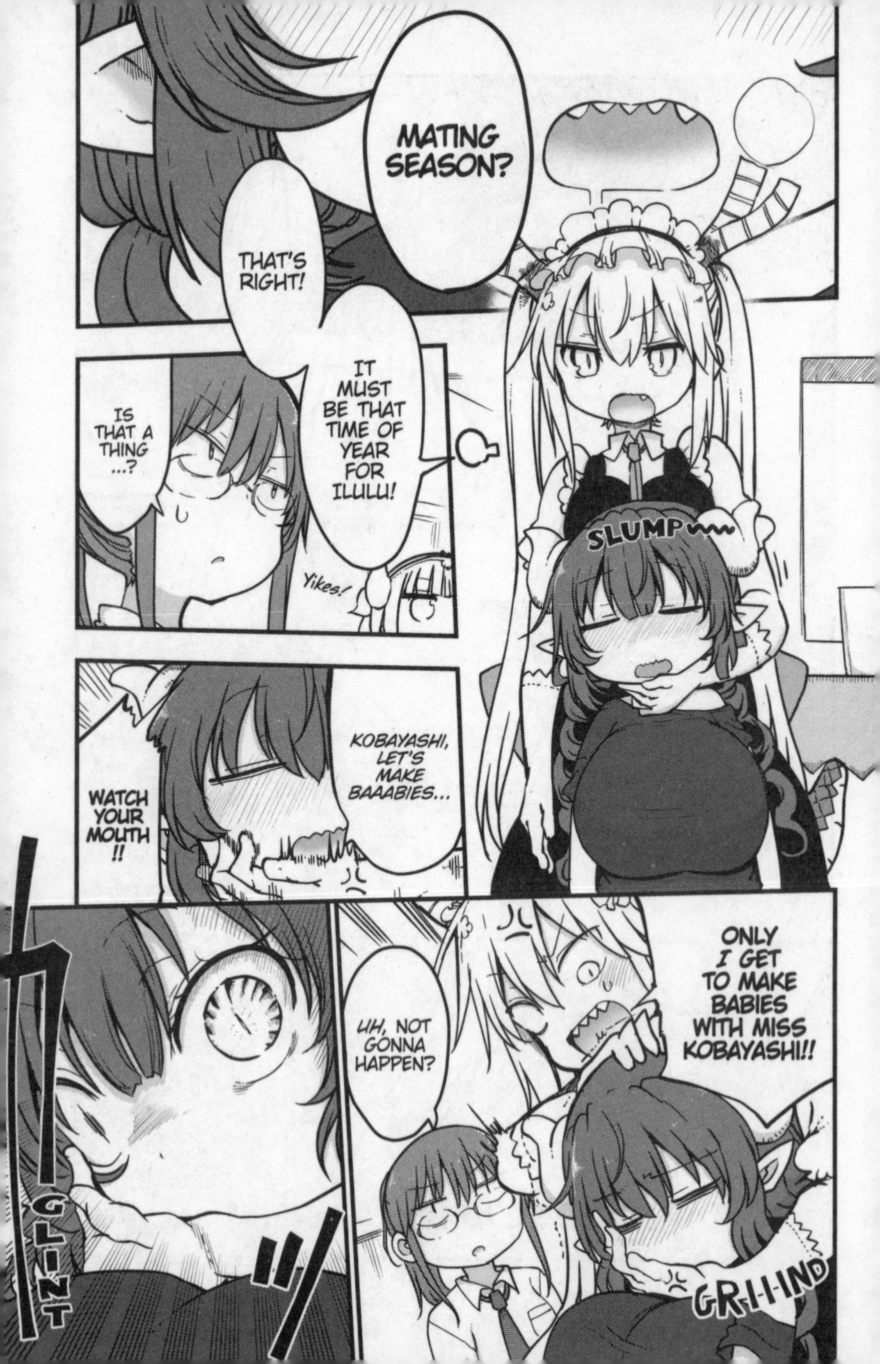
MATING SEASON?
THAT'S RIGHT!
SLUMP
IT MUST BE THAT TIME OF YEAR FOR ILULU!
IS THAT A THING ...?
Yikes!
KOBAYASHI, LET'S MAKE BAAABIES...
WATCH YOUR MOUTH !!
ONLY I GET TO MAKE BABIES WITH MISS KOBAYASHI!!
UH, NOT GONNA HAPPEN?
GR-I-I-IND
GLINT

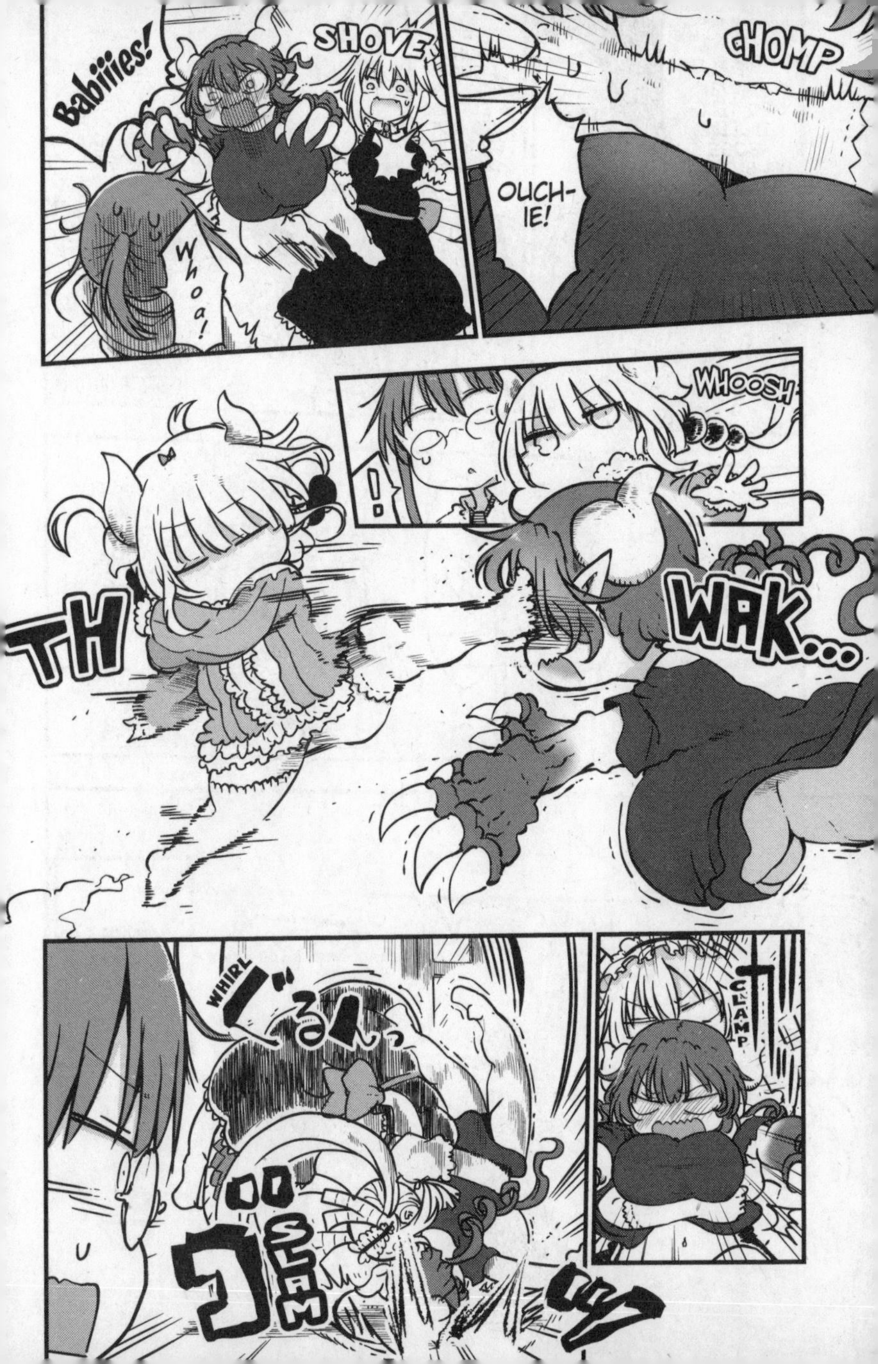
CHOMP
OUCH-
IE!
SHOVE
Babiiies!
Whoa!
WHOOSH
!
TH
WAK...
CLAMP
WHIRL
SLAM

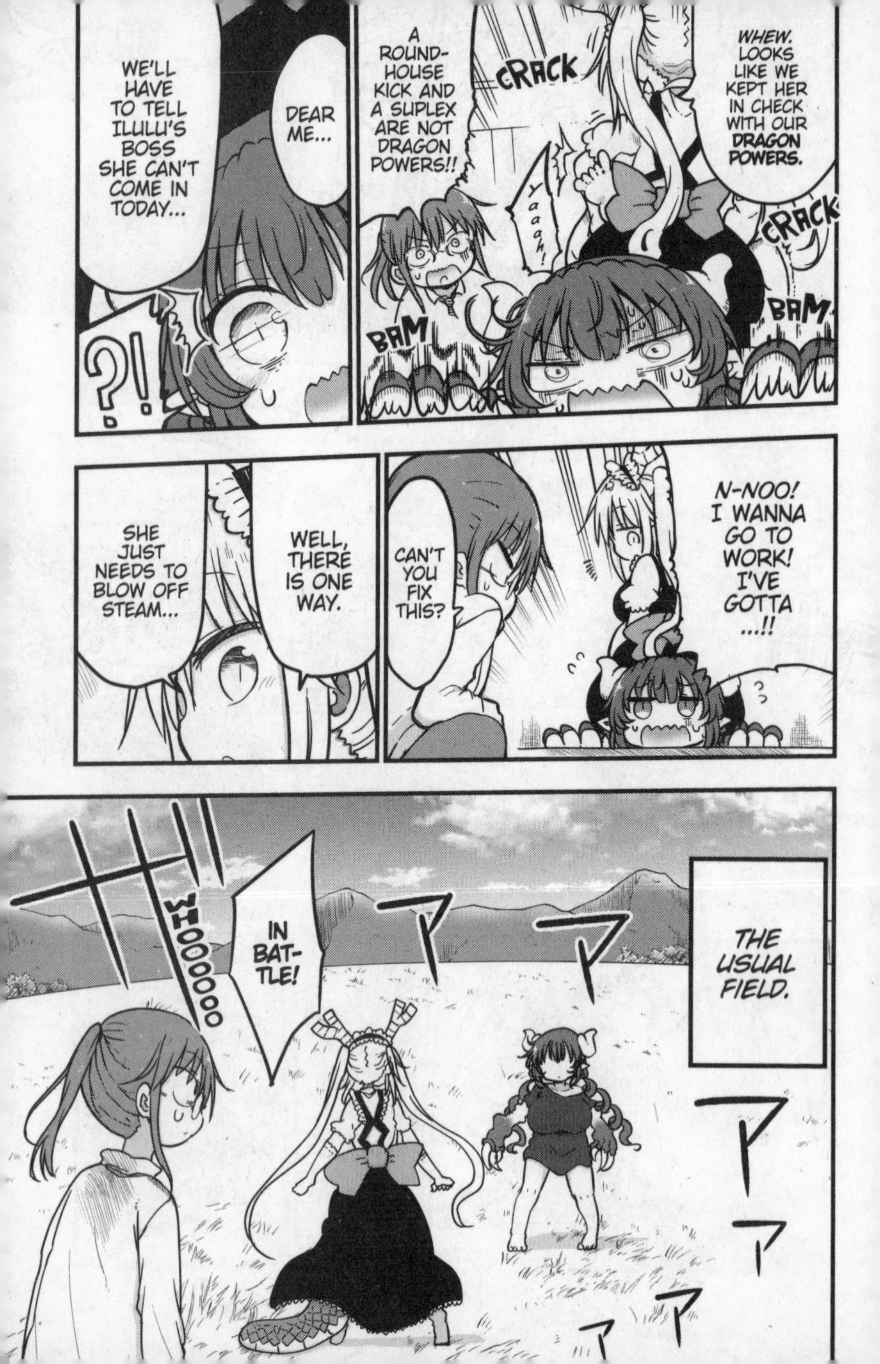
WHEW. LOOKS LIKE WE KEPT HER IN CHECK WITH OUR DRAGON POWERS.
CRACK
CRACK
Yaaah!
A ROUND-HOUSE KICK AND A SUPLEX ARE NOT DRAGON POWERS!!
BAM
BAM
DEAR ME...
WE'LL HAVE TO TELL ILULU'S BOSS SHE CAN'T COME IN TODAY...
?!
N-NOO! I WANNA GO TO WORK! I'VE GOTTA ...!!
CAN'T YOU FIX THIS?
WELL, THERE IS ONE WAY.
SHE JUST NEEDS TO BLOW OFF STEAM...
THE USUAL FIELD.
IN BAT-TLE!
WHOOOOOOO

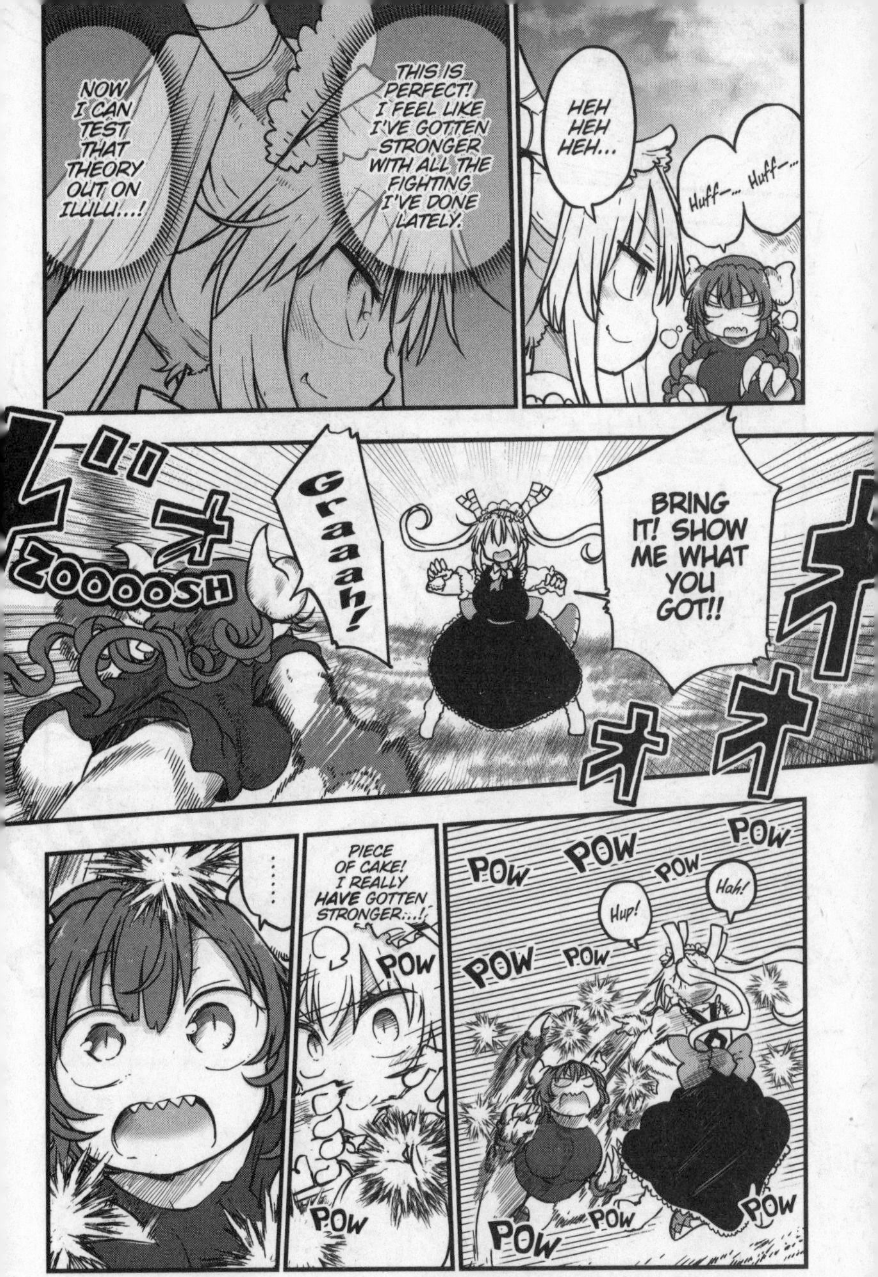
HEH HEH HEH...
Huff—... Huff—...
THIS IS PERFECT! I FEEL LIKE I'VE GOTTEN STRONGER WITH ALL THE FIGHTING I'VE DONE LATELY.
NOW I CAN TEST THAT THEORY OUT ON ILULU...!
BRING IT! SHOW ME WHAT YOU GOT!!
Graaah!
ZOOOOOSH
POW POW POW POW
Hah!
Hup!
POW POW
POW POW POW POW
PIECE OF CAKE! I REALLY HAVE GOTTEN STRONGER...!
POW
POW
......

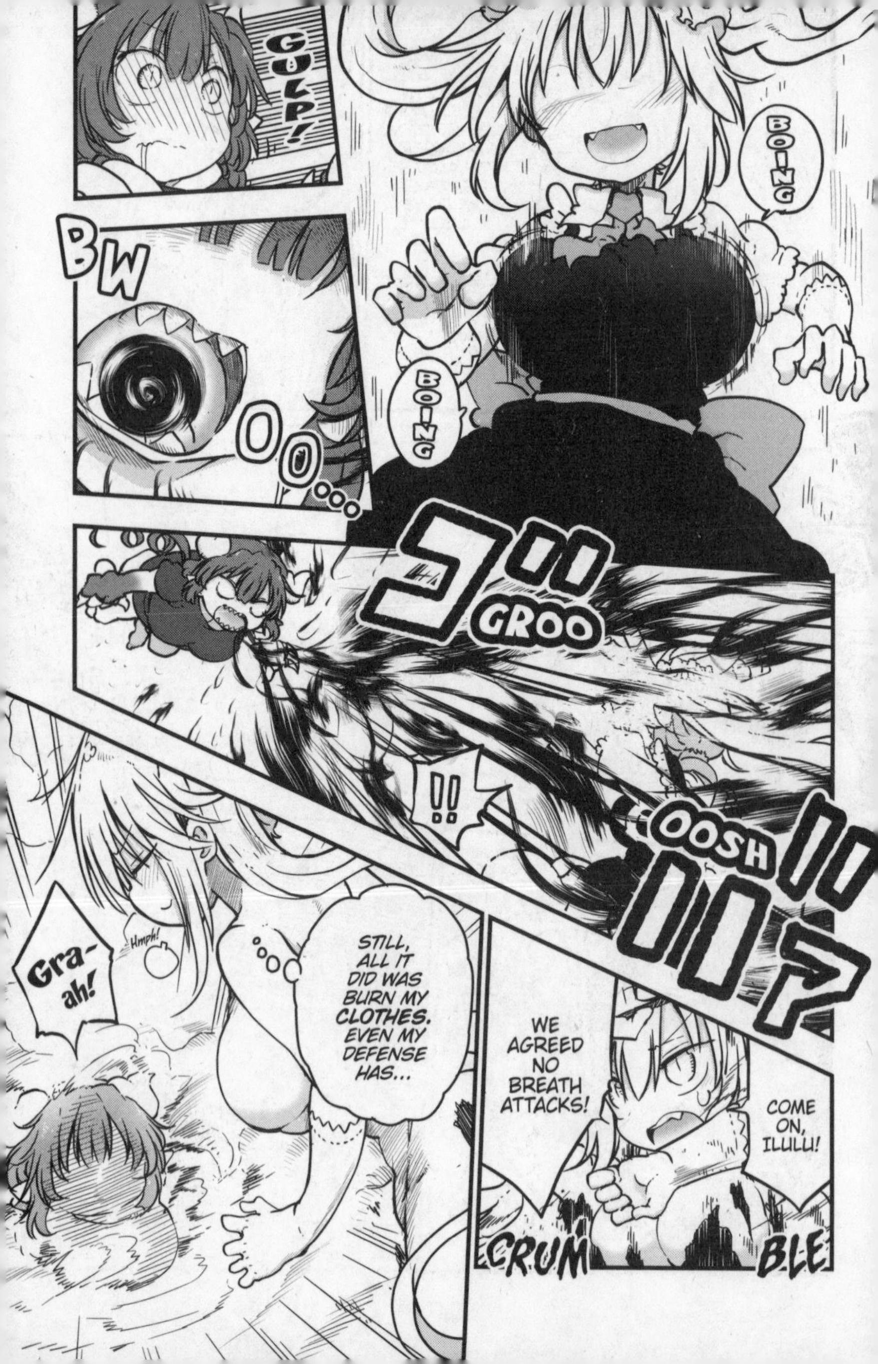
BOING
BOING
GULP!
BWOOO...
GROO
!!
OOSH
WE AGREED NO BREATH ATTACKS!
COME ON, ILULU!
CRUMBLE
STILL, ALL IT DID WAS BURN MY CLOTHES. EVEN MY DEFENSE HAS...
Hmph!
Gra-ah!

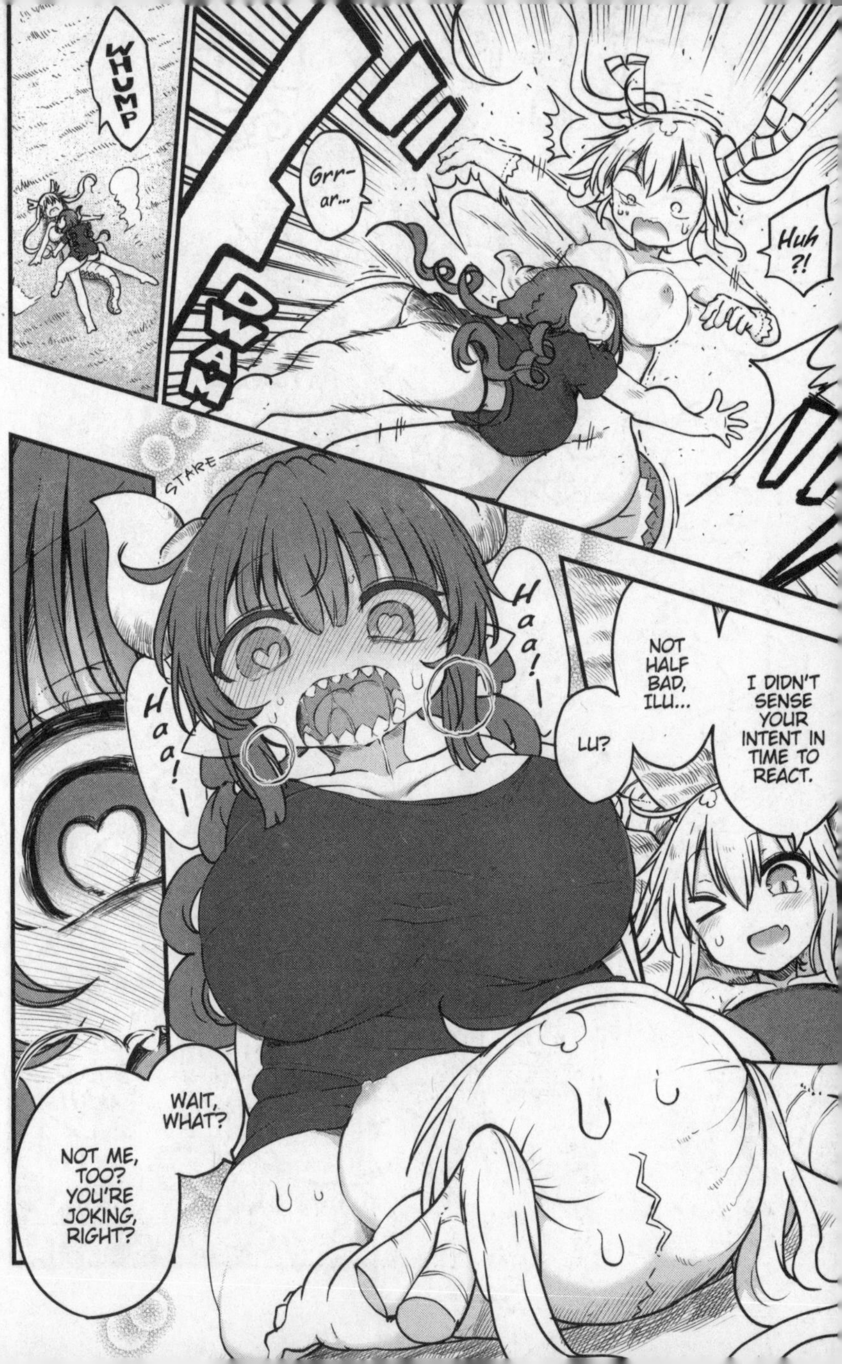
Huh ?!
Grr-ar...
DWAM
WHUMP
I DIDN'T SENSE YOUR INTENT IN TIME TO REACT.
NOT HALF BAD, ILU...
LU?
STARE
Haa!
Haa!
WAIT, WHAT?
NOT ME, TOO? YOU'RE JOKING, RIGHT?

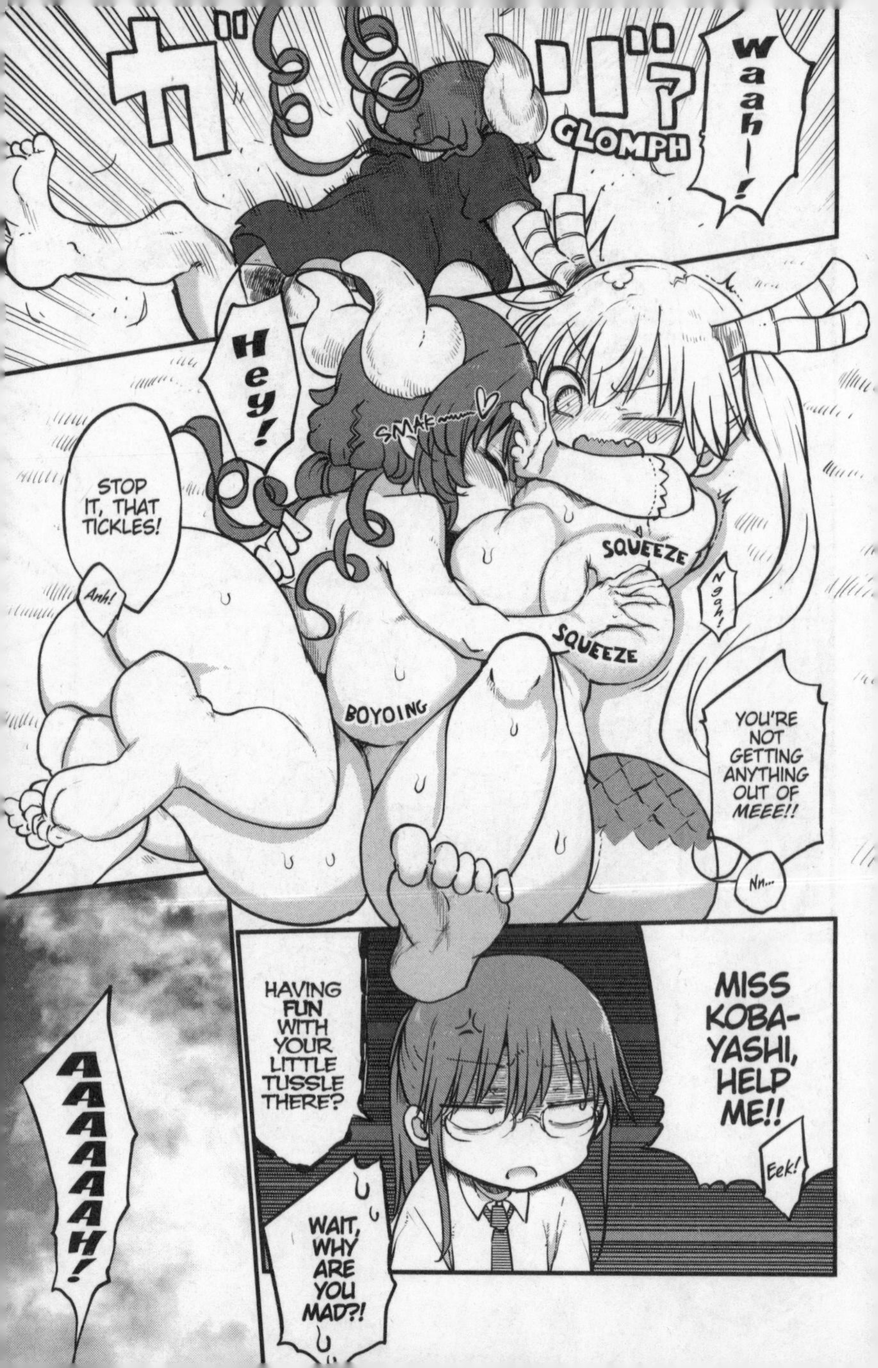
Waah--!
GLOMPH
Hey!
SMAK~
STOP IT, THAT TICKLES!
SQUEEZE
Ngah!
Anh!
SQUEEZE
BOYOING
YOU'RE NOT GETTING ANYTHING OUT OF MEEE!!
Nn...
MISS KOBAYASHI, HELP ME!!
HAVING FUN WITH YOUR LITTLE TUSSLE THERE?
Eek!
WAIT, WHY ARE YOU MAD?!
AAAAAAAH!

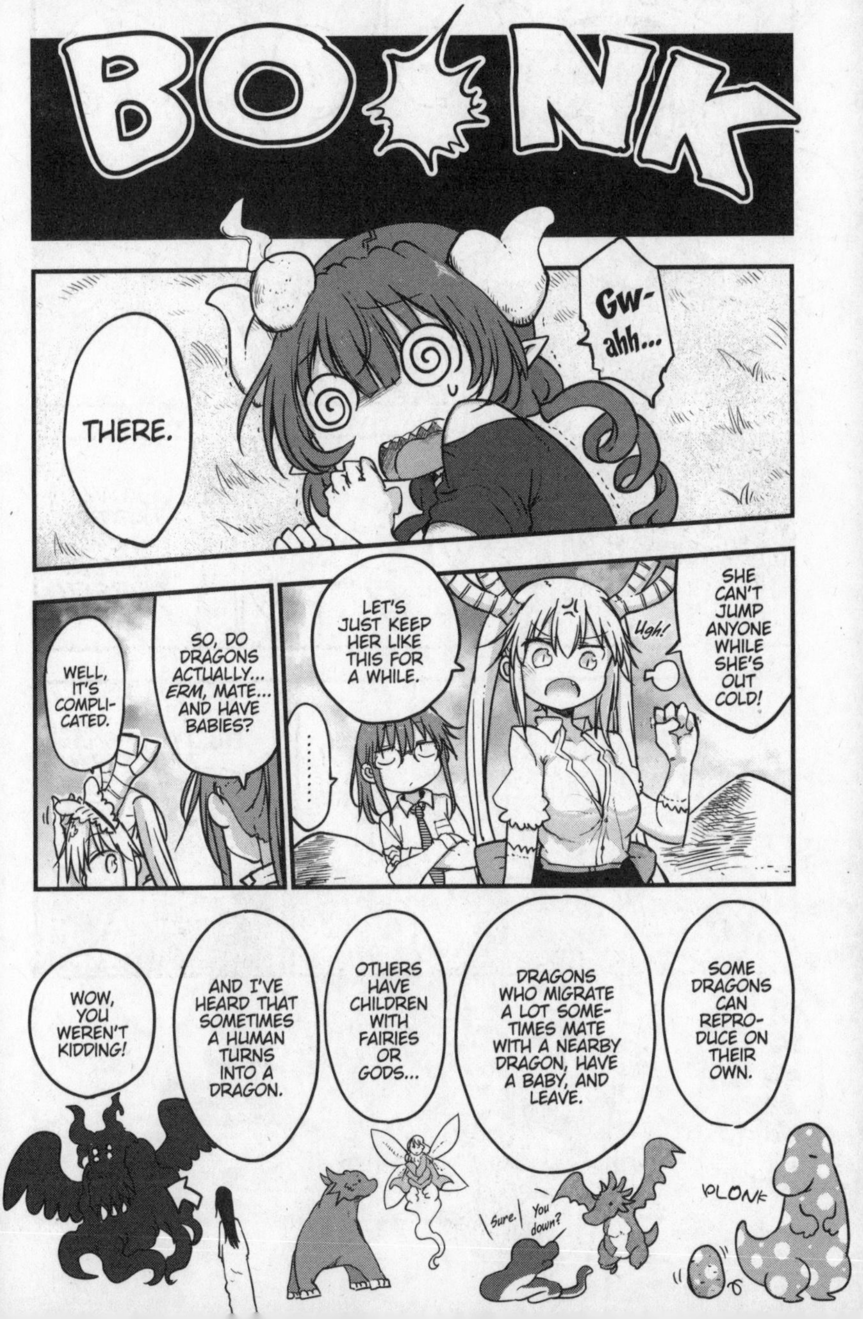
BONK
Gw-ahh...
THERE.
SHE CAN'T JUMP ANYONE WHILE SHE'S OUT COLD!
Ugh!
LET'S JUST KEEP HER LIKE THIS FOR A WHILE.
......
SO, DO DRAGONS ACTUALLY... ERM, MATE... AND HAVE BABIES?
WELL, IT'S COMPLICATED.
SOME DRAGONS CAN REPRODUCE ON THEIR OWN.
PLONK
DRAGONS WHO MIGRATE A LOT SOMETIMES MATE WITH A NEARBY DRAGON, HAVE A BABY, AND LEAVE.
You down?
Sure.
OTHERS HAVE CHILDREN WITH FAIRIES OR GODS...
AND I'VE HEARD THAT SOMETIMES A HUMAN TURNS INTO A DRAGON.
WOW, YOU WEREN'T KIDDING!

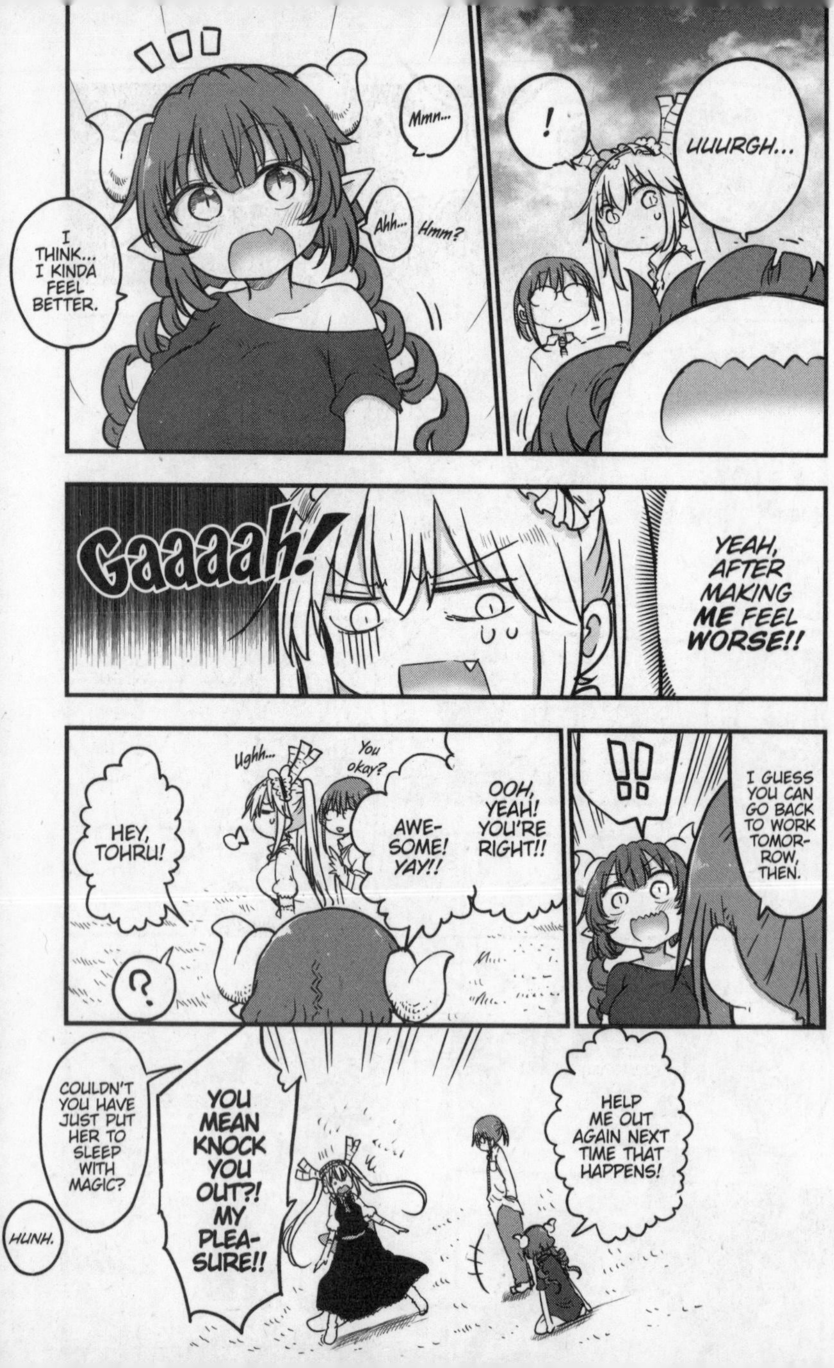
UUURGH...
!
Mmn...
Ahh...
Hmm?
I THINK... I KINDA FEEL BETTER.
YEAH, AFTER MAKING ME FEEL WORSE!!
Gaaaah!
!!
I GUESS YOU CAN GO BACK TO WORK TOMORROW, THEN.
OOH, YEAH! YOU'RE RIGHT!!
AWE-SOME! YAY!!
You okay?
Ughh...
HEY, TOHRU!
?
HELP ME OUT AGAIN NEXT TIME THAT HAPPENS!
YOU MEAN KNOCK YOU OUT?! MY PLEA-SURE!!
COULDN'T YOU HAVE JUST PUT HER TO SLEEP WITH MAGIC?
HUNH.

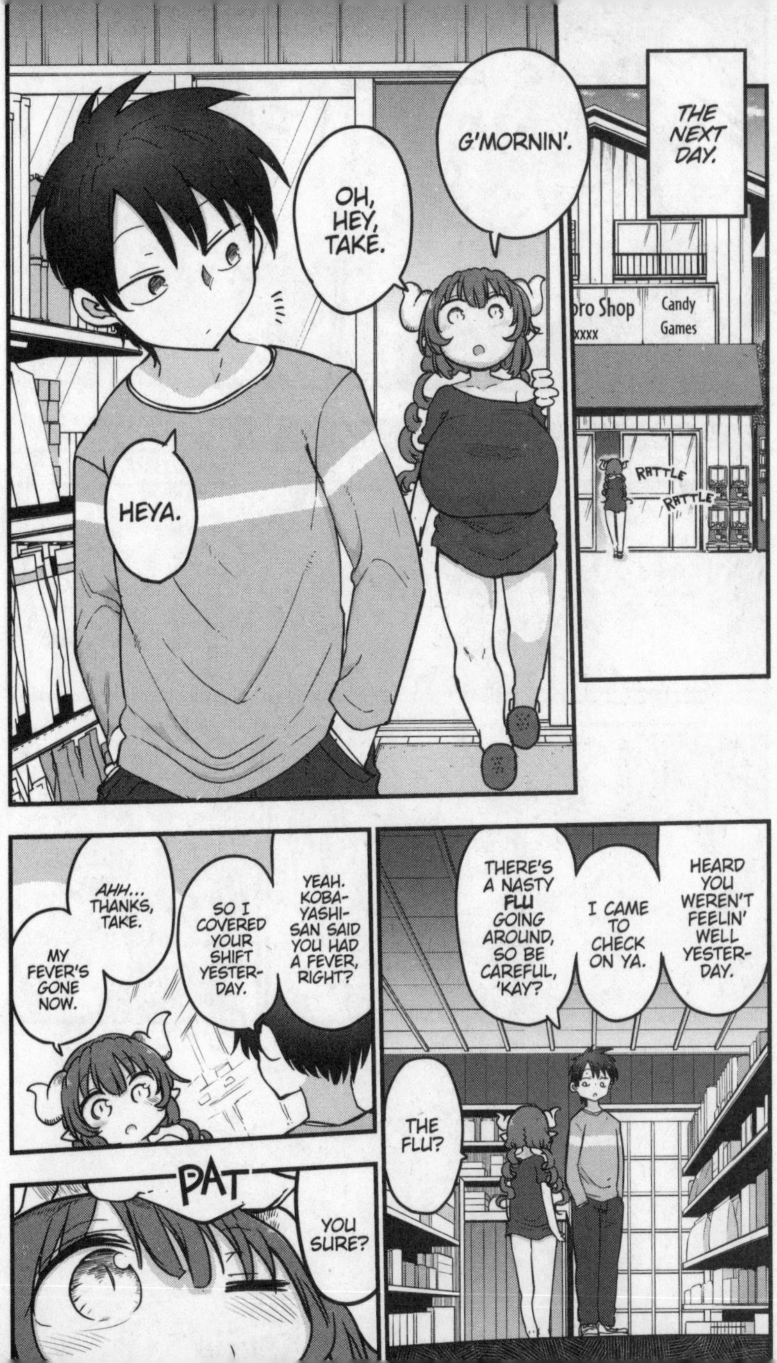
THE NEXT DAY.
ro Shop
Candy Games
RATTLE RATTLE
G'MORNIN'.
OH, HEY, TAKE.
HEYA.
HEARD YOU WEREN'T FEELIN' WELL YESTER-DAY.
I CAME TO CHECK ON YA.
THERE'S A NASTY FLU GOING AROUND, SO BE CAREFUL, 'KAY?
THE FLU?
YEAH. KOBA-YASHI-SAN SAID YOU HAD A FEVER, RIGHT?
SO I COVERED YOUR SHIFT YESTER-DAY.
AHH... THANKS, TAKE.
MY FEVER'S GONE NOW.
PAT
YOU SURE?

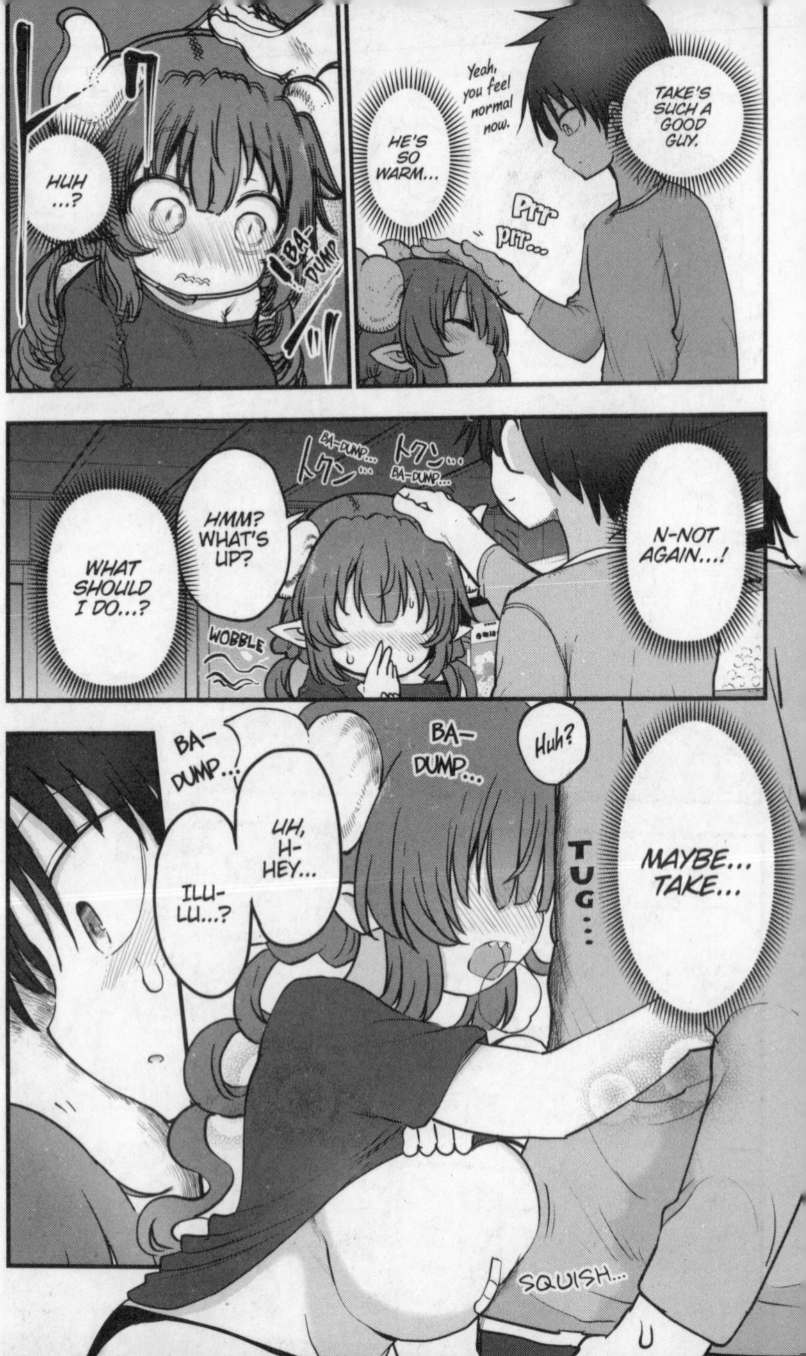
TAKE'S SUCH A GOOD GUY.
Yeah, you feel normal now.
HE'S SO WARM...
Prrr prrr...
HUH ...?
BA-DUMP
N-NOT AGAIN...!
トクン... BA-DUMP...
BA-DUMP... トクン...
HMM? WHAT'S UP?
WHAT SHOULD I DO...?
WOBBLE
MAYBE... TAKE...
Huh?
BA-DUMP...
TUG...
BA-DUMP...
UH, H-HEY...
ILU-LU...?
SQUISH...

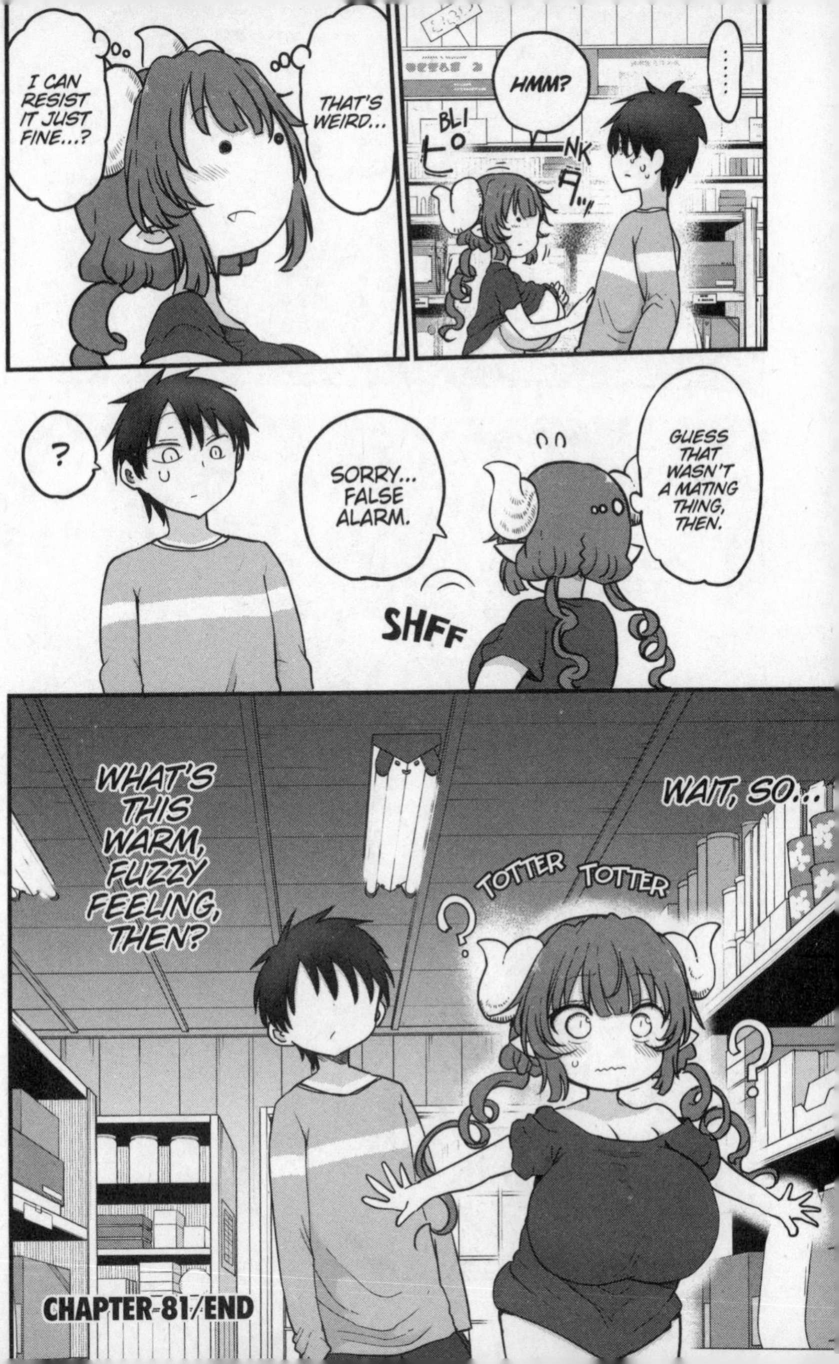
......
HMM?
BLINK
ダッ
THAT'S WEIRD...
I CAN RESIST IT JUST FINE...?
GUESS THAT WASN'T A MATING THING, THEN.
SORRY... FALSE ALARM.
?
SHFF
WAIT, SO...
WHAT'S THIS WARM, FUZZY FEELING, THEN?
TOTTER TOTTER
CHAPTER 81/END

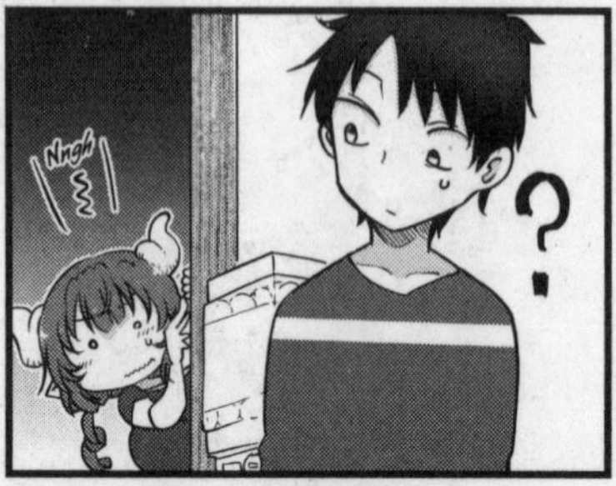
Nngh

Miss Kobayashi's Dragon Maid

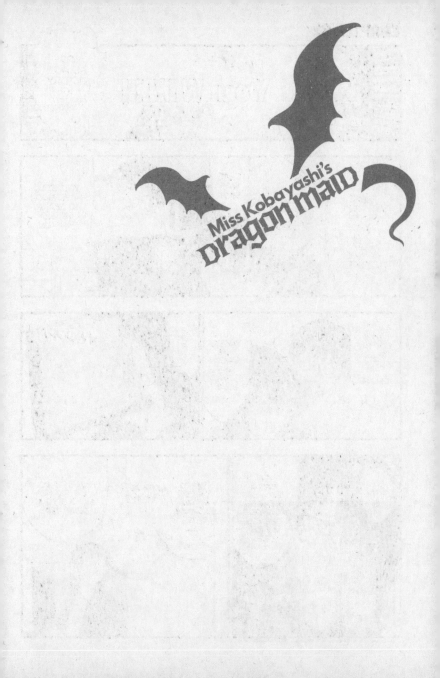

CHAPTER 82

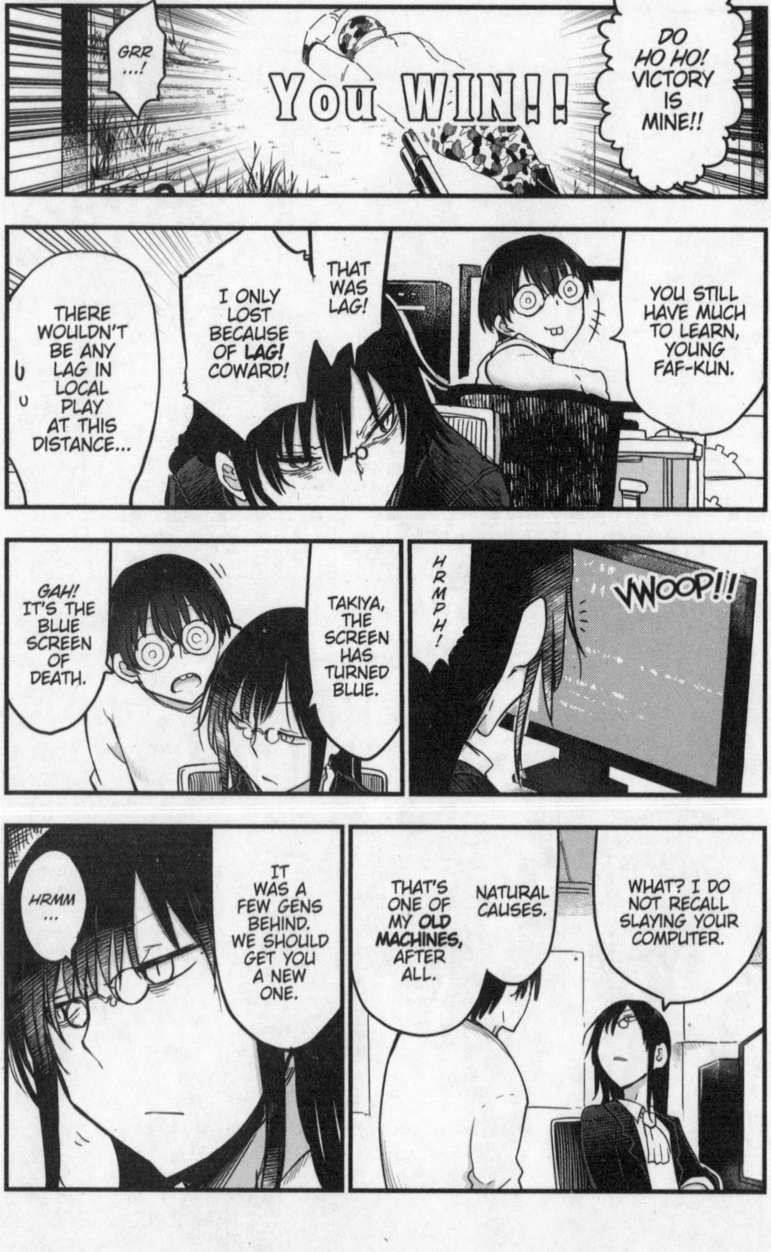
DO HO HO! VICTORY IS MINE!!
You WIN!!
GRR ...!
YOU STILL HAVE MUCH TO LEARN, YOUNG FAF-KUN.
THAT WAS LAG!
I ONLY LOST BECAUSE OF **LAG!** COWARD!
THERE WOULDN'T BE ANY LAG IN LOCAL PLAY AT THIS DISTANCE...
VWOOP!!
HRMPH!
TAKIYA, THE SCREEN HAS TURNED BLUE.
GAH! IT'S THE BLUE SCREEN OF DEATH.
WHAT? I DO NOT RECALL SLAYING YOUR COMPUTER.
NATURAL CAUSES.
THAT'S ONE OF MY **OLD MACHINES,** AFTER ALL.
IT WAS A FEW GENS BEHIND. WE SHOULD GET YOU A NEW ONE.
HRMM ...

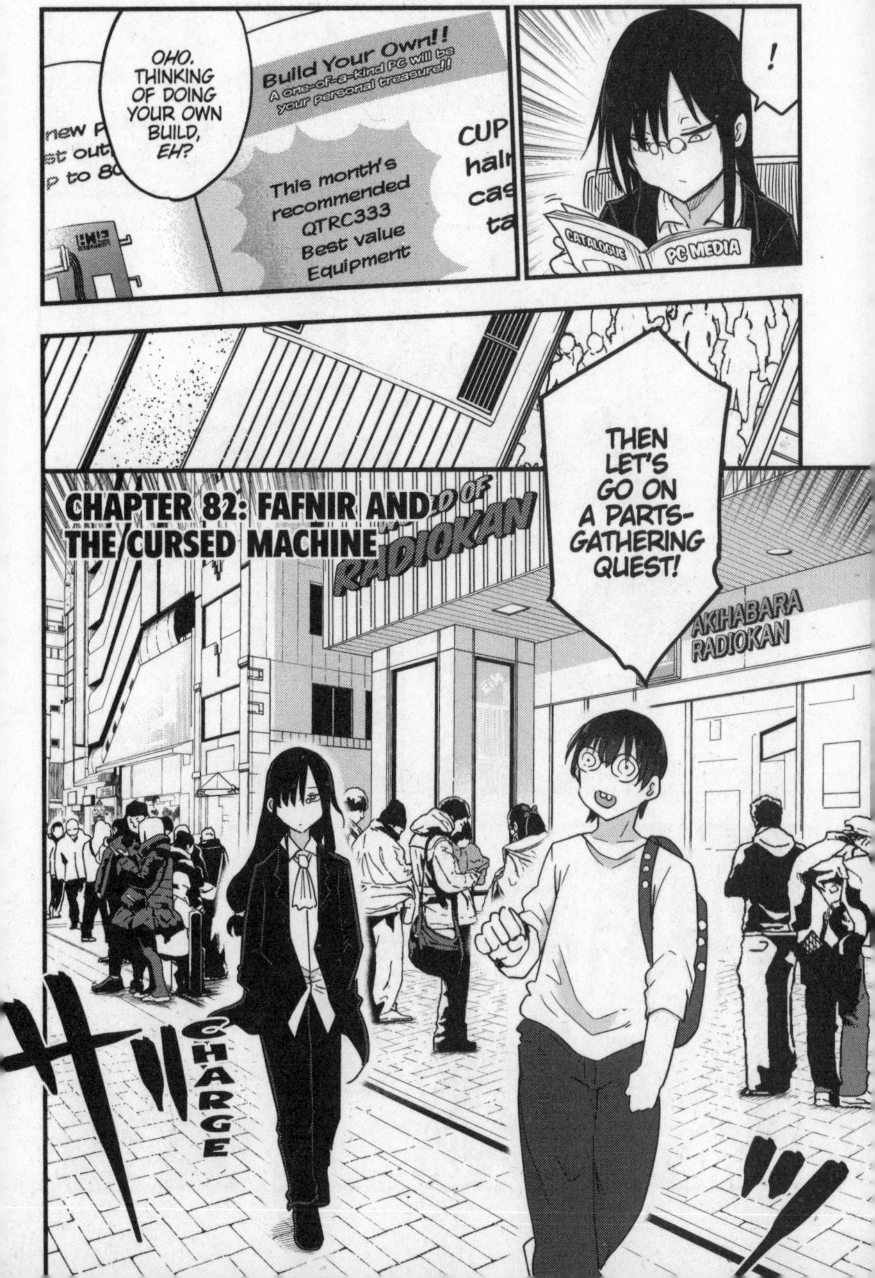
!
CATALOGUE
PC MEDIA
OHO. THINKING OF DOING YOUR OWN BUILD, EH?
Build Your Own!!
A One-of-a-kind PC will be your personal treasure!!
This month's recommended QTRC333 Best value Equipment
THEN LET'S GO ON A PARTS-GATHERING QUEST!
CHAPTER 82: FAFNIR AND THE CURSED MACHINE
RADIOKAN
AKIHABARA RADIOKAN
CHARGE

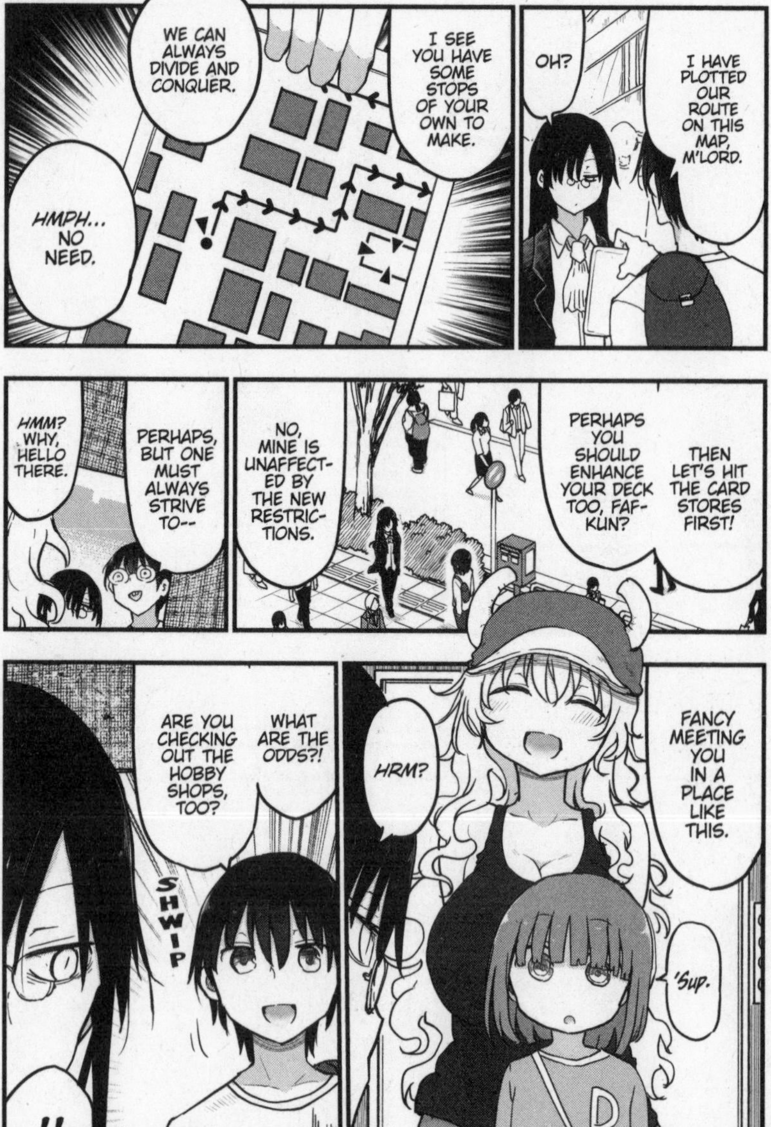
I HAVE PLOTTED OUR ROUTE ON THIS MAP, M'LORD.
OH?
I SEE YOU HAVE SOME STOPS OF YOUR OWN TO MAKE.
WE CAN ALWAYS DIVIDE AND CONQUER.
HMPH... NO NEED.
THEN LET'S HIT THE CARD STORES FIRST!
PERHAPS YOU SHOULD ENHANCE YOUR DECK TOO, FAF-KUN?
NO, MINE IS UNAFFECTED BY THE NEW RESTRICTIONS.
PERHAPS, BUT ONE MUST ALWAYS STRIVE TO--
HMM? WHY, HELLO THERE.
FANCY MEETING YOU IN A PLACE LIKE THIS.
HRM?
'Sup.
WHAT ARE THE ODDS?!
ARE YOU CHECKING OUT THE HOBBY SHOPS, TOO?
SHWIP
!!

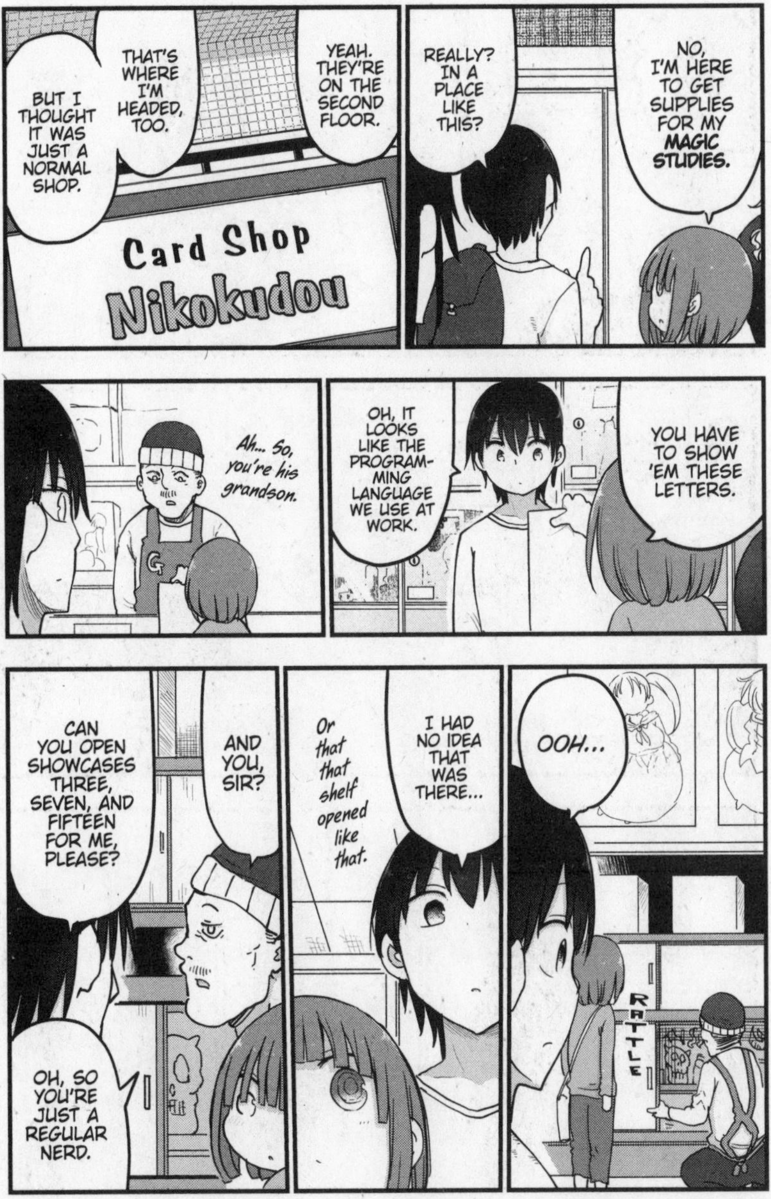
NO, I'M HERE TO GET SUPPLIES FOR MY **MAGIC STUDIES.**
REALLY? IN A PLACE LIKE THIS?
YEAH. THEY'RE ON THE SECOND FLOOR.
THAT'S WHERE I'M HEADED, TOO.
BUT I THOUGHT IT WAS JUST A NORMAL SHOP.
Card Shop Nikokudou
YOU HAVE TO SHOW 'EM THESE LETTERS.
OH, IT LOOKS LIKE THE PROGRAMMING LANGUAGE WE USE AT WORK.
Ah... So, you're his grandson.
OOH...
RATTLE
I HAD NO IDEA THAT WAS THERE...
Or that that shelf opened like that.
...
AND YOU, SIR?
CAN YOU OPEN SHOWCASES THREE, SEVEN, AND FIFTEEN FOR ME, PLEASE?
OH, SO YOU'RE JUST A REGULAR NERD.

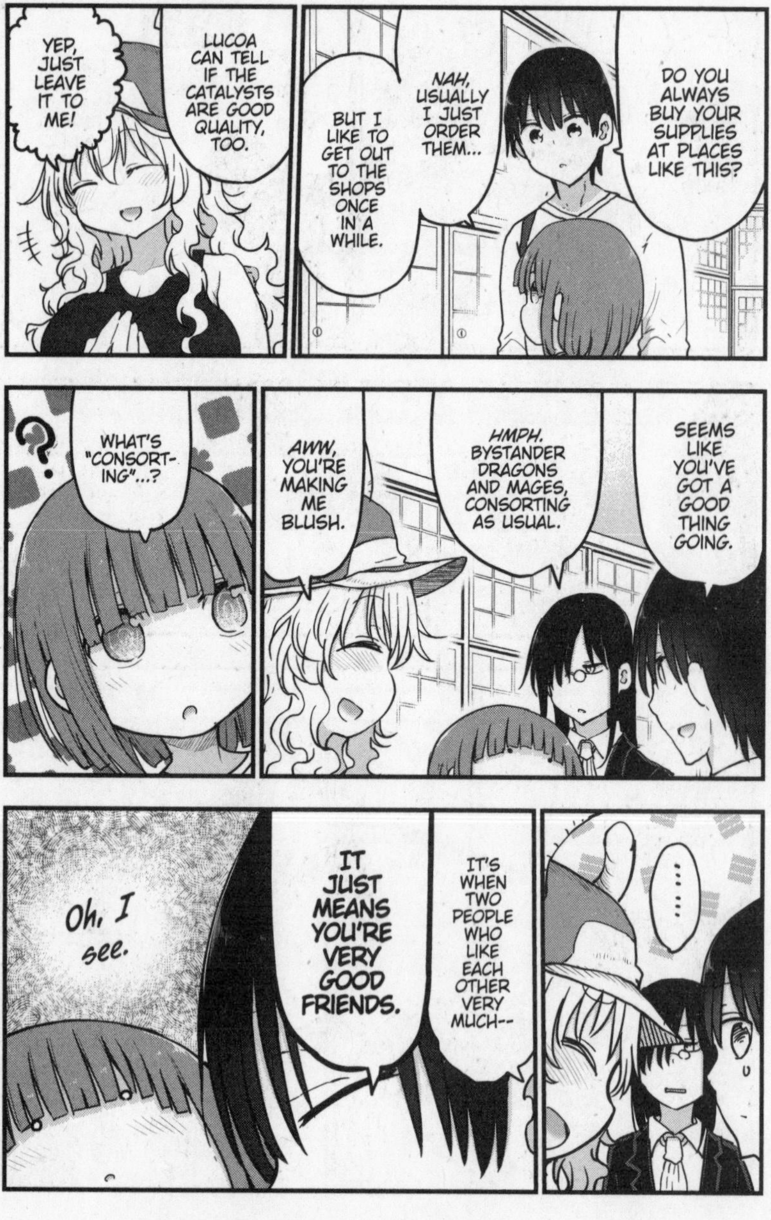
DO YOU ALWAYS BUY YOUR SUPPLIES AT PLACES LIKE THIS?
NAH, USUALLY I JUST ORDER THEM...
BUT I LIKE TO GET OUT TO THE SHOPS ONCE IN A WHILE.
LUCOA CAN TELL IF THE CATALYSTS ARE GOOD QUALITY, TOO.
YEP, JUST LEAVE IT TO ME!
SEEMS LIKE YOU'VE GOT A GOOD THING GOING.
HMPH. BYSTANDER DRAGONS AND MAGES, CONSORTING AS USUAL.
AWW, YOU'RE MAKING ME BLUSH.
?
WHAT'S "CONSORTING"...?
......
IT'S WHEN TWO PEOPLE WHO LIKE EACH OTHER VERY MUCH--
IT JUST MEANS YOU'RE VERY GOOD FRIENDS.
Oh, I see.

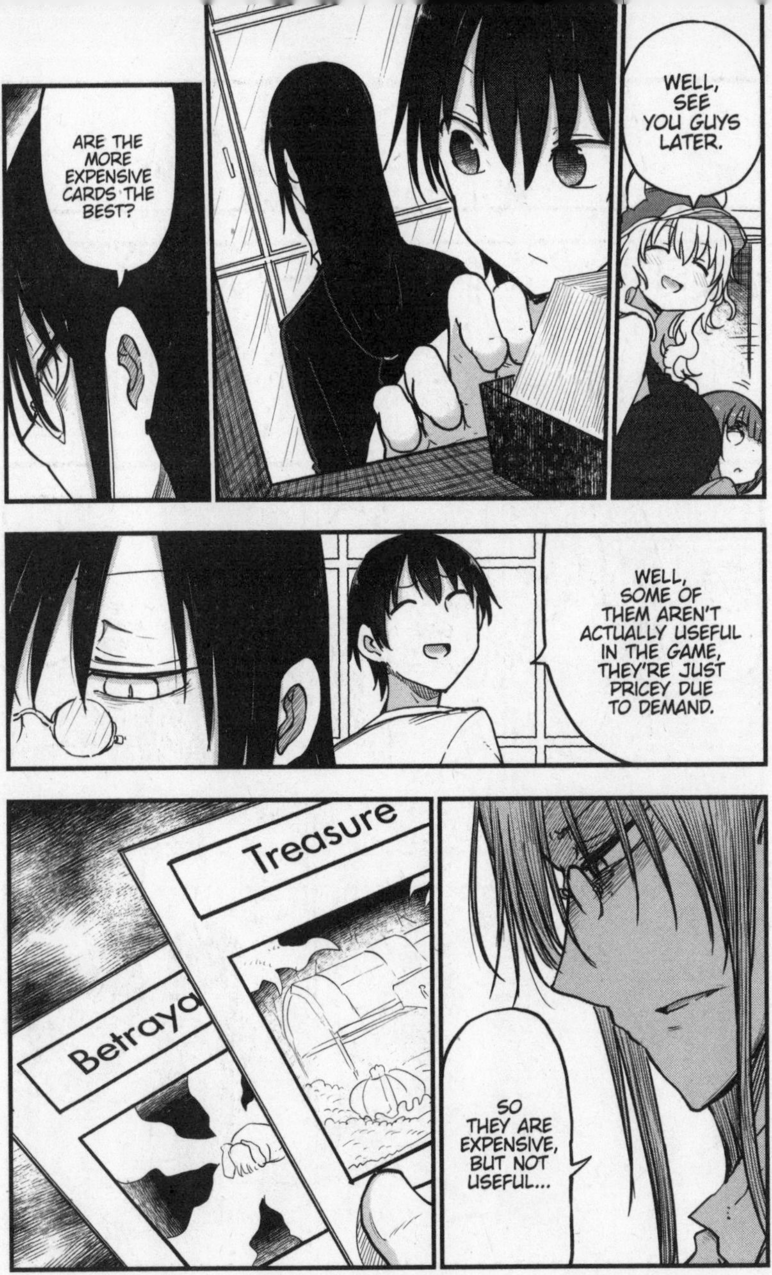
WELL, SEE YOU GUYS LATER.
ARE THE MORE EXPENSIVE CARDS THE BEST?
WELL, SOME OF THEM AREN'T ACTUALLY USEFUL IN THE GAME, THEY'RE JUST PRICEY DUE TO DEMAND.
SO THEY ARE EXPENSIVE, BUT NOT USEFUL...
Treasure
Betraya

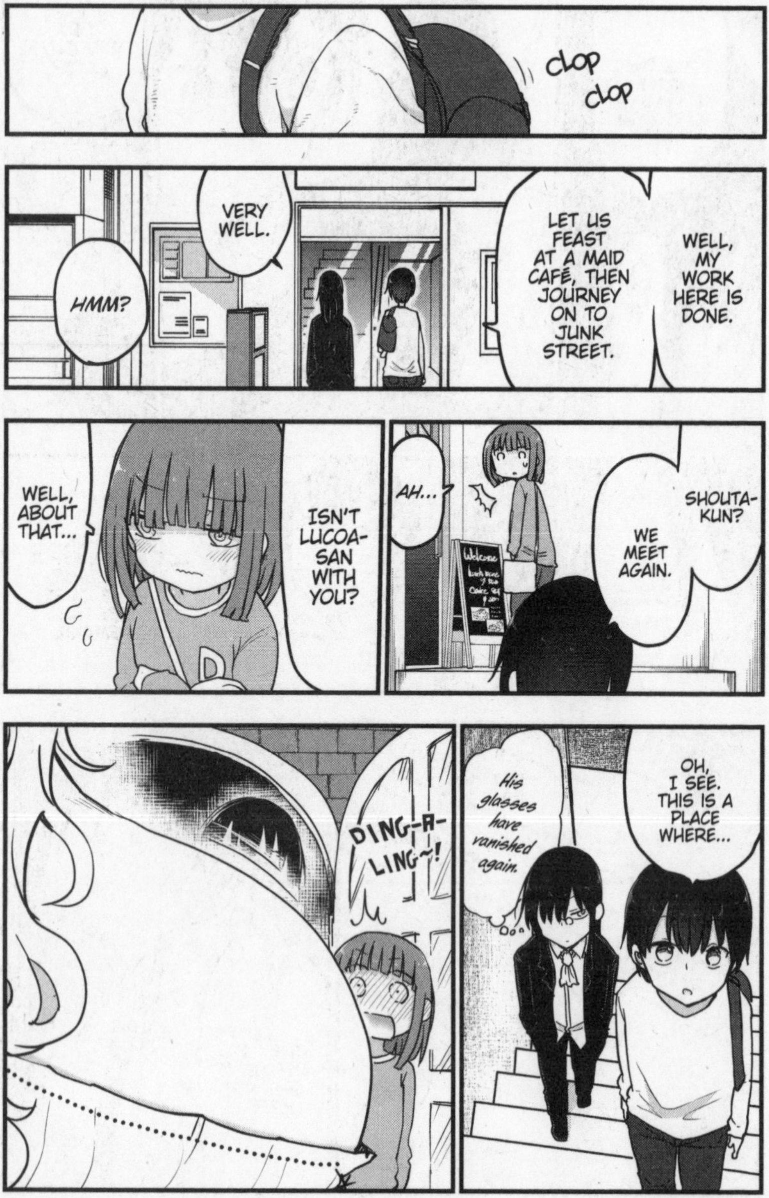
CLOP
CLOP
WELL, MY WORK HERE IS DONE.
LET US FEAST AT A MAID CAFÉ, THEN JOURNEY ON TO JUNK STREET.
VERY WELL.
HMM?
SHOUTA-KUN?
WE MEET AGAIN.
AH...
ISN'T LUCOA-SAN WITH YOU?
WELL, ABOUT THAT...
OH, I SEE. THIS IS A PLACE WHERE...
His glasses have vanished again.
DING-A-LING~!

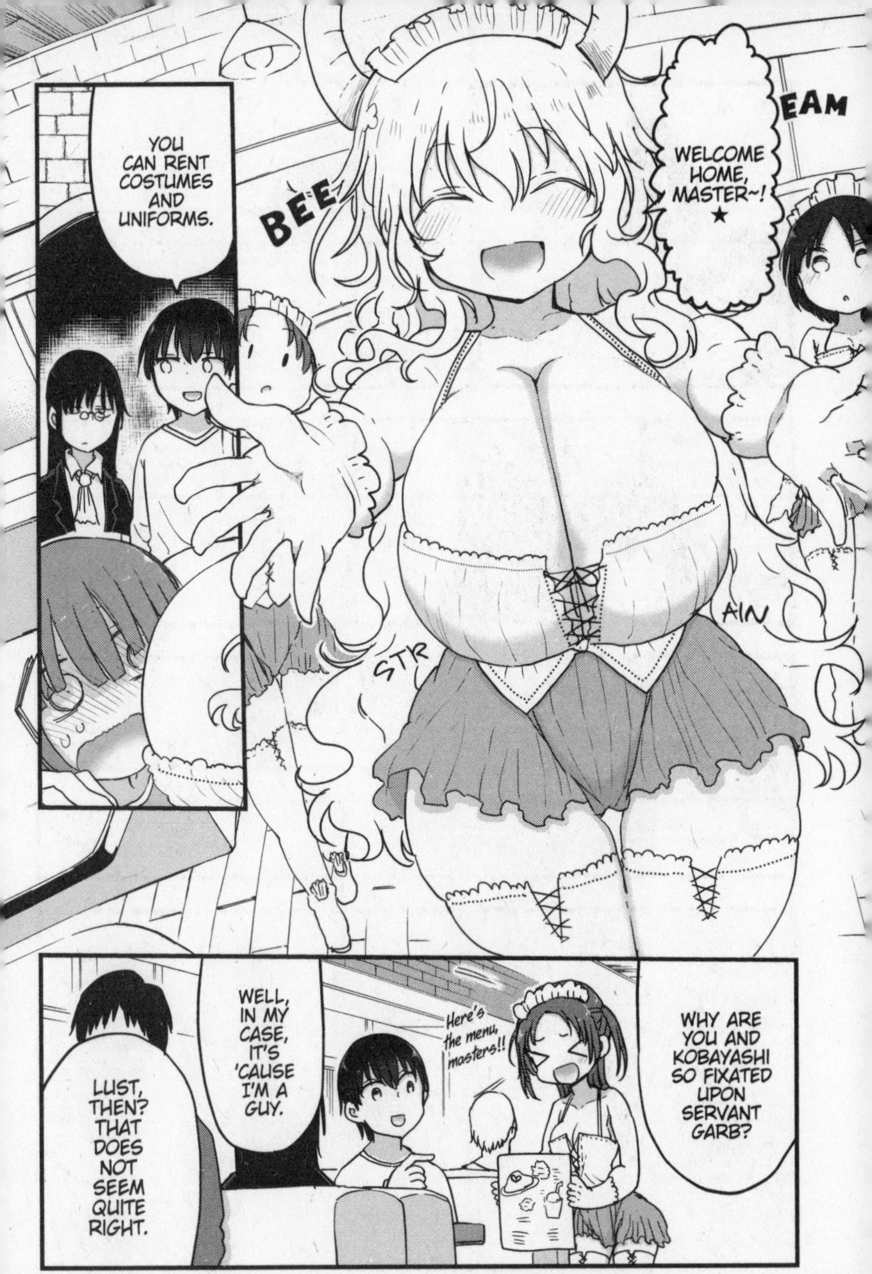
WELCOME HOME, MASTER~! ★
EAM
BEE
AIN
STR
YOU CAN RENT COSTUMES AND UNIFORMS.
WHY ARE YOU AND KOBAYASHI SO FIXATED UPON SERVANT GARB?
Here's the menu, masters!!
WELL, IN MY CASE, IT'S 'CAUSE I'M A GUY.
LUST, THEN? THAT DOES NOT SEEM QUITE RIGHT.

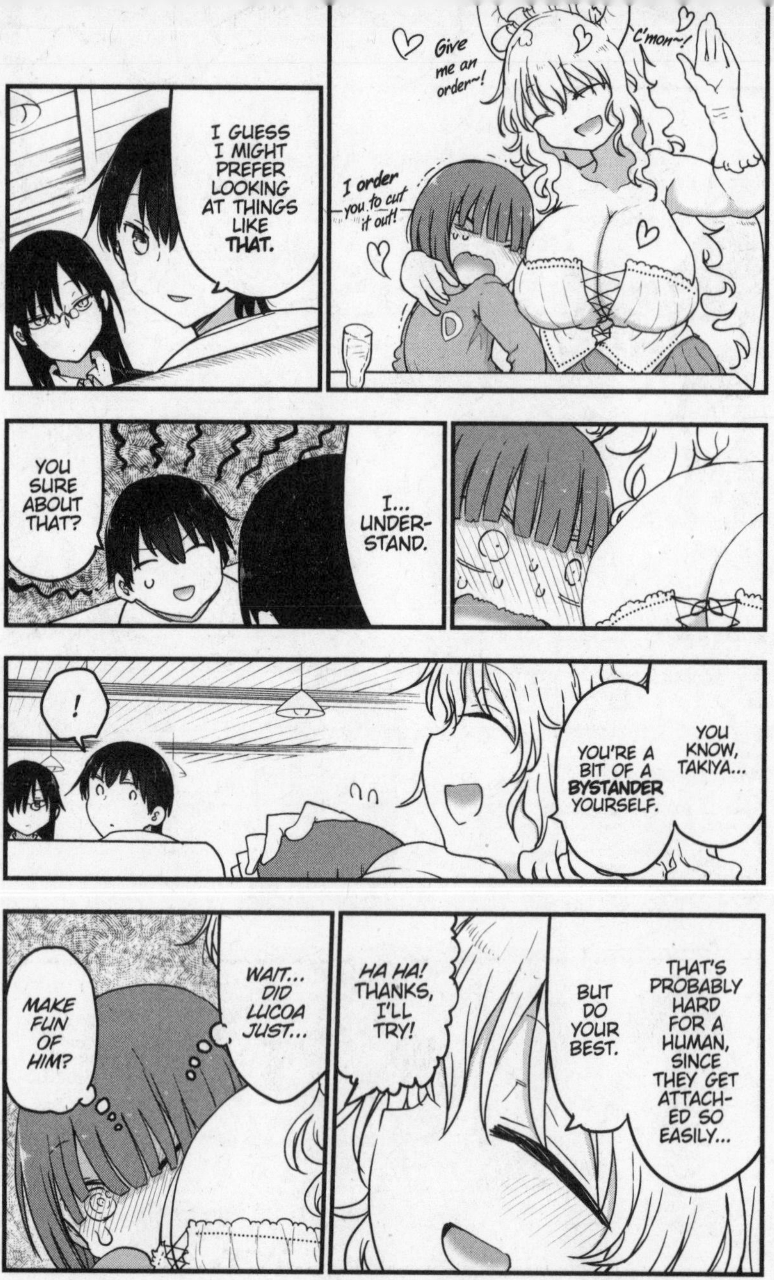
C'mon~!
Give me an order~!
I order you to cut it out!
I GUESS I MIGHT PREFER LOOKING AT THINGS LIKE **THAT.**
I... UNDERSTAND.
YOU SURE ABOUT THAT?
YOU KNOW, TAKIYA...
YOU'RE A BIT OF A **BYSTANDER** YOURSELF.
!
THAT'S PROBABLY HARD FOR A HUMAN, SINCE THEY GET ATTACHED SO EASILY...
BUT DO YOUR BEST.
HA HA! THANKS, I'LL TRY!
WAIT... DID LUCOA JUST...
MAKE FUN OF HIM?

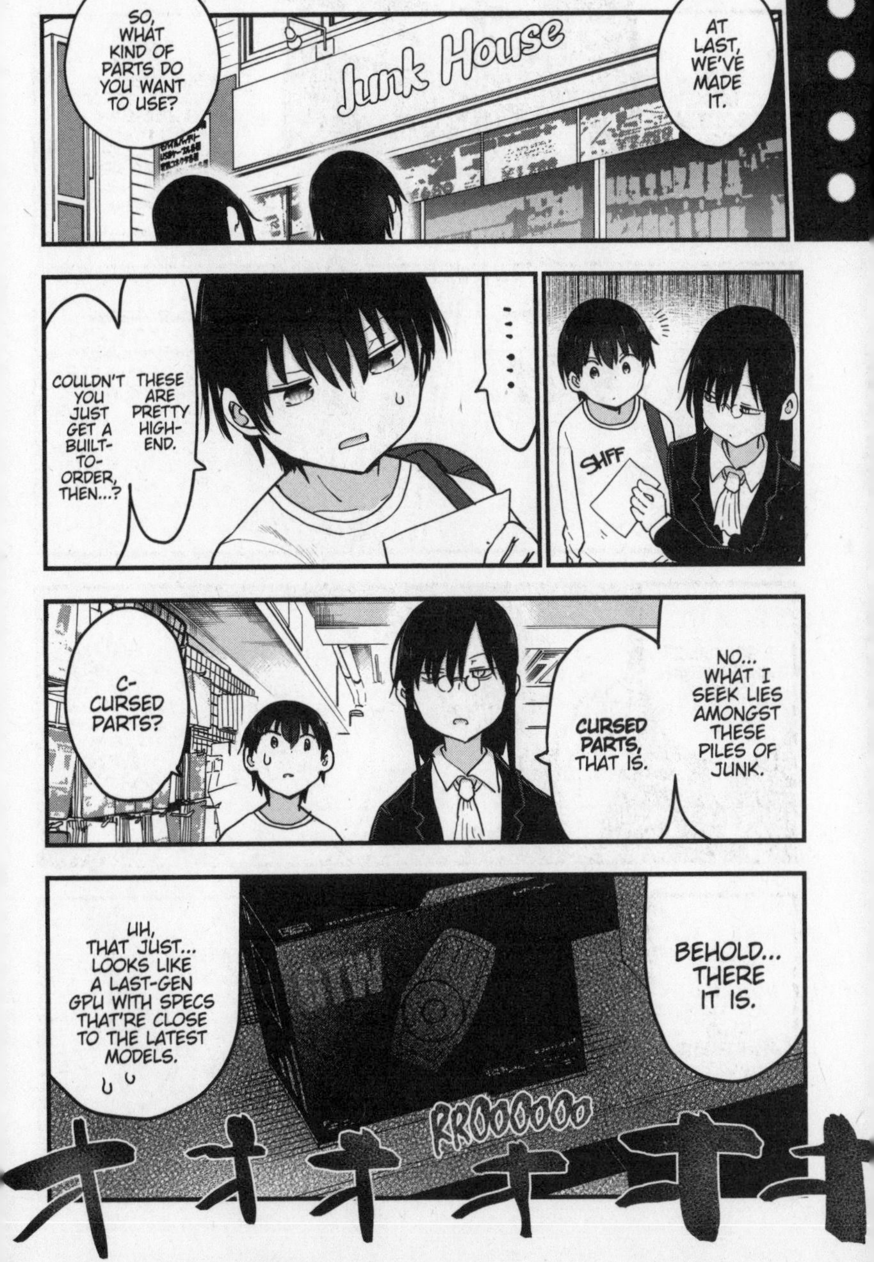
AT LAST, WE'VE MADE IT.
Junk House
SO, WHAT KIND OF PARTS DO YOU WANT TO USE?
SHFF
......
THESE ARE PRETTY HIGH-END.
COULDN'T YOU JUST GET A BUILT-TO-ORDER, THEN...?
NO... WHAT I SEEK LIES AMONGST THESE PILES OF JUNK.
CURSED PARTS, THAT IS.
C-CURSED PARTS?
BEHOLD... THERE IT IS.
KROOOOOO
UH, THAT JUST... LOOKS LIKE A LAST-GEN GPU WITH SPECS THAT'RE CLOSE TO THE LATEST MODELS.

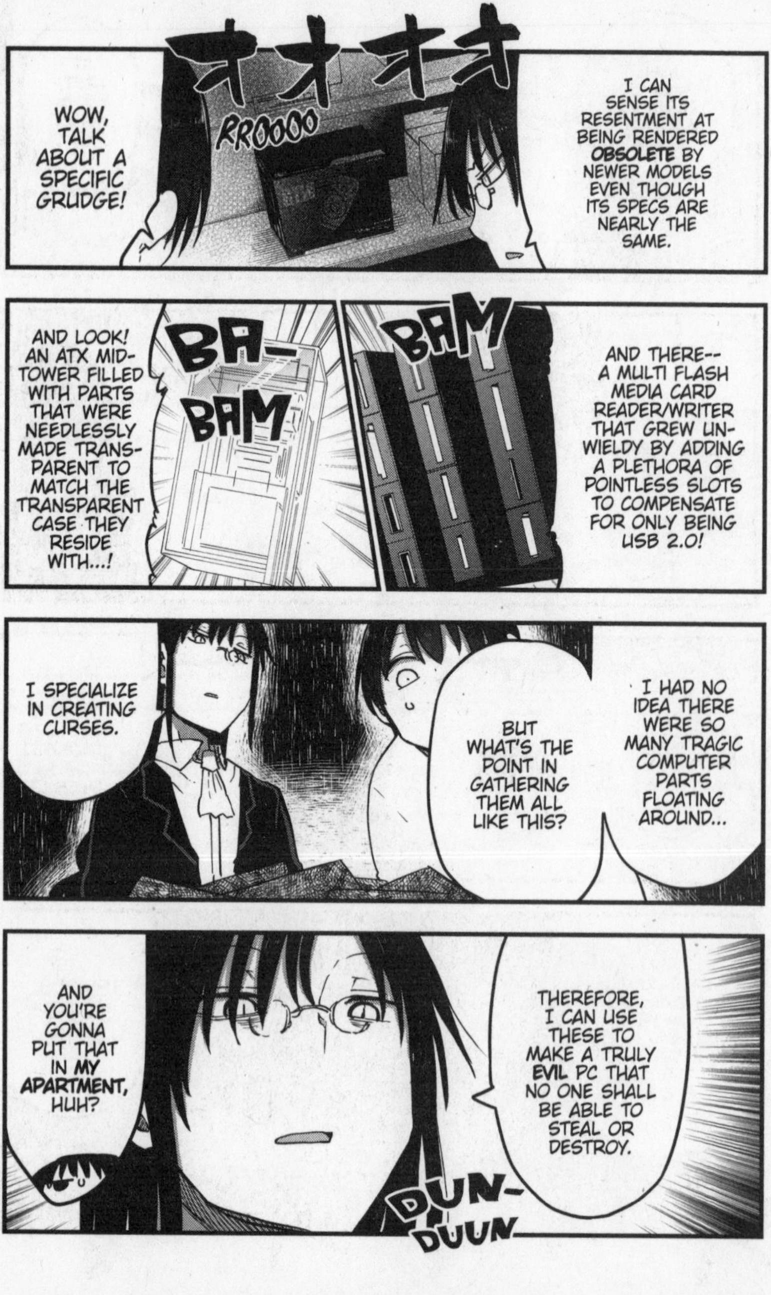
オオオオ
I CAN SENSE ITS RESENTMENT AT BEING RENDERED **OBSOLETE** BY NEWER MODELS EVEN THOUGH ITS SPECS ARE NEARLY THE SAME.
KROOOO
WOW, TALK ABOUT A SPECIFIC GRUDGE!
BAM
AND THERE-- A MULTI FLASH MEDIA CARD READER/WRITER THAT GREW UNWIELDY BY ADDING A PLETHORA OF POINTLESS SLOTS TO COMPENSATE FOR ONLY BEING USB 2.0!
BA-BAM
AND LOOK! AN ATX MID-TOWER FILLED WITH PARTS THAT WERE NEEDLESSLY MADE TRANSPARENT TO MATCH THE TRANSPARENT CASE THEY RESIDE WITH...!
I HAD NO IDEA THERE WERE SO MANY TRAGIC COMPUTER PARTS FLOATING AROUND...
BUT WHAT'S THE POINT IN GATHERING THEM ALL LIKE THIS?
I SPECIALIZE IN CREATING CURSES.
THEREFORE, I CAN USE THESE TO MAKE A TRULY **EVIL** PC THAT NO ONE SHALL BE ABLE TO STEAL OR DESTROY.
DUN-DUUN
AND YOU'RE GONNA PUT THAT IN **MY APARTMENT**, HUH?

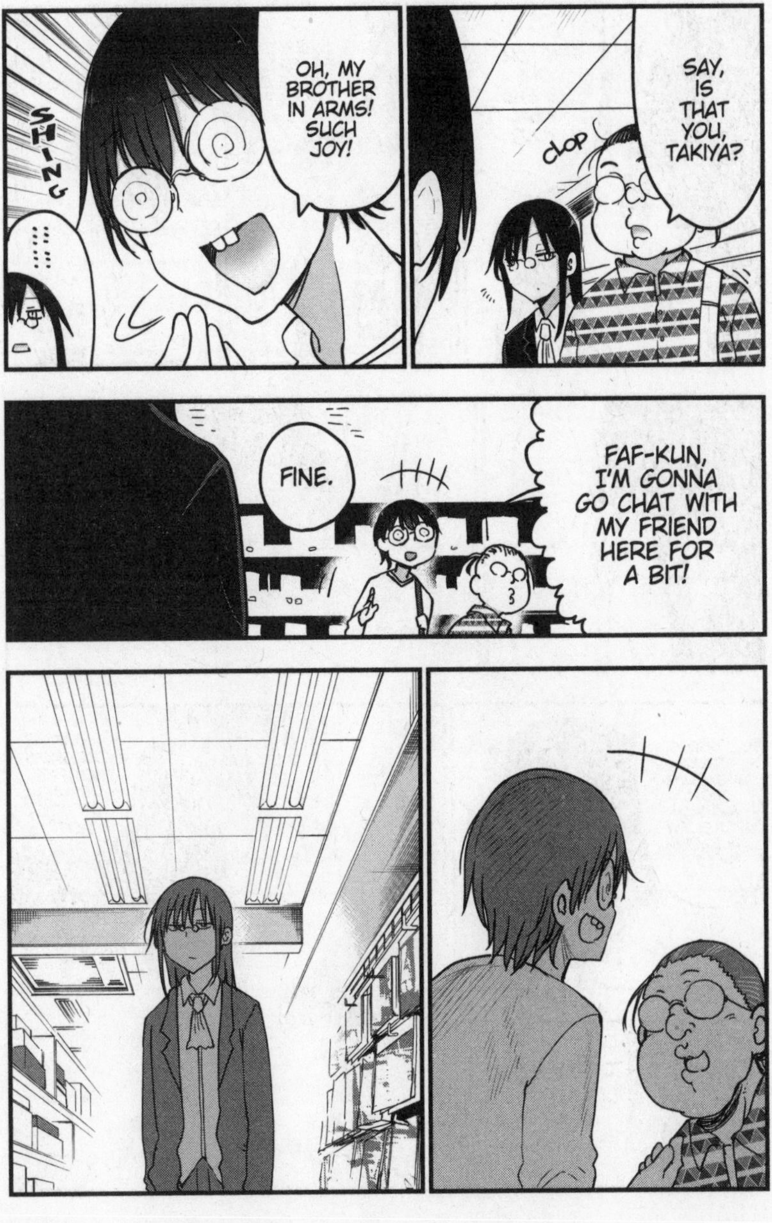
SAY, IS THAT YOU, TAKIYA?
CLOP
OH, MY BROTHER IN ARMS! SUCH JOY!
SHING
FAF-KUN, I'M GONNA GO CHAT WITH MY FRIEND HERE FOR A BIT!
FINE.

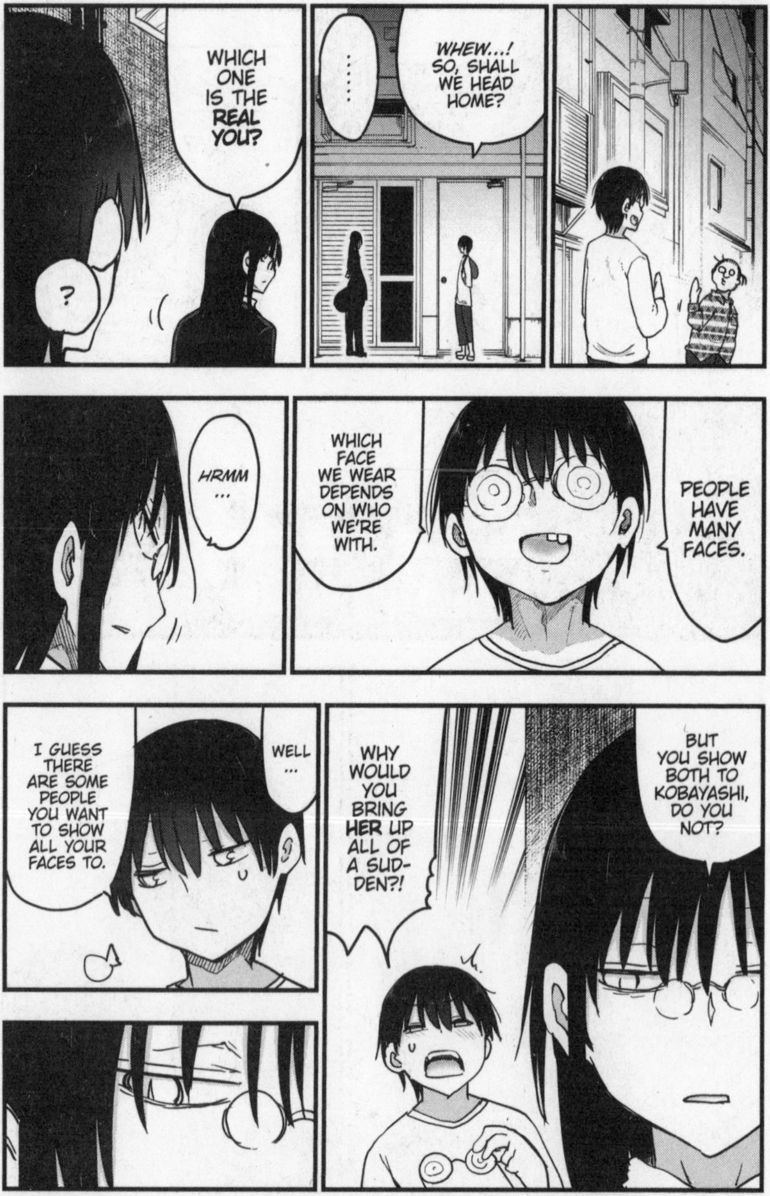
WHEW...! SO, SHALL WE HEAD HOME?
......
WHICH ONE IS THE REAL YOU?
?
PEOPLE HAVE MANY FACES.
WHICH FACE WE WEAR DEPENDS ON WHO WE'RE WITH.
HRMM...
BUT YOU SHOW BOTH TO KOBAYASHI, DO YOU NOT?
WHY WOULD YOU BRING HER UP ALL OF A SUDDEN?!
WELL...
I GUESS THERE ARE SOME PEOPLE YOU WANT TO SHOW ALL YOUR FACES TO.

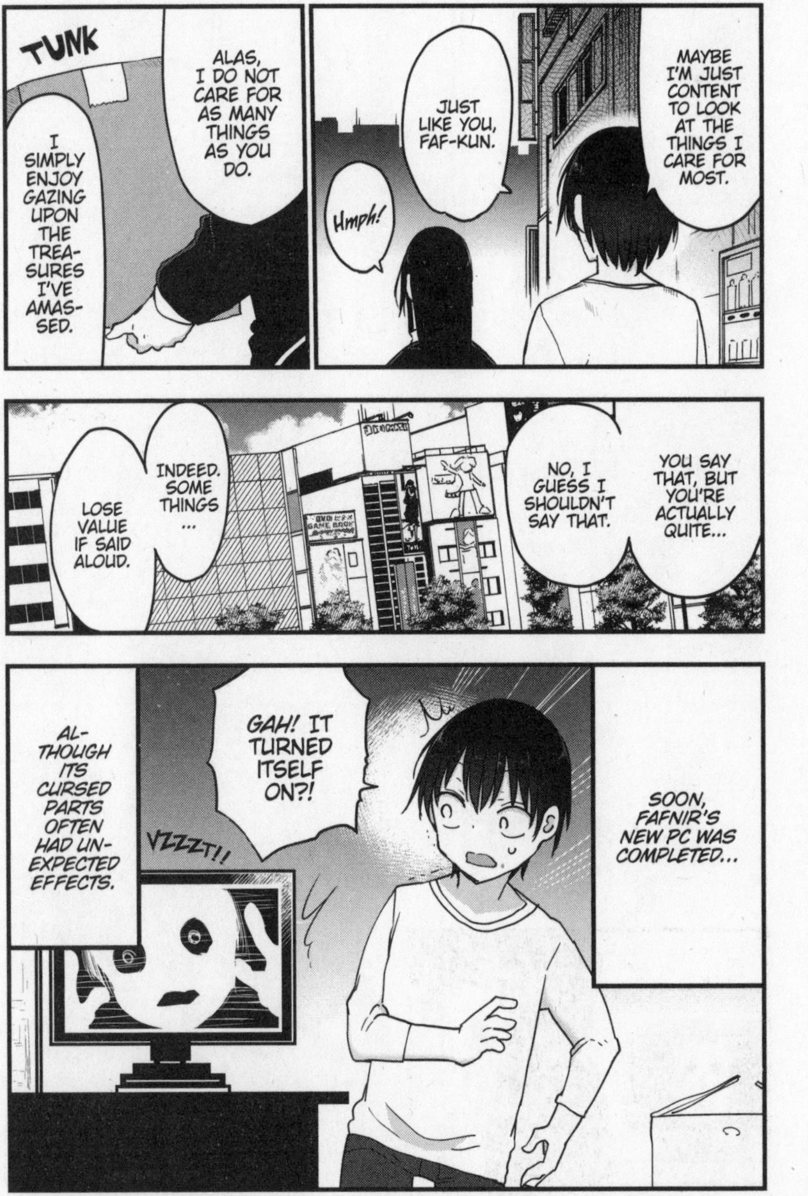
MAYBE I'M JUST CONTENT TO LOOK AT THE THINGS I CARE FOR MOST.
JUST LIKE YOU, FAF-KUN.
Hmph!
TUNK
ALAS, I DO NOT CARE FOR AS MANY THINGS AS YOU DO.
I SIMPLY ENJOY GAZING UPON THE TREA-SURES I'VE AMAS-SED.
YOU SAY THAT, BUT YOU'RE ACTUALLY QUITE...
NO, I GUESS I SHOULDN'T SAY THAT.
INDEED. SOME THINGS ...
LOSE VALUE IF SAID ALOUD.
SOON, FAFNIR'S NEW PC WAS COMPLETED...
GAH! IT TURNED ITSELF ON?!
VZZZT!!
AL-THOUGH ITS CURSED PARTS OFTEN HAD UN-EXPECTED EFFECTS.

CHAPTER 82/END

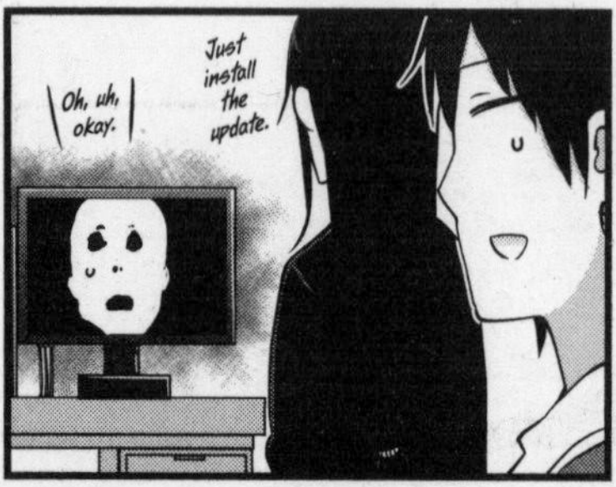
Just install the update.
Oh, uh, okay.

Miss Kobayashi's
DRAGON MAID

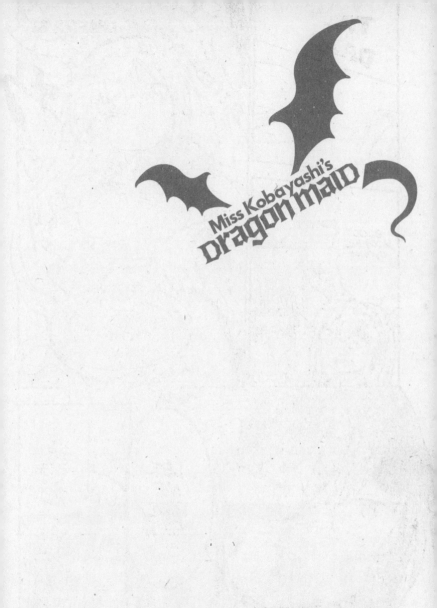

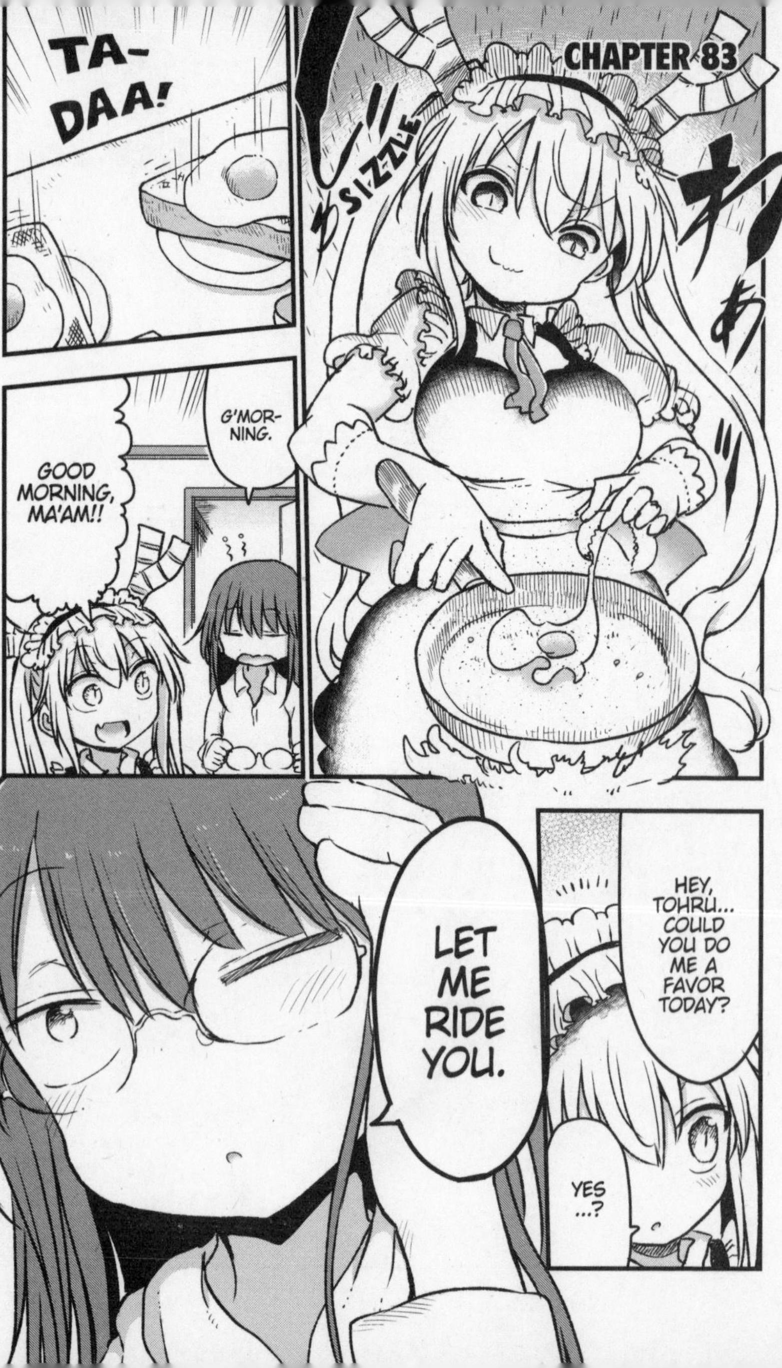
CHAPTER 83
SIZZLE
TA-DAA!
G'MOR-NING.
GOOD MORNING, MA'AM!!
HEY, TOHRU... COULD YOU DO ME A FAVOR TODAY?
YES ...?
LET ME RIDE YOU.

CHAPTER 83: KOBAYASHI AND THE FINAL BATTLE

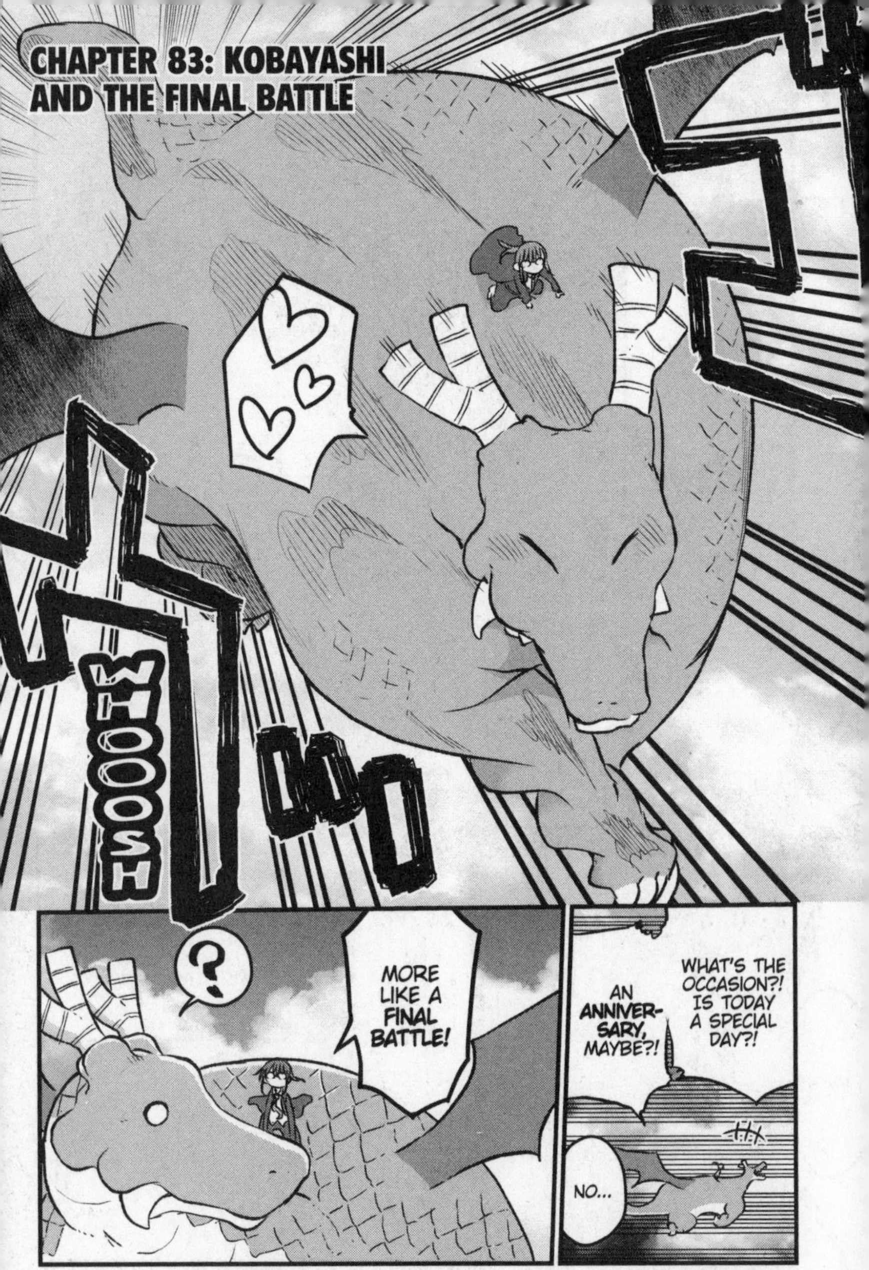
WHOOOSH
WHAT'S THE OCCASION?! IS TODAY A SPECIAL DAY?!
AN ANNIVERSARY, MAYBE?!
NO...
MORE LIKE A FINAL BATTLE!
?

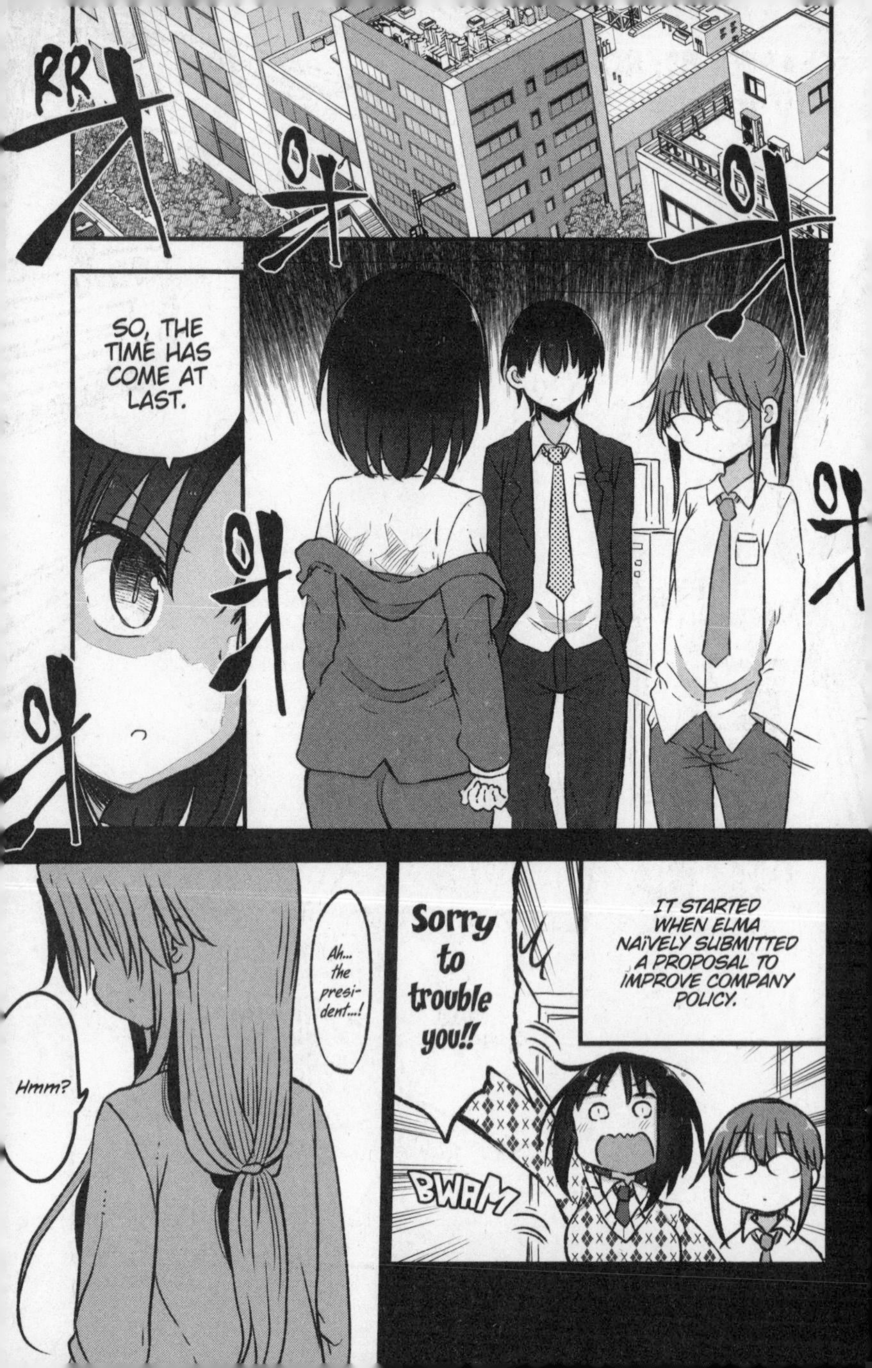
RR
SO, THE TIME HAS COME AT LAST.
IT STARTED WHEN ELMA NAÏVELY SUBMITTED A PROPOSAL TO IMPROVE COMPANY POLICY.
Sorry to trouble you!!
BWAM
Ah... the presi-dent...!
Hmm?

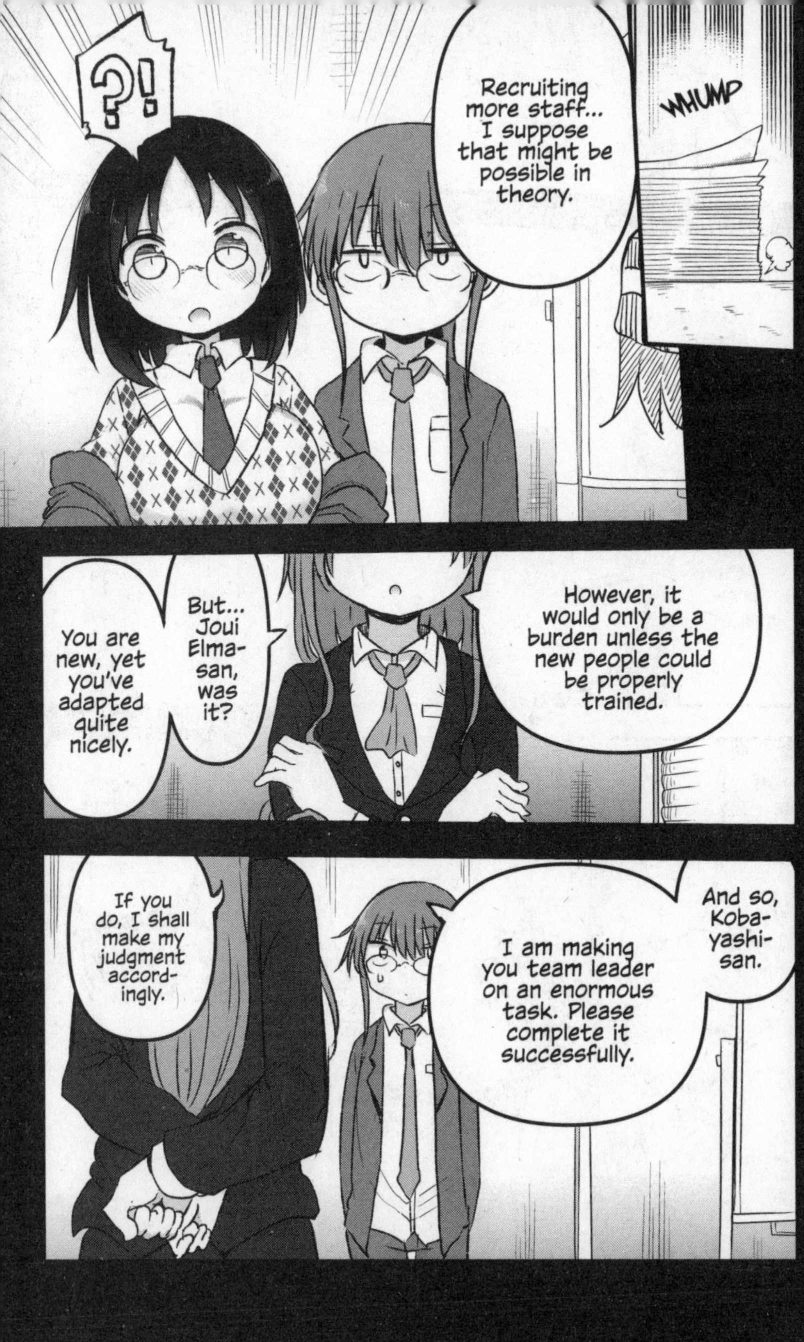
WHUMP
Recruiting more staff... I suppose that might be possible in theory.
?!
However, it would only be a burden unless the new people could be properly trained.
But... Joui Elma-san, was it?
You are new, yet you've adapted quite nicely.
And so, Koba-yashi-san.
I am making you team leader on an enormous task. Please complete it successfully.
If you do, I shall make my judgment accord-ingly.

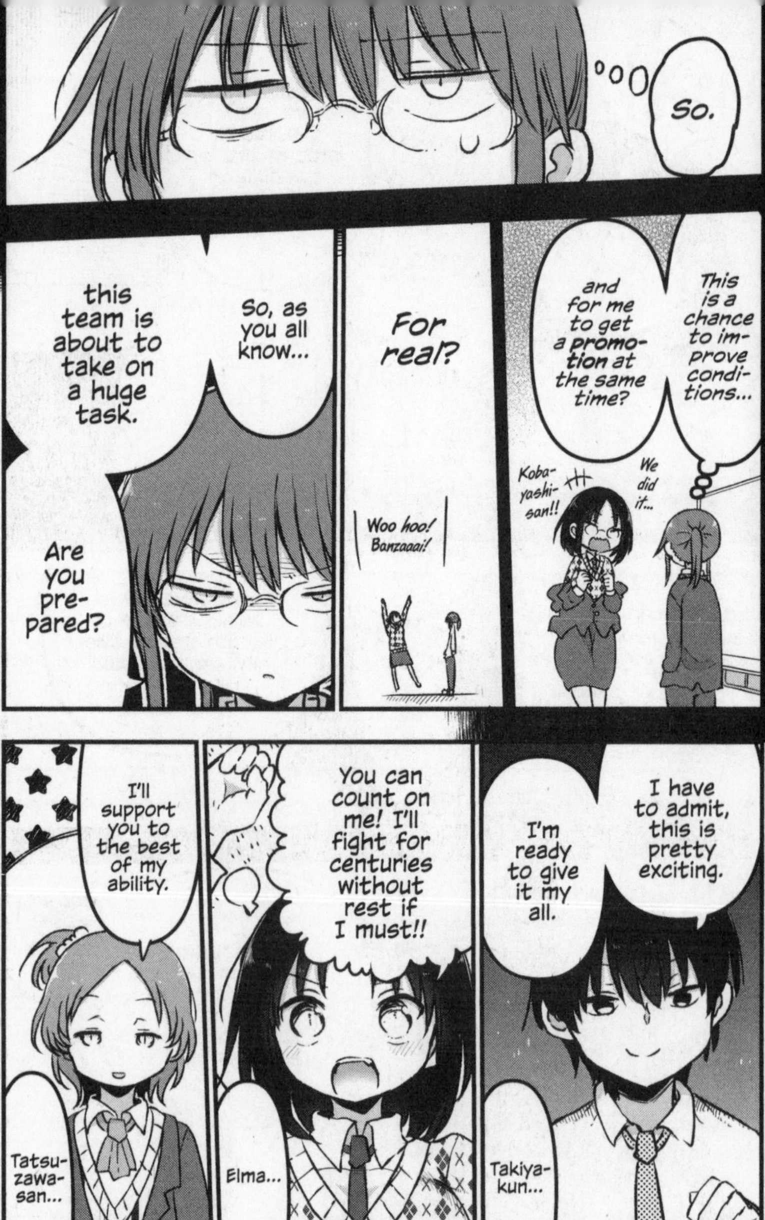
So.
This is a chance to improve conditions...
and for me to get a **promotion** at the same time?
We did it...
Kobayashi-san!!
For real?
Woo hoo! Banzaaai!
So, as you all know...
this team is about to take on a huge task.
Are you prepared?
I have to admit, this is pretty exciting.
I'm ready to give it my all.
Takiya-kun...
You can count on me! I'll fight for centuries without rest if I must!!
Elma...
I'll support you to the best of my ability.
Tatsuzawa-san...

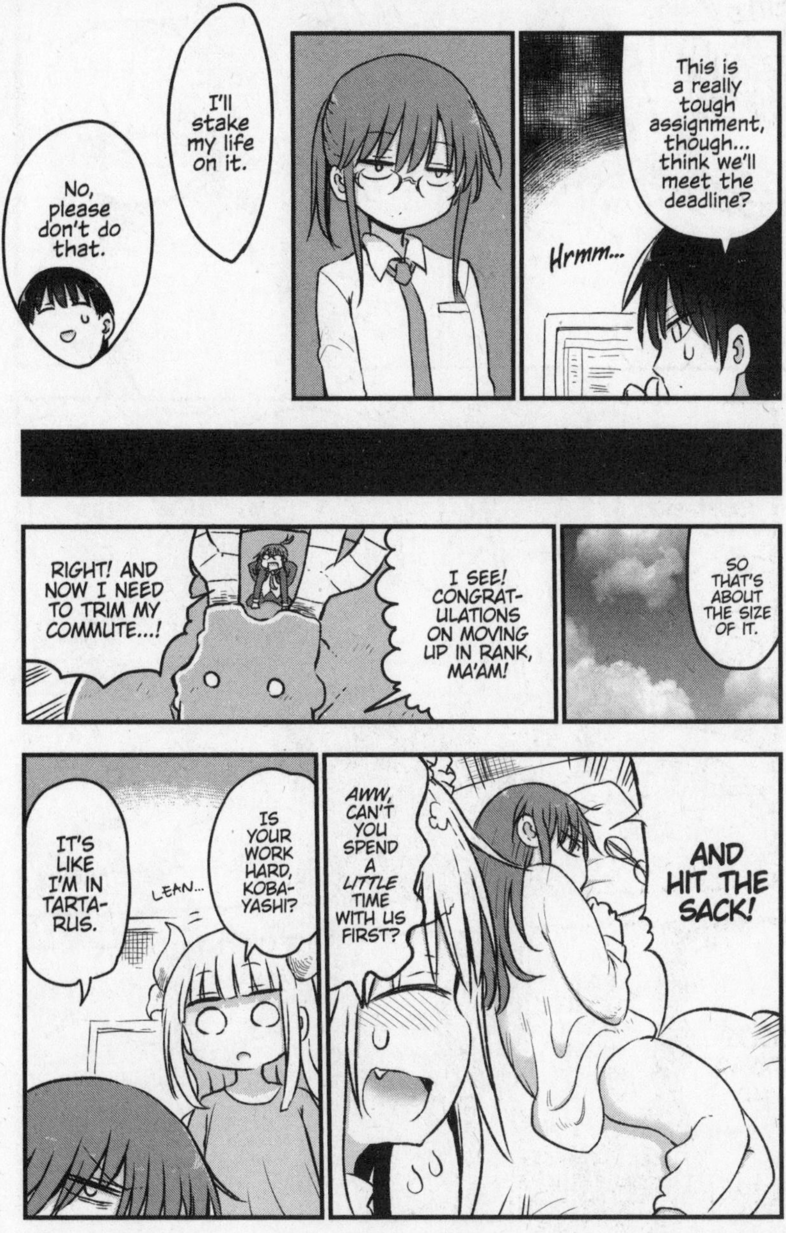
This is a really tough assignment, though... think we'll meet the deadline?
Hrmm...
I'll stake my life on it.
No, please don't do that.
SO THAT'S ABOUT THE SIZE OF IT.
I SEE! CONGRATULATIONS ON MOVING UP IN RANK, MA'AM!
RIGHT! AND NOW I NEED TO TRIM MY COMMUTE...!
AND HIT THE SACK!
AWW, CAN'T YOU SPEND A *LITTLE* TIME WITH US FIRST?
IS YOUR WORK HARD, KOBAYASHI?
LEAN...
IT'S LIKE I'M IN TARTARUS.

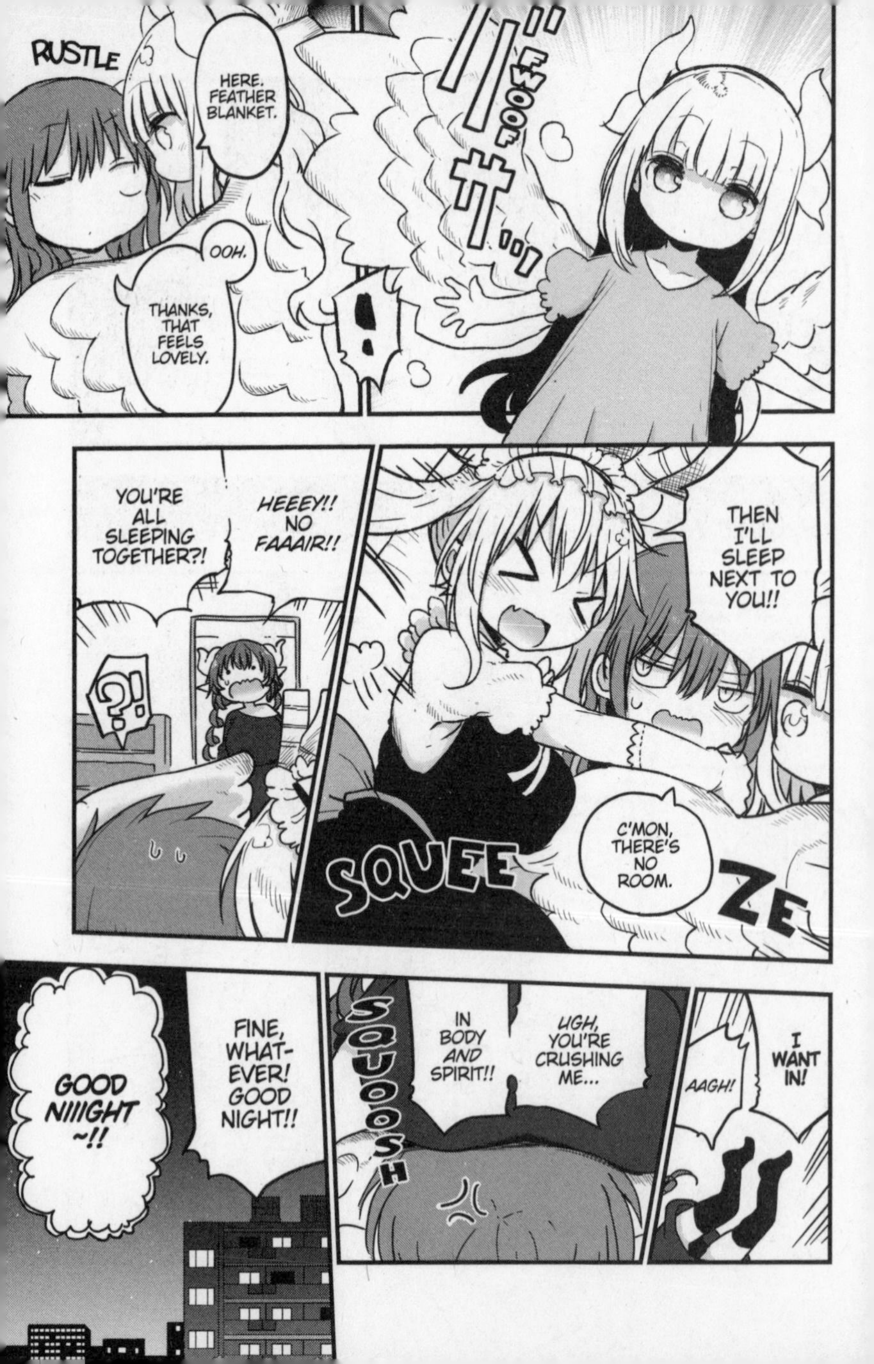
FWOOF
ザッ
HERE. FEATHER BLANKET.
RUSTLE
!
OOH.
THANKS, THAT FEELS LOVELY.
THEN I'LL SLEEP NEXT TO YOU!!
C'MON, THERE'S NO ROOM.
ZE
SQUEE
HEEEY!! NO FAAAIR!!
YOU'RE ALL SLEEPING TOGETHER?!
?!
I WANT IN!
AAGH!
UGH, YOU'RE CRUSHING ME...
IN BODY AND SPIRIT!!
SQUOOOSH
FINE, WHAT-EVER! GOOD NIGHT!!
GOOD NIIIGHT ~!!

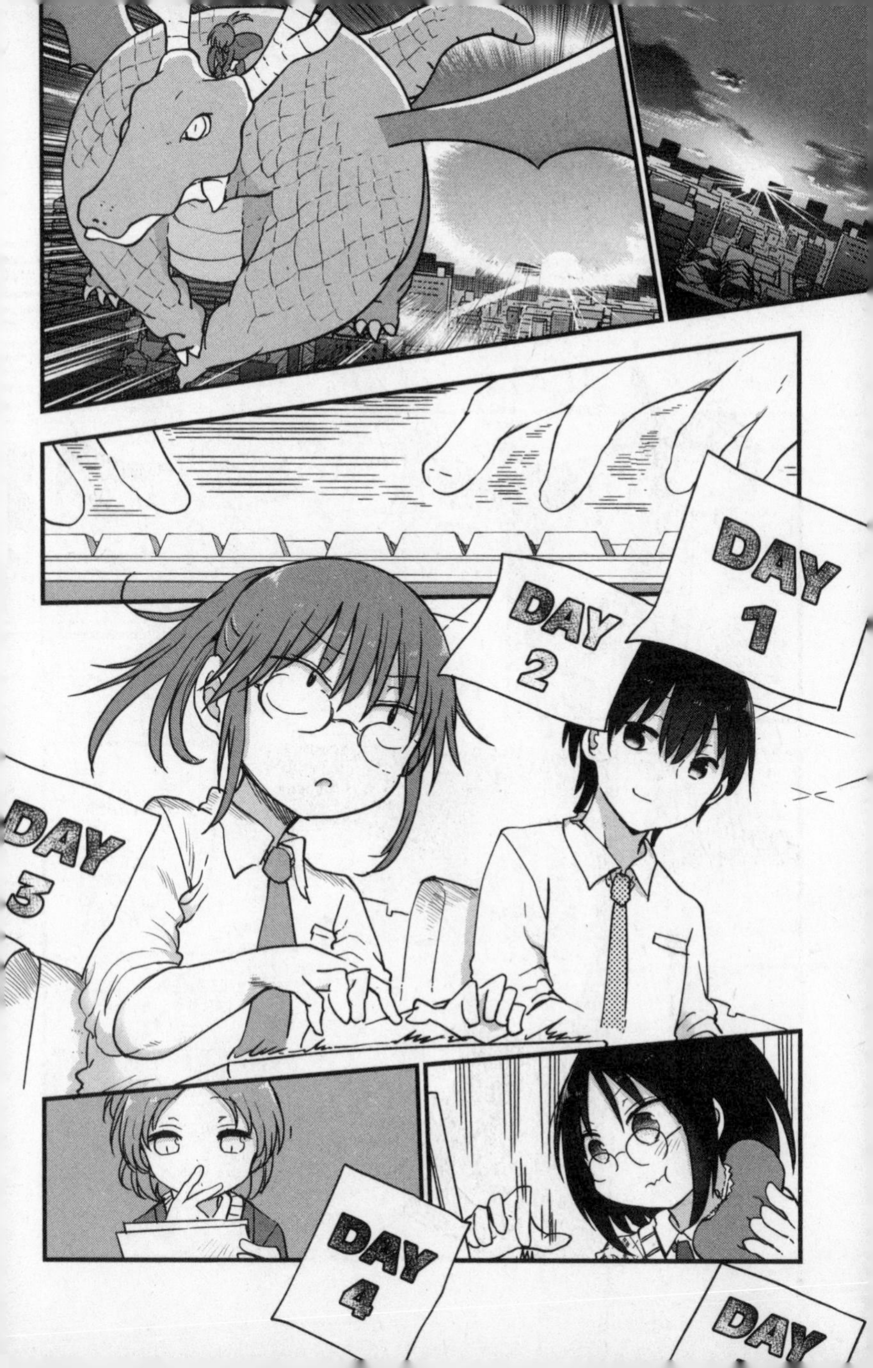
DAY 1
DAY 2
DAY 3
DAY 4
DAY

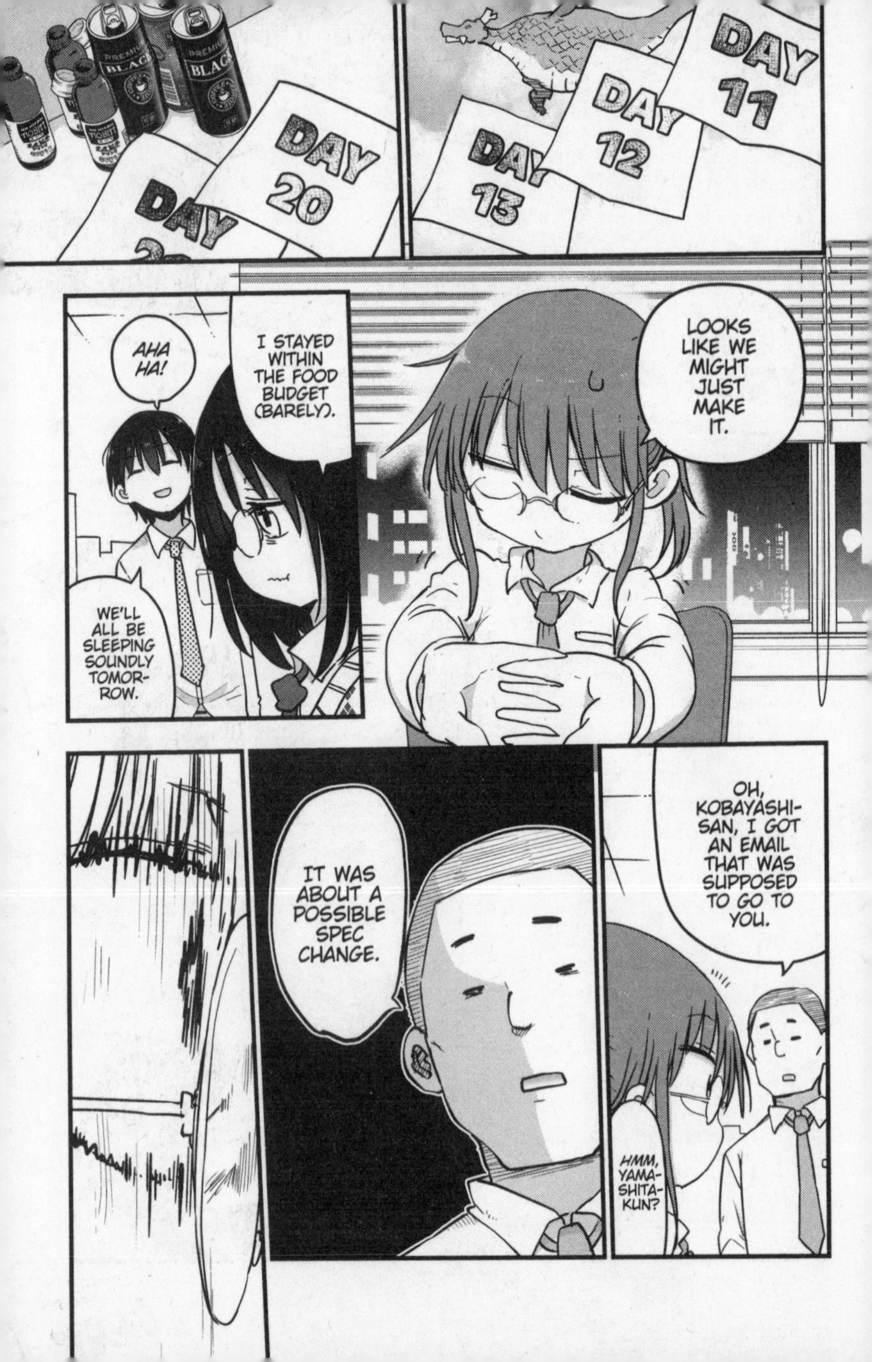
DAY 11
DAY 12
DAY 13
DAY 20
DAY
LOOKS LIKE WE MIGHT JUST MAKE IT.
I STAYED WITHIN THE FOOD BUDGET (BARELY).
AHA HA!
WE'LL ALL BE SLEEPING SOUNDLY TOMORROW.
OH, KOBAYASHI-SAN, I GOT AN EMAIL THAT WAS SUPPOSED TO GO TO YOU.
HMM, YAMASHITA-KUN?
IT WAS ABOUT A POSSIBLE SPEC CHANGE.

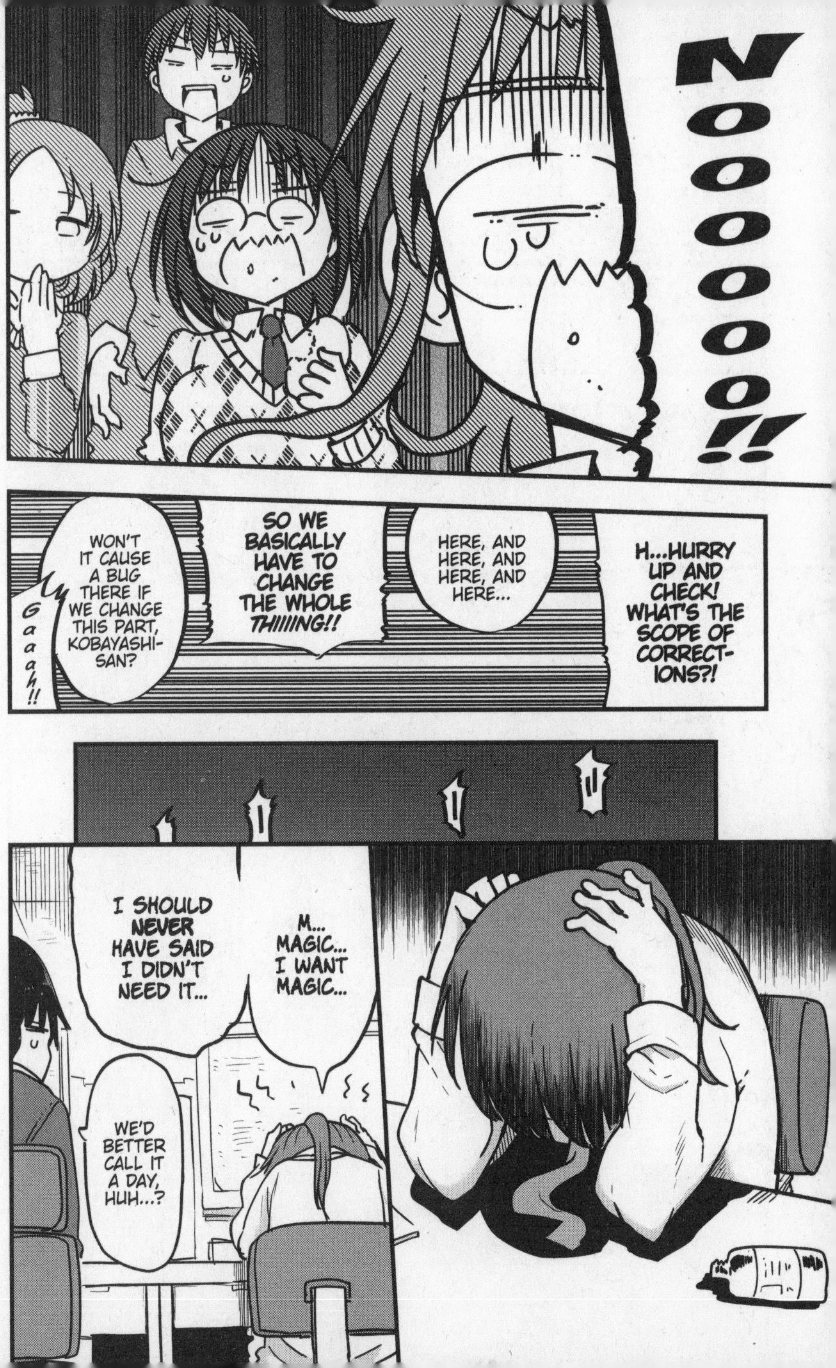
NOOOOOO!!
H...HURRY UP AND CHECK! WHAT'S THE SCOPE OF CORRECT-IONS?!
HERE, AND HERE, AND HERE, AND HERE...
SO WE BASICALLY HAVE TO CHANGE THE WHOLE THIIIING!!
WON'T IT CAUSE A BUG THERE IF WE CHANGE THIS PART, KOBAYASHI-SAN?
Gaaah!!
M... MAGIC... I WANT MAGIC...
I SHOULD NEVER HAVE SAID I DIDN'T NEED IT...
WE'D BETTER CALL IT A DAY, HUH...?

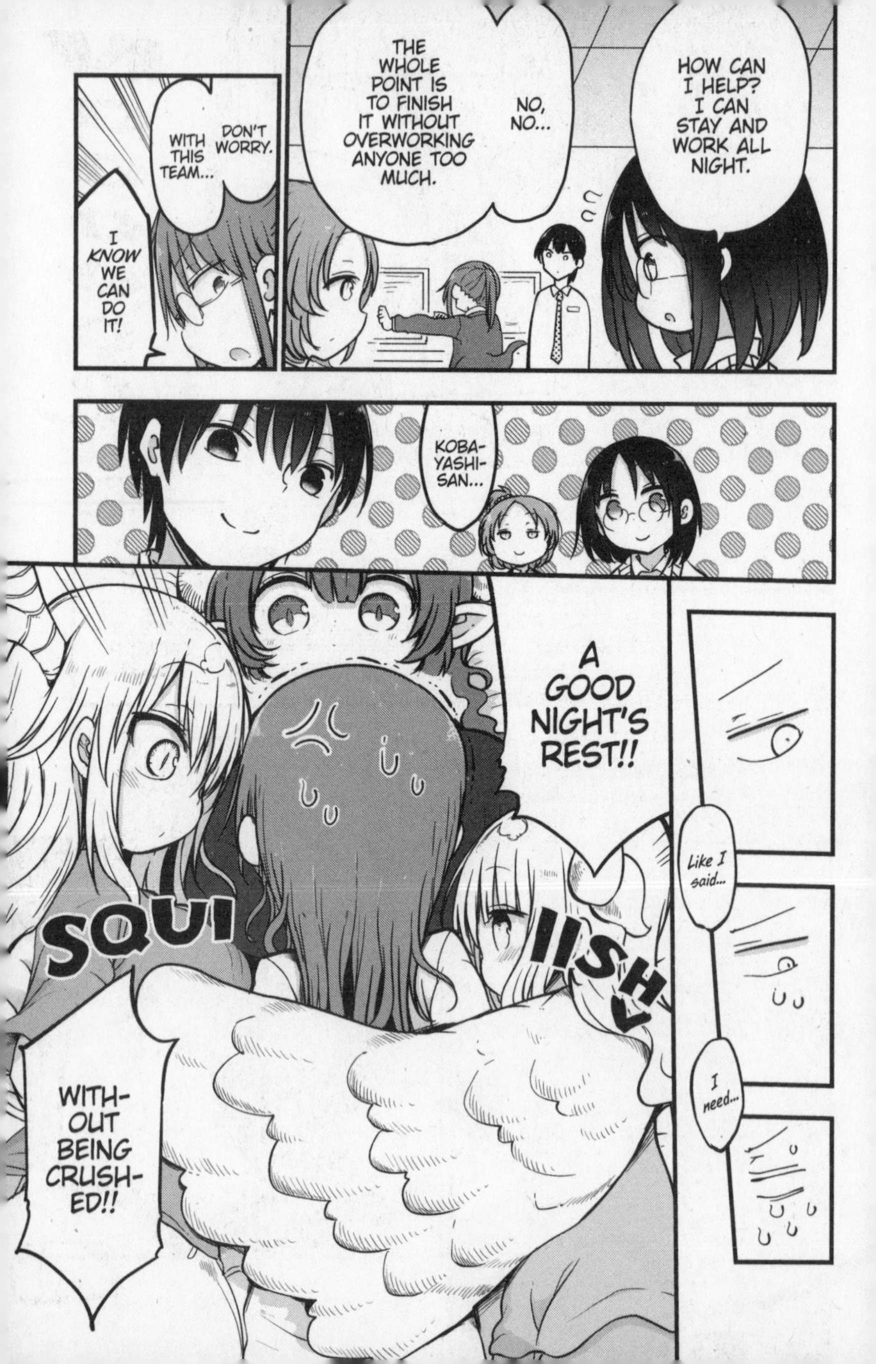
HOW CAN I HELP? I CAN STAY AND WORK ALL NIGHT.
NO, NO...
THE WHOLE POINT IS TO FINISH IT WITHOUT OVERWORKING ANYONE TOO MUCH.
DON'T WORRY.
WITH THIS TEAM...
I KNOW WE CAN DO IT!
KOBA-YASHI-SAN...
Like I said...
I need...
A GOOD NIGHT'S REST!!
SQUI
IISH
WITH-OUT BEING CRUSH-ED!!

ONE SHEEP ... TWO SHEEP ...

Haa...

RUSTLE...

BOYOING BOYOING

BUT THIS IS THE MOST COMFORTABLE WAY TO SLEEP!!

EX-CUSE ME?

NUZZLE NUZZLE

UGH...

BUT SOME-HOW, THE TEAM GOT THROUGH IT ALL.

Uuuurghh...

SNORE

PLUS THE MOUNTAIN OF BUGS THAT FOL-LOWED...

IT'S LIKE BATTLING A TYPHON...

DOOOOOOM

CORRECTIONS, CORRECTIONS, AND MORE CORRECTIONS...

THE NEXT DAY...

Refreshed.

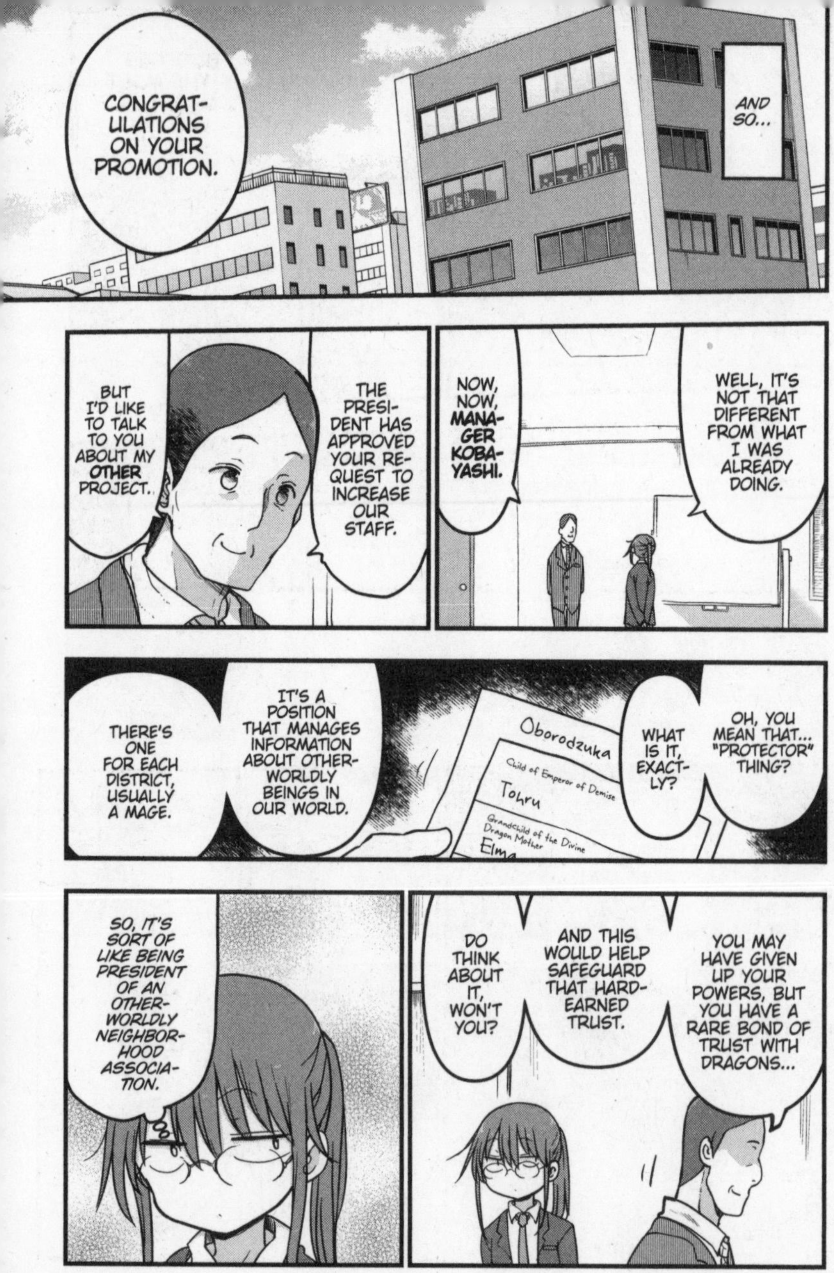
AND SO...
CONGRATULATIONS ON YOUR PROMOTION.
WELL, IT'S NOT THAT DIFFERENT FROM WHAT I WAS ALREADY DOING.
NOW, NOW, **MANAGER KOBAYASHI.**
THE PRESIDENT HAS APPROVED YOUR REQUEST TO INCREASE OUR STAFF.
BUT I'D LIKE TO TALK TO YOU ABOUT MY **OTHER** PROJECT.
OH, YOU MEAN THAT... "PROTECTOR" THING?
WHAT IS IT, EXACTLY?
Oborodzuka
Child of Emperor of Demise
Tohru
Grandchild of the Divine Dragon Mother
IT'S A POSITION THAT MANAGES INFORMATION ABOUT OTHERWORLDLY BEINGS IN OUR WORLD.
THERE'S ONE FOR EACH DISTRICT, USUALLY A MAGE.
YOU MAY HAVE GIVEN UP YOUR POWERS, BUT YOU HAVE A RARE BOND OF TRUST WITH DRAGONS...
AND THIS WOULD HELP SAFEGUARD THAT HARD-EARNED TRUST.
DO THINK ABOUT IT, WON'T YOU?
SO, IT'S SORT OF LIKE BEING PRESIDENT OF AN OTHERWORLDLY NEIGHBORHOOD ASSOCIATION.

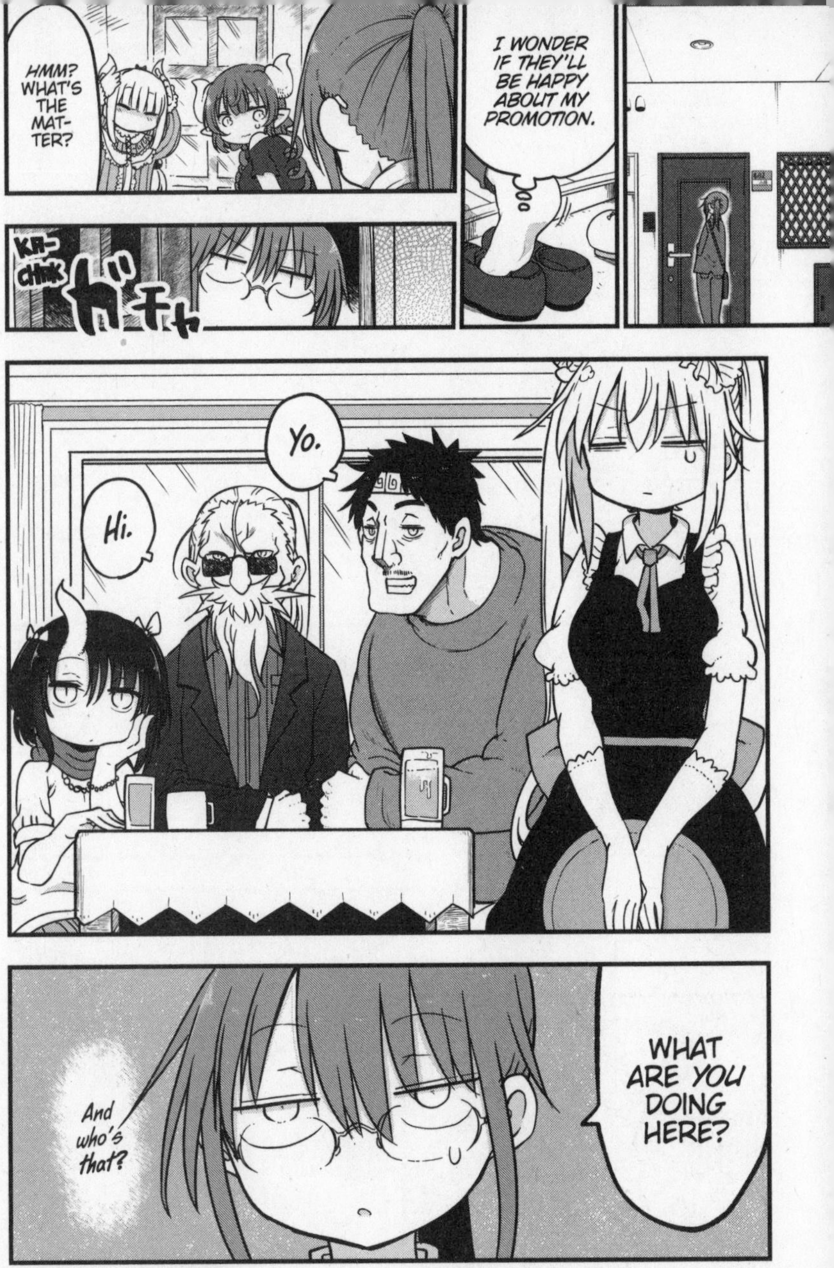
I WONDER IF THEY'LL BE HAPPY ABOUT MY PROMOTION.
HMM? WHAT'S THE MAT-TER?
KA-CHINK
ガチャ
Yo.
Hi.
WHAT ARE YOU DOING HERE?
And who's that?

CHAPTER 83/END

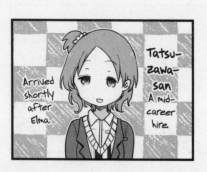

Tatsu-zawa-san
A mid-career hire.
Arrived shortly after Elma.

Miss Kobayashi's
Dragon Maid

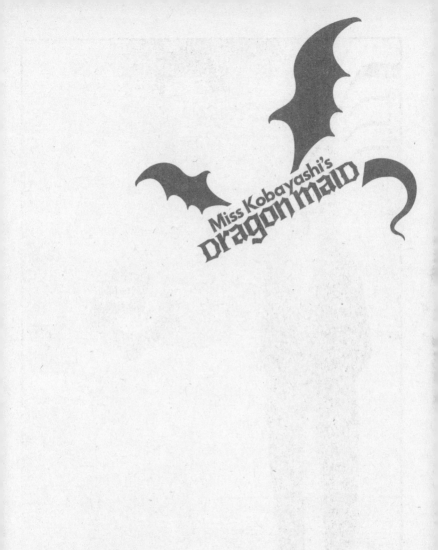

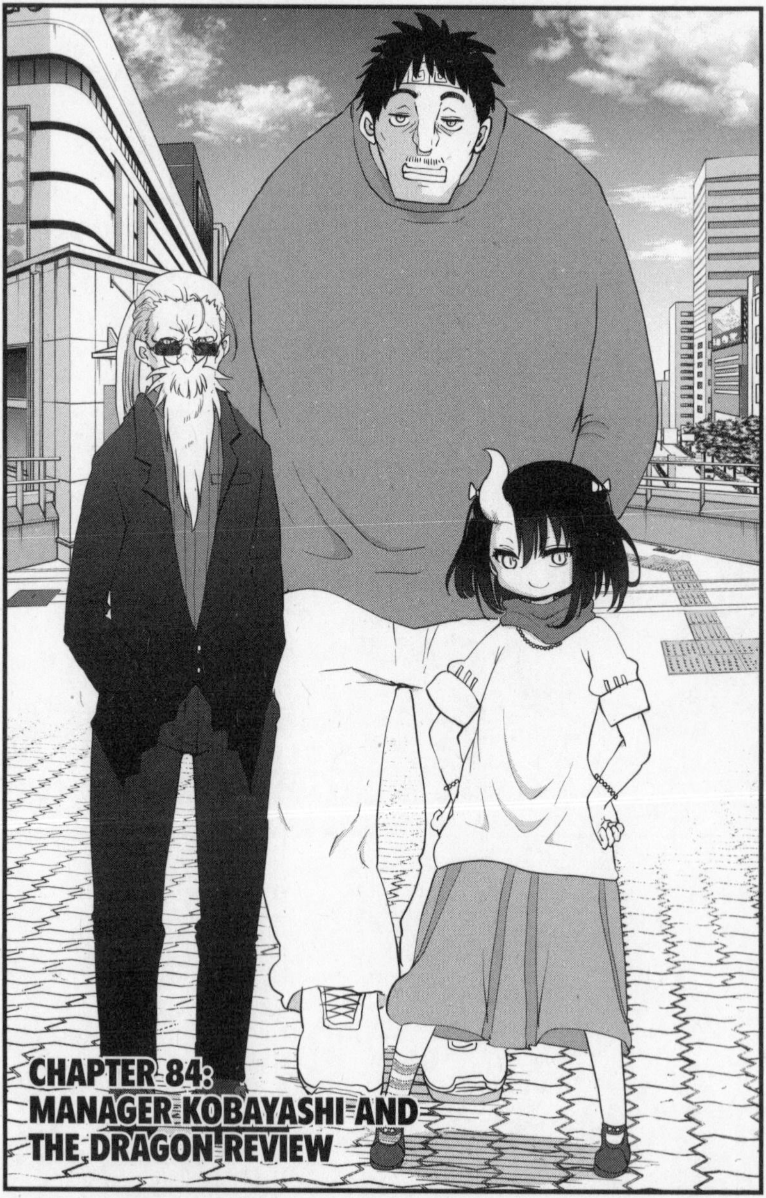
CHAPTER 84:
MANAGER KOBAYASHI AND
THE DRAGON REVIEW

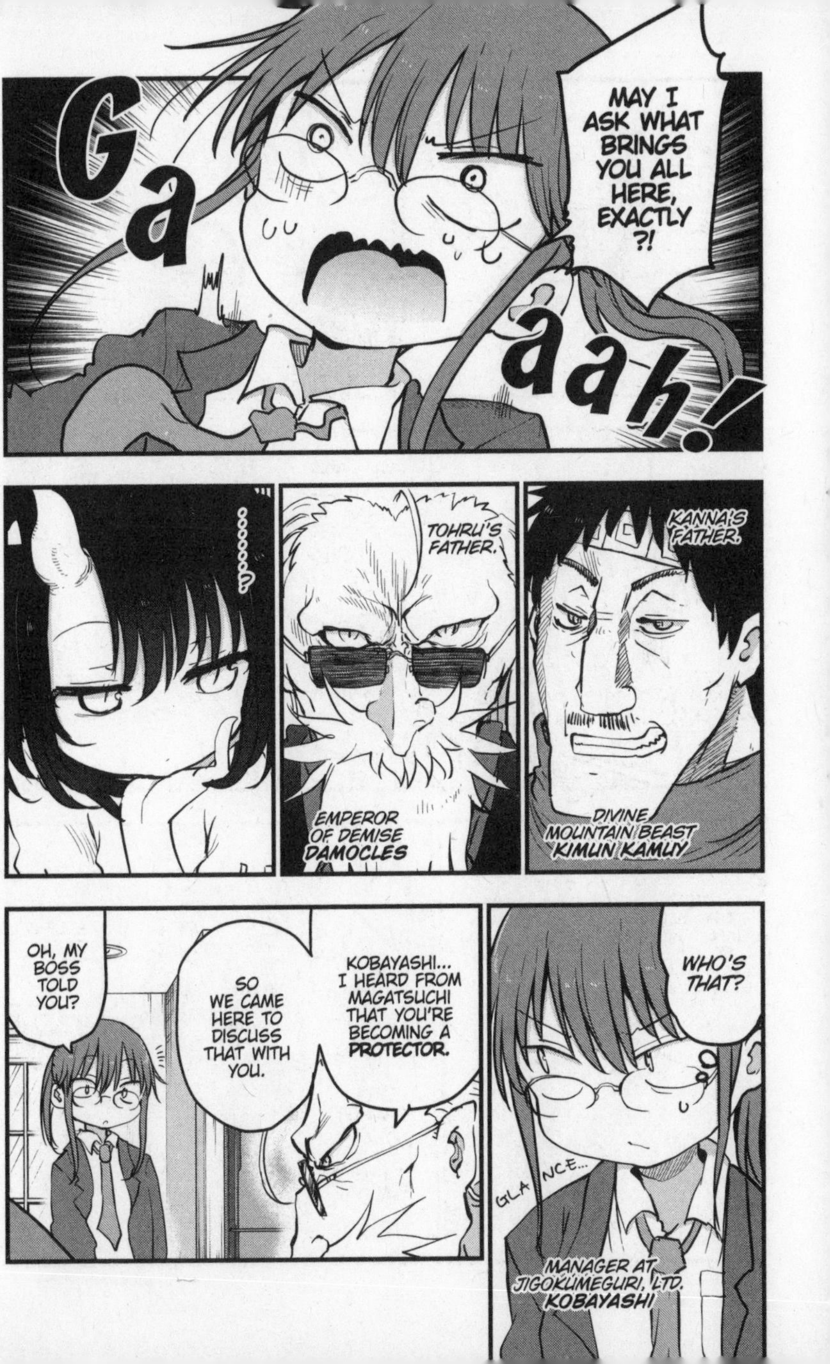
MAY I ASK WHAT BRINGS YOU ALL HERE, EXACTLY?!
Gaaah!!
KANNA'S FATHER.
DIVINE MOUNTAIN BEAST KIMUN KAMUY
TOHRU'S FATHER.
EMPEROR OF DEMISE DAMOCLES
oooooo?
WHO'S THAT?
GLANCE...
MANAGER AT JIGOKUMEGURI, LTD. KOBAYASHI
KOBAYASHI... I HEARD FROM MAGATSUCHI THAT YOU'RE BECOMING A PROTECTOR.
SO WE CAME HERE TO DISCUSS THAT WITH YOU.
OH, MY BOSS TOLD YOU?

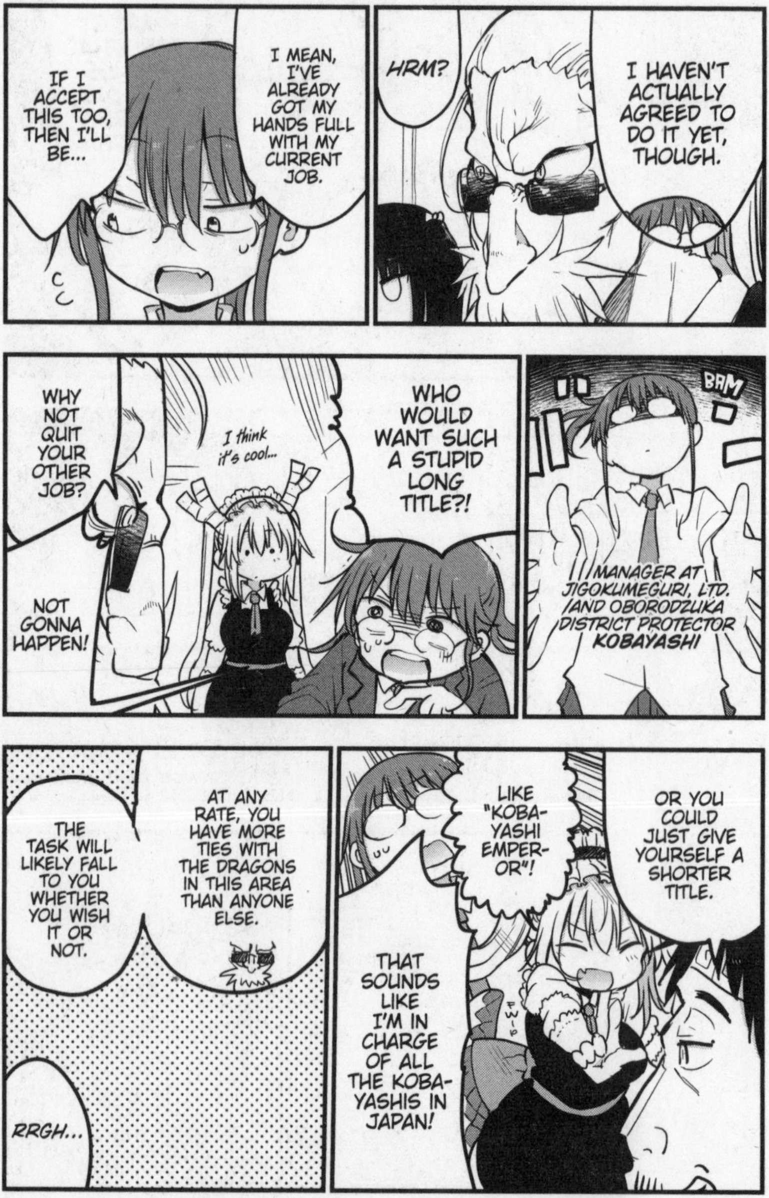
I HAVEN'T ACTUALLY AGREED TO DO IT YET, THOUGH.
HRM?
I MEAN, I'VE ALREADY GOT MY HANDS FULL WITH MY CURRENT JOB.
IF I ACCEPT THIS TOO, THEN I'LL BE...
BAM
MANAGER AT JIGOKUMEGURI, LTD. /AND OBORODZUKA DISTRICT PROTECTOR KOBAYASHI
WHO WOULD WANT SUCH A STUPID LONG TITLE?!
I think it's cool...
WHY NOT QUIT YOUR OTHER JOB?
NOT GONNA HAPPEN!
OR YOU COULD JUST GIVE YOURSELF A SHORTER TITLE.
LIKE "KOBA-YASHI EMPER-OR"!
THAT SOUNDS LIKE I'M IN CHARGE OF ALL THE KOBA-YASHIS IN JAPAN!
FWIP
AT ANY RATE, YOU HAVE MORE TIES WITH THE DRAGONS IN THIS AREA THAN ANYONE ELSE.
THE TASK WILL LIKELY FALL TO YOU WHETHER YOU WISH IT OR NOT.
RRGH...

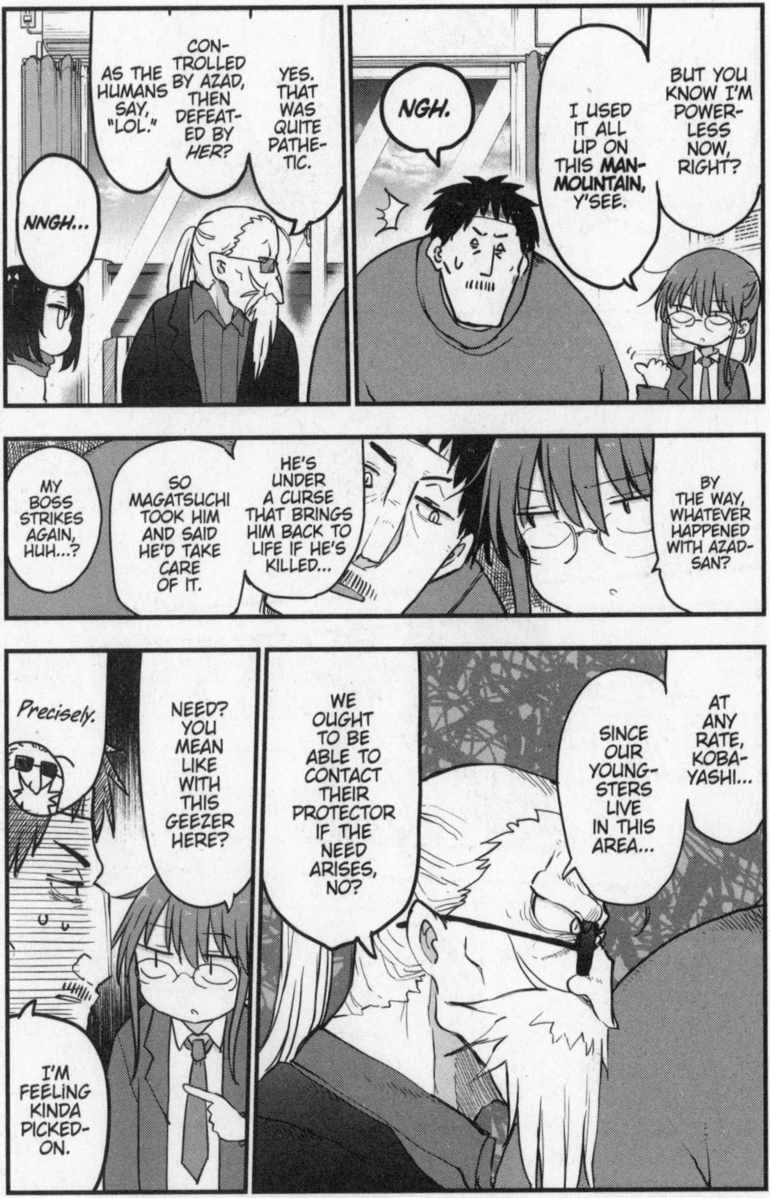
BUT YOU KNOW I'M POWERLESS NOW, RIGHT?
I USED IT ALL UP ON THIS **MAN-MOUNTAIN**, Y'SEE.
NGH.
YES. THAT WAS QUITE PATHETIC.
CONTROLLED BY AZAD, THEN DEFEATED BY *HER*?
AS THE HUMANS SAY, "LOL."
NNGH...
BY THE WAY, WHATEVER HAPPENED WITH AZAD-SAN?
HE'S UNDER A CURSE THAT BRINGS HIM BACK TO LIFE IF HE'S KILLED...
SO MAGATSUCHI TOOK HIM AND SAID HE'D TAKE CARE OF IT.
MY BOSS STRIKES AGAIN, HUH...?
AT ANY RATE, KOBAYASHI...
SINCE OUR YOUNGSTERS LIVE IN THIS AREA...
WE OUGHT TO BE ABLE TO CONTACT THEIR PROTECTOR IF THE NEED ARISES, NO?
NEED? YOU MEAN LIKE WITH THIS GEEZER HERE?
Precisely.
I'M FEELING KINDA PICKED-ON.

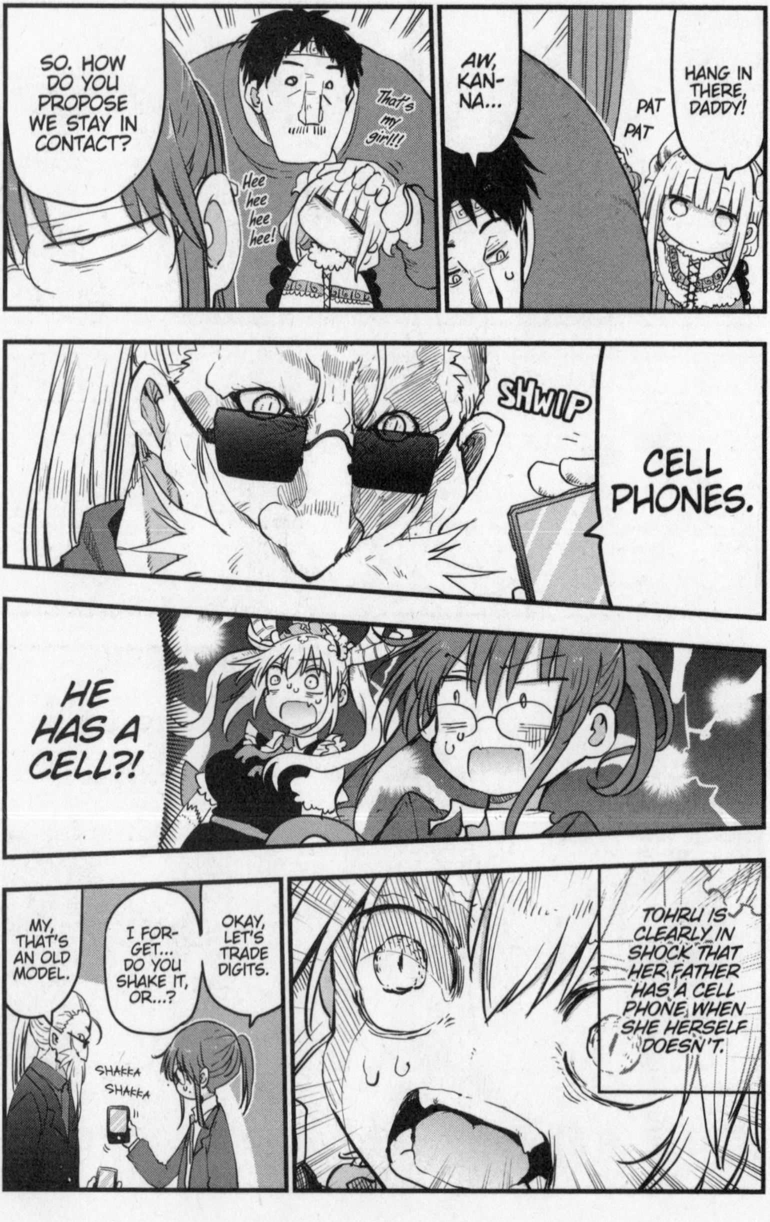
HANG IN THERE, DADDY!
PAT PAT
AW, KAN-NA...
That's my girl!!!
SO. HOW DO YOU PROPOSE WE STAY IN CONTACT?
Hee hee hee hee!
SHWIP
CELL PHONES.
HE HAS A CELL?!
TOHRU IS CLEARLY IN SHOCK THAT HER FATHER HAS A CELL PHONE WHEN SHE HERSELF DOESN'T.
OKAY, LET'S TRADE DIGITS.
I FOR-GET... DO YOU SHAKE IT, OR...?
MY, THAT'S AN OLD MODEL.
SHAKKA SHAKKA

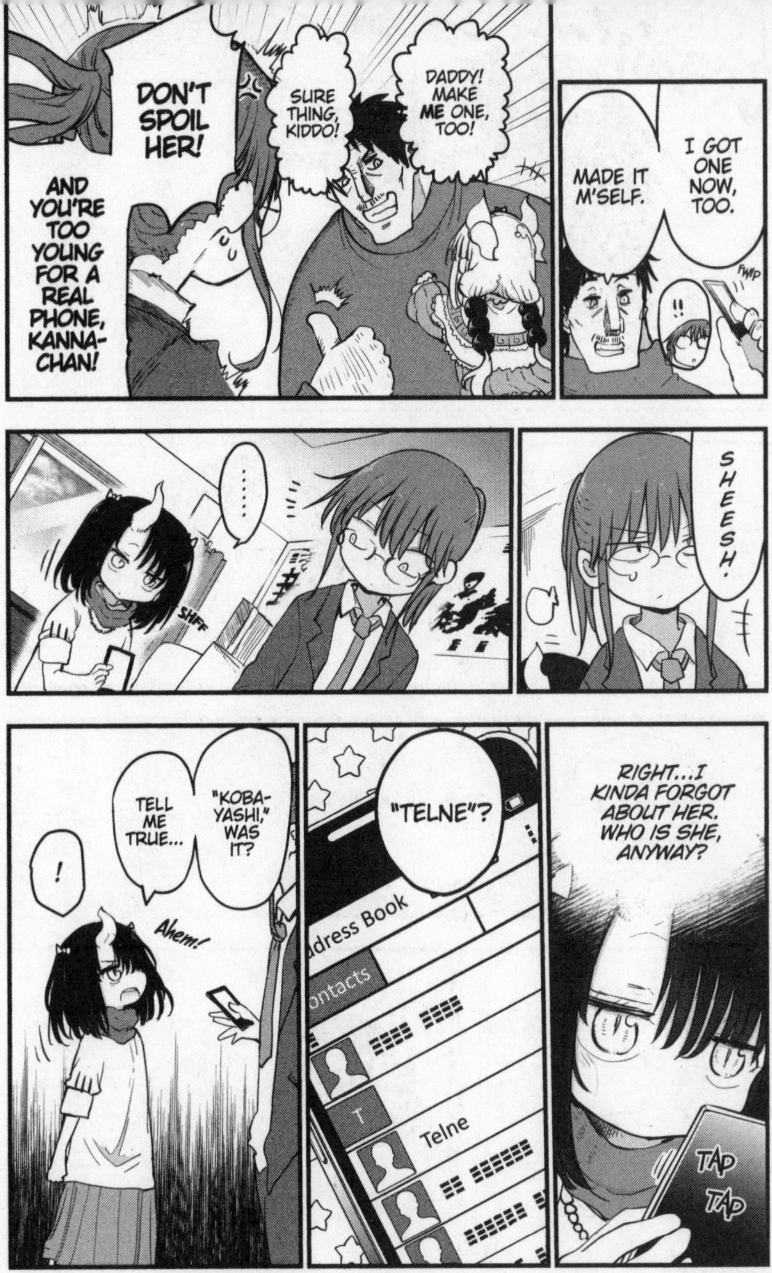
I GOT ONE NOW, TOO.
MADE IT M'SELF.
!!
FWIP
DADDY! MAKE ME ONE, TOO!
SURE THING, KIDDO!
DON'T SPOIL HER!
AND YOU'RE TOO YOUNG FOR A REAL PHONE, KANNA-CHAN!
SHEESH!
......
SHFF
RIGHT...I KINDA FORGOT ABOUT HER. WHO IS SHE, ANYWAY?
TAP
TAP
"TELNE"?
dress Book
ontacts
T
Telne
"KOBA-YASHI," WAS IT?
TELL ME TRUE...
!
Ahem!

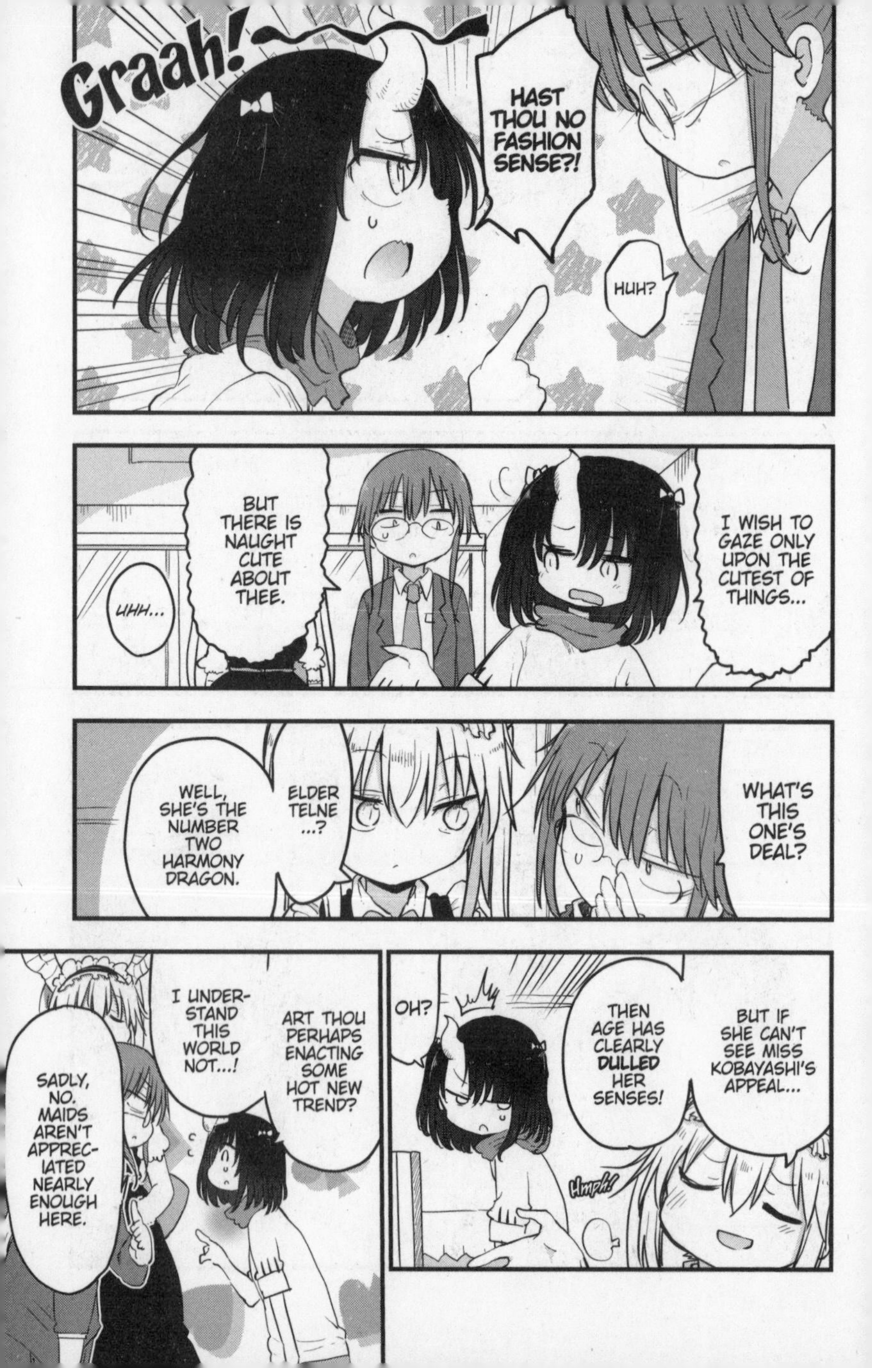
Graah!
HAST THOU NO FASHION SENSE?!
HUH?
I WISH TO GAZE ONLY UPON THE CUTEST OF THINGS...
BUT THERE IS NAUGHT CUTE ABOUT THEE.
UHH...
WHAT'S THIS ONE'S DEAL?
ELDER TELNE ...?
WELL, SHE'S THE NUMBER TWO HARMONY DRAGON.
BUT IF SHE CAN'T SEE MISS KOBAYASHI'S APPEAL...
THEN AGE HAS CLEARLY DULLED HER SENSES!
OH?
Hmph!
ART THOU PERHAPS ENACTING SOME HOT NEW TREND?
I UNDER-STAND THIS WORLD NOT...!
SADLY, NO. MAIDS AREN'T APPREC-IATED NEARLY ENOUGH HERE.

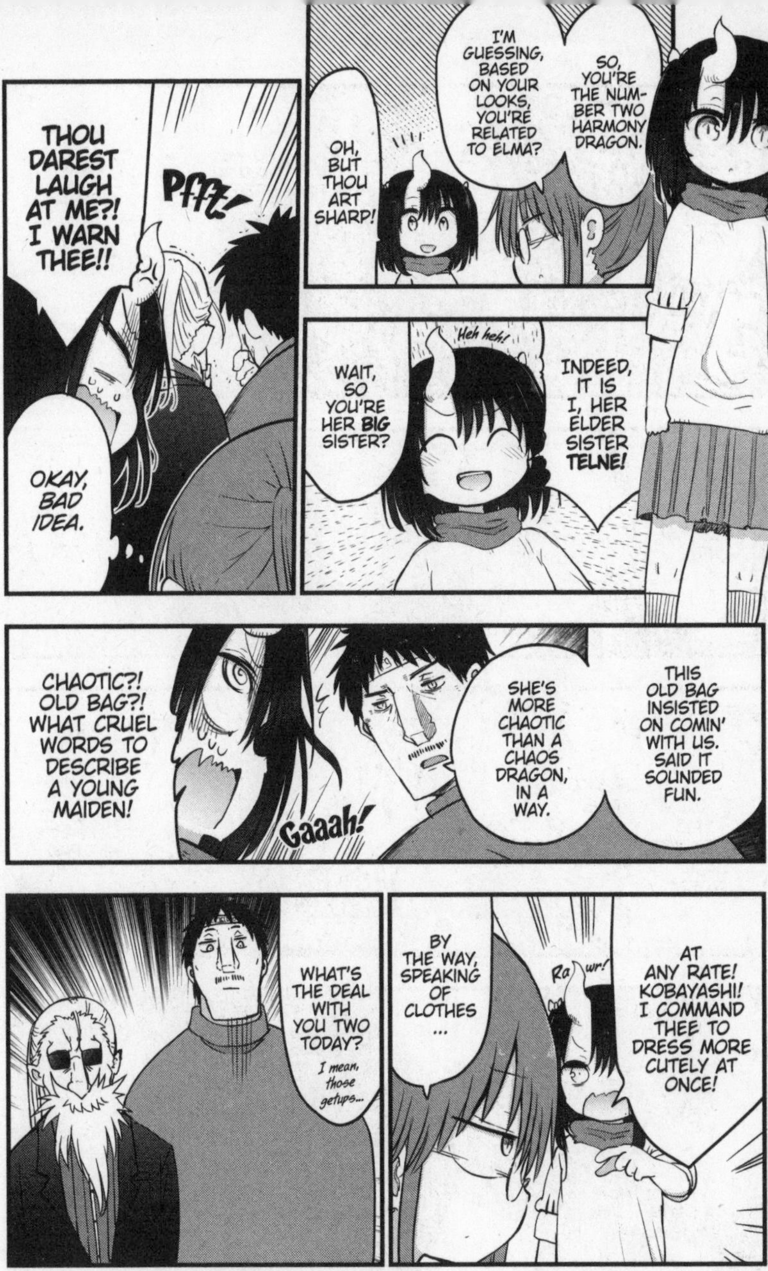
SO, YOU'RE THE NUMBER TWO HARMONY DRAGON.
I'M GUESSING, BASED ON YOUR LOOKS, YOU'RE RELATED TO ELMA?
OH, BUT THOU ART SHARP!
WAIT, SO YOU'RE HER BIG SISTER?
Heh heh!
INDEED, IT IS I, HER ELDER SISTER TELNE!
Pfft!
THOU DAREST LAUGH AT ME?! I WARN THEE!!
OKAY, BAD IDEA.
THIS OLD BAG INSISTED ON COMIN' WITH US. SAID IT SOUNDED FUN.
SHE'S MORE CHAOTIC THAN A CHAOS DRAGON, IN A WAY.
Gaaah!
CHAOTIC?! OLD BAG?! WHAT CRUEL WORDS TO DESCRIBE A YOUNG MAIDEN!
AT ANY RATE! KOBAYASHI! I COMMAND THEE TO DRESS MORE CUTELY AT ONCE!
Rawr!
BY THE WAY, SPEAKING OF CLOTHES...
WHAT'S THE DEAL WITH YOU TWO TODAY?
I mean, those getups...

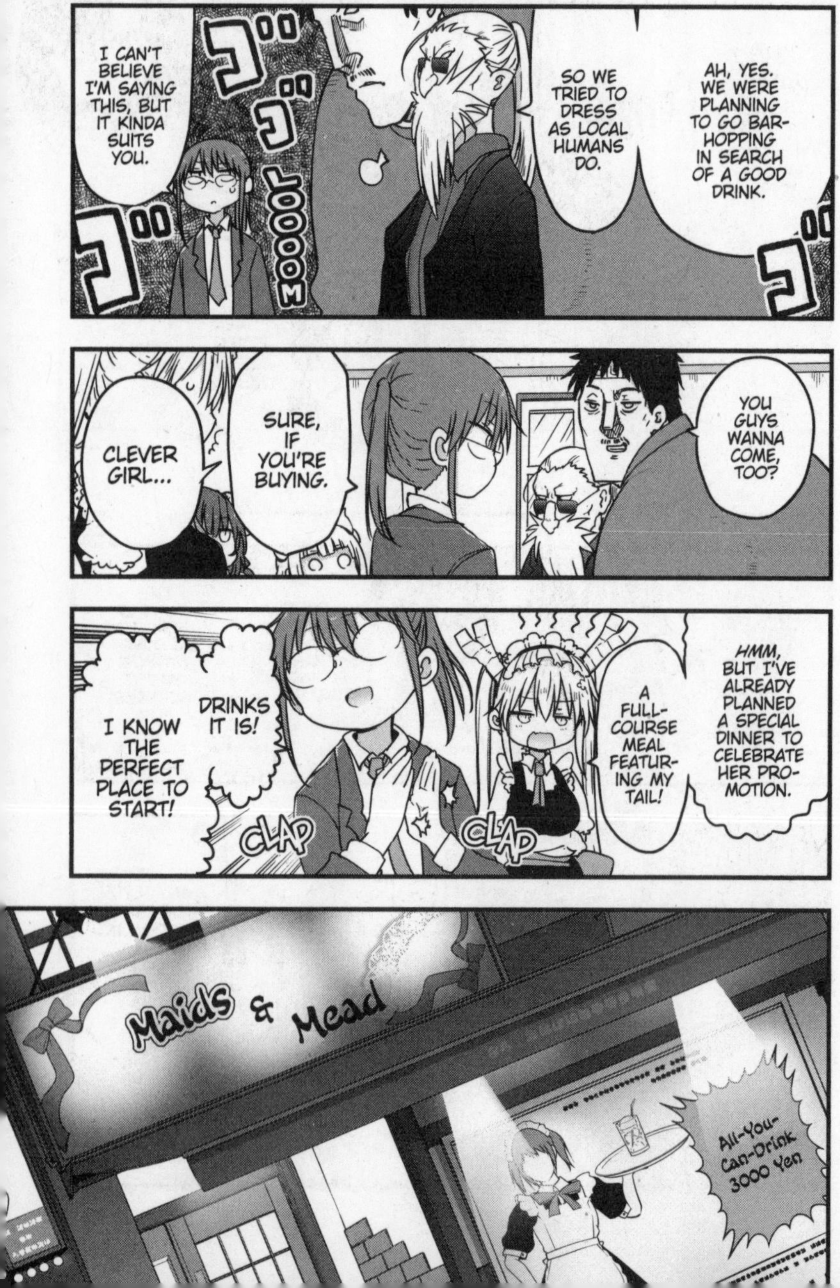
AH, YES. WE WERE PLANNING TO GO BAR-HOPPING IN SEARCH OF A GOOD DRINK.
SO WE TRIED TO DRESS AS LOCAL HUMANS DO.
WOOOOOM
I CAN'T BELIEVE I'M SAYING THIS, BUT IT KINDA SUITS YOU.
YOU GUYS WANNA COME, TOO?
SURE, IF YOU'RE BUYING.
CLEVER GIRL...
HMM, BUT I'VE ALREADY PLANNED A SPECIAL DINNER TO CELEBRATE HER PROMOTION.
A FULL-COURSE MEAL FEATURING MY TAIL!
CLAP
CLAP
DRINKS IT IS!
I KNOW THE PERFECT PLACE TO START!
Maids & Mead
All-You-Can-Drink 3000 Yen

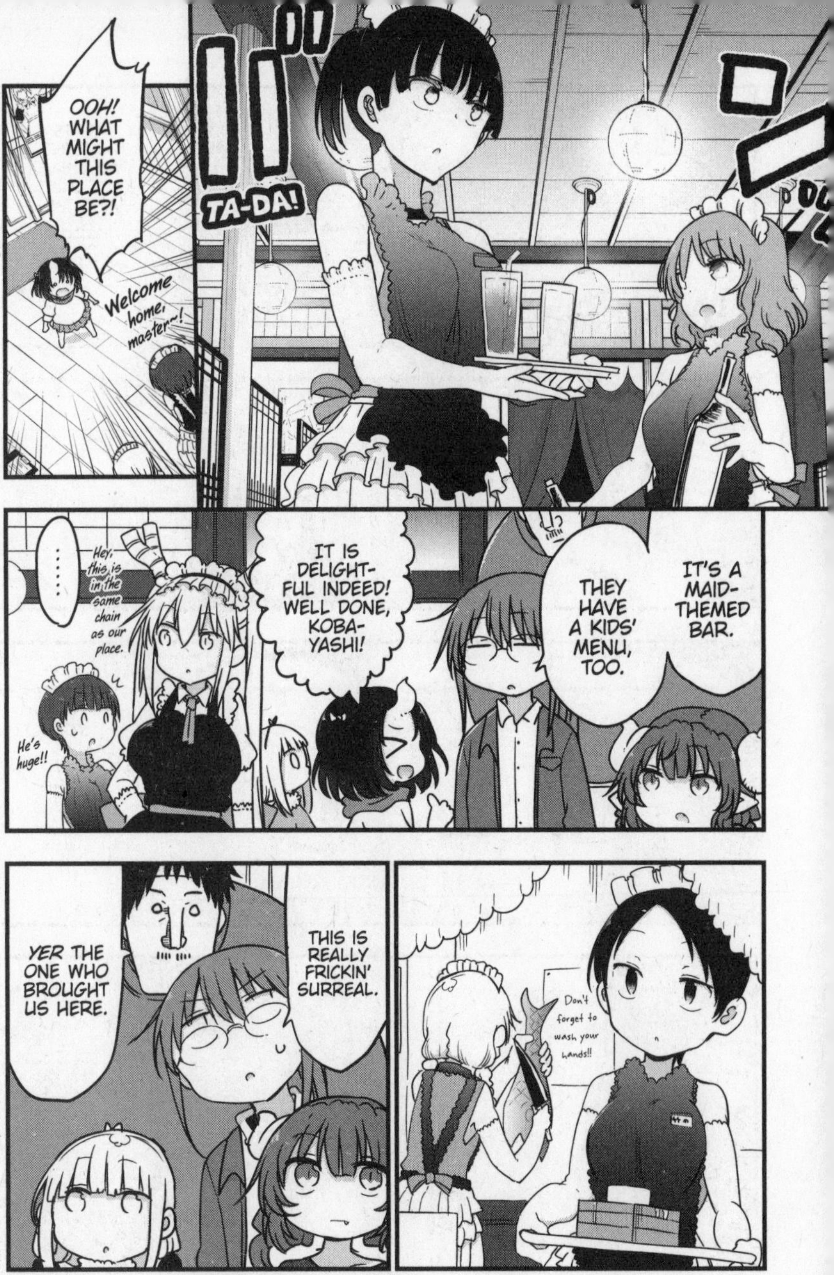
TA-DA!
OOH! WHAT MIGHT THIS PLACE BE?!
Welcome home, master~!
IT'S A MAID-THEMED BAR.
THEY HAVE A KIDS' MENU, TOO.
IT IS DELIGHTFUL INDEED! WELL DONE, KOBAYASHI!
Hey, this is in the same chain as our place.
......
He's huge!!
Don't forget to wash your hands!!
THIS IS REALLY FRICKIN' SURREAL.
YER THE ONE WHO BROUGHT US HERE.

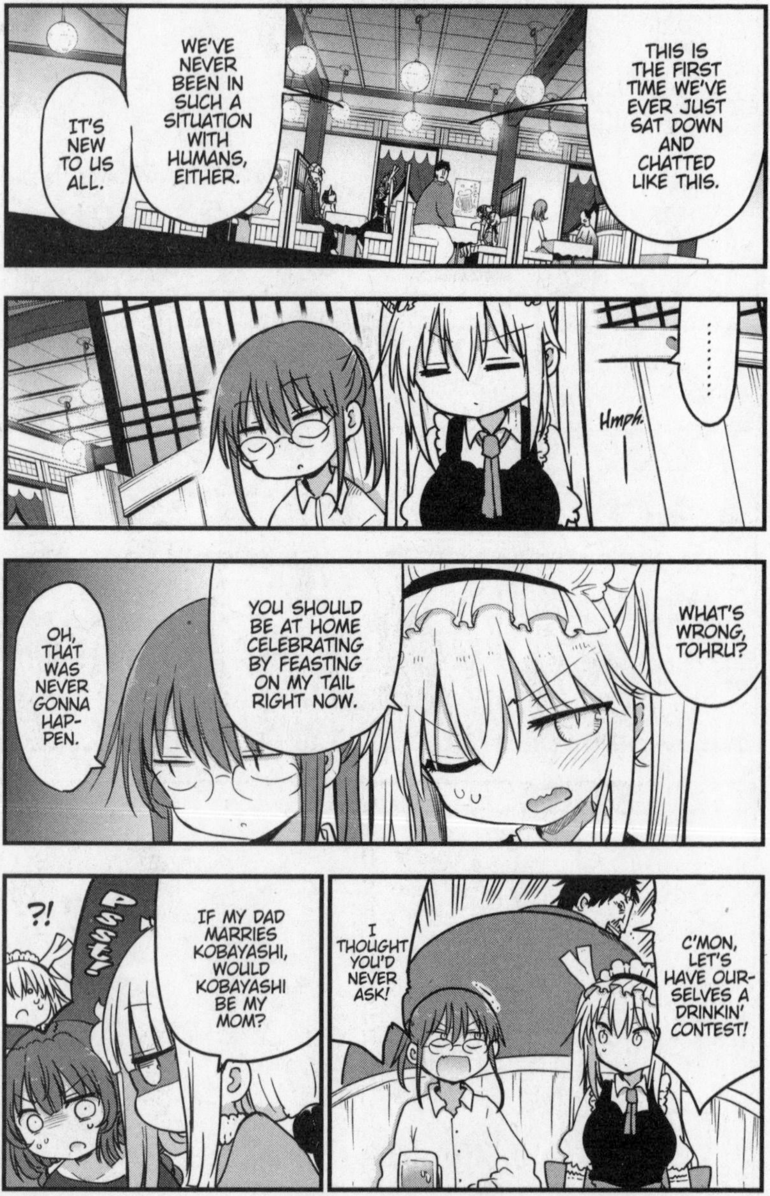
THIS IS THE FIRST TIME WE'VE EVER JUST SAT DOWN AND CHATTED LIKE THIS.
WE'VE NEVER BEEN IN SUCH A SITUATION WITH HUMANS, EITHER.
IT'S NEW TO US ALL.
......
Hmph.
WHAT'S WRONG, TOHRU?
YOU SHOULD BE AT HOME CELEBRATING BY FEASTING ON MY TAIL RIGHT NOW.
OH, THAT WAS NEVER GONNA HAP-PEN.
C'MON, LET'S HAVE OUR-SELVES A DRINKIN' CONTEST!
I THOUGHT YOU'D NEVER ASK!
IF MY DAD MARRIES KOBAYASHI, WOULD KOBAYASHI BE MY MOM?
PSST!
?!

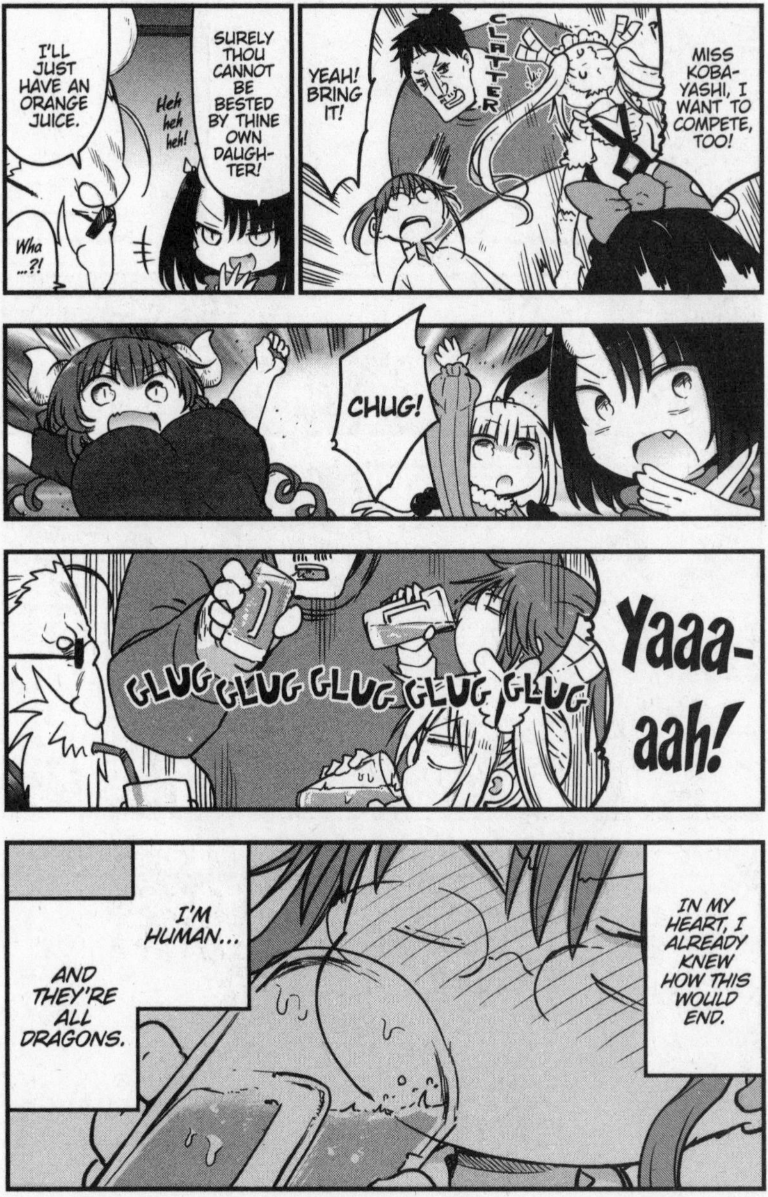
MISS KOBA-YASHI, I WANT TO COMPETE, TOO!
CLATTER
YEAH! BRING IT!
SURELY THOU CANNOT BE BESTED BY THINE OWN DAUGH-TER!
Heh heh heh!
I'LL JUST HAVE AN ORANGE JUICE.
Wha ...?!
CHUG!
Yaaa-aah!
GLUG GLUG GLUG GLUG GLUG
IN MY HEART, I ALREADY KNEW HOW THIS WOULD END.
I'M HUMAN...
AND THEY'RE ALL DRAGONS.

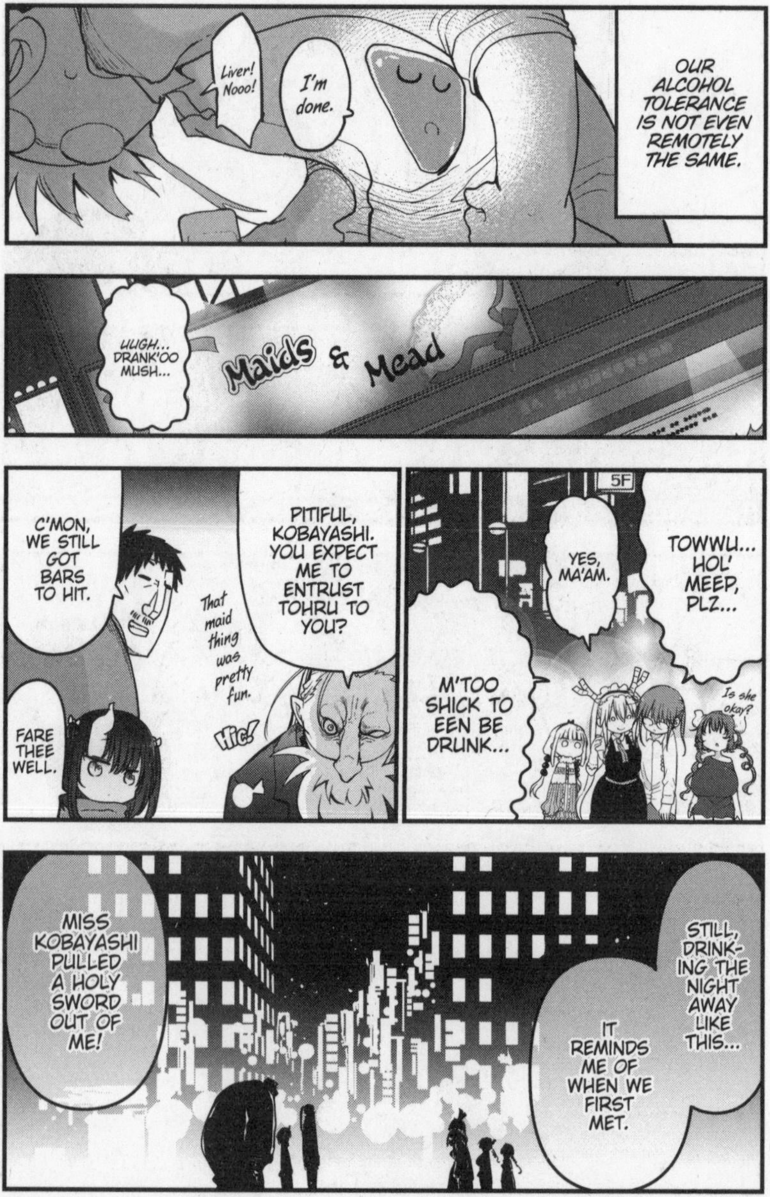
OUR ALCOHOL TOLERANCE IS NOT EVEN REMOTELY THE SAME.
I'm done.
Liver! Nooo!
UUGH... DRANK'OO MUSH...
Maids & Mead
5F
TOWWU... HOL' MEEP, PLZ...
YES, MA'AM.
Is she okay?
M'TOO SHICK TO EEN BE DRUNK...
PITIFUL, KOBAYASHI. YOU EXPECT ME TO ENTRUST TOHRU TO YOU?
That maid thing was pretty fun.
Hic!
C'MON, WE STILL GOT BARS TO HIT.
FARE THEE WELL.
STILL, DRINK-ING THE NIGHT AWAY LIKE THIS...
IT REMINDS ME OF WHEN WE FIRST MET.
MISS KOBAYASHI PULLED A HOLY SWORD OUT OF ME!

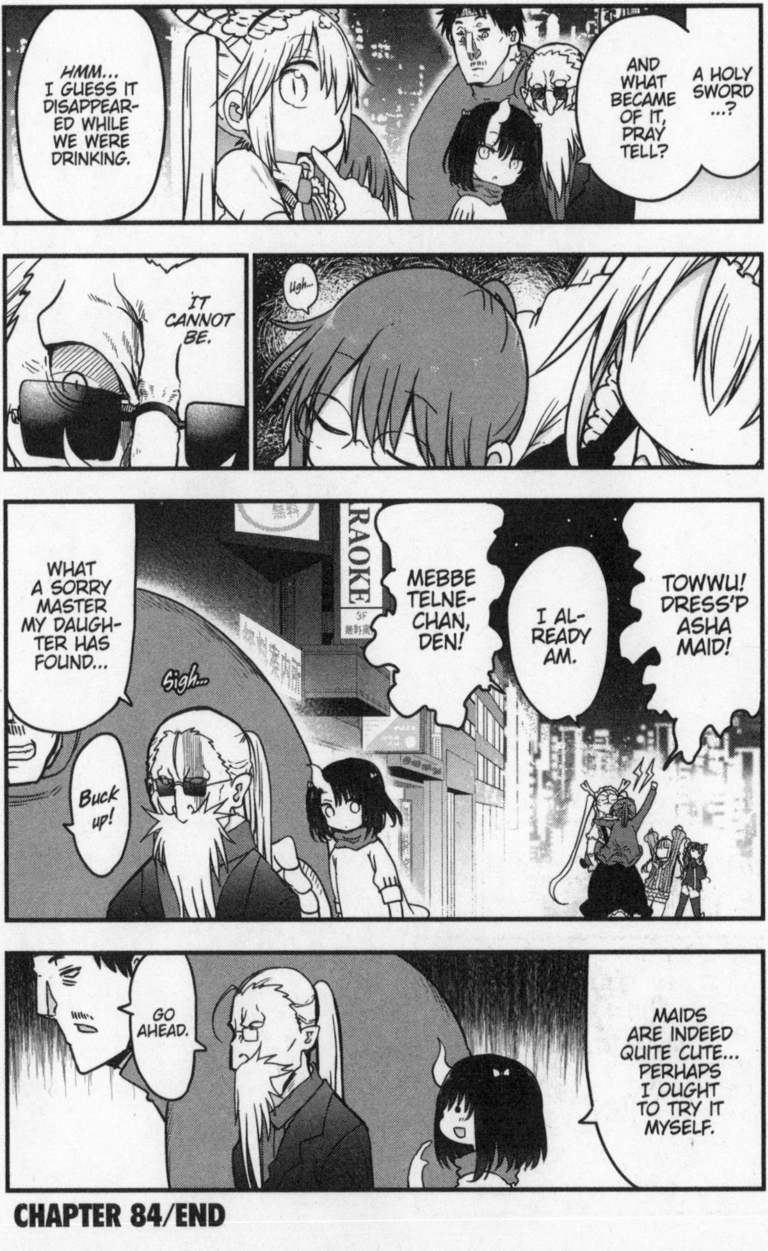
A HOLY SWORD ...?
AND WHAT BECAME OF IT, PRAY TELL?
HMM... I GUESS IT DISAPPEARED WHILE WE WERE DRINKING.
Ugh...
IT CANNOT BE.
TOWWU! DRESS'P ASHA MAID!
I ALREADY AM.
MEBBE TELNE-CHAN, DEN!
RAOKE
3F
WHAT A SORRY MASTER MY DAUGHTER HAS FOUND...
Sigh...
Buck up!
MAIDS ARE INDEED QUITE CUTE... PERHAPS I OUGHT TO TRY IT MYSELF.
GO AHEAD.

CHAPTER 84/END

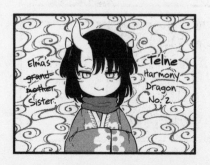

Telne Harmony Dragon No. 2.
Elma's grandmother Sister.

Miss Kobayashi's
Dragon Maid

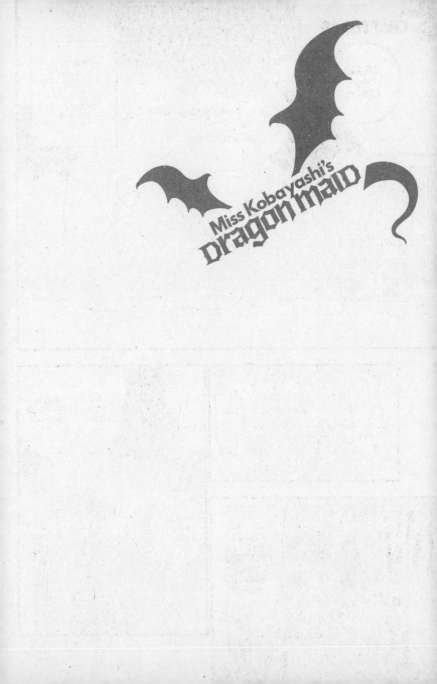

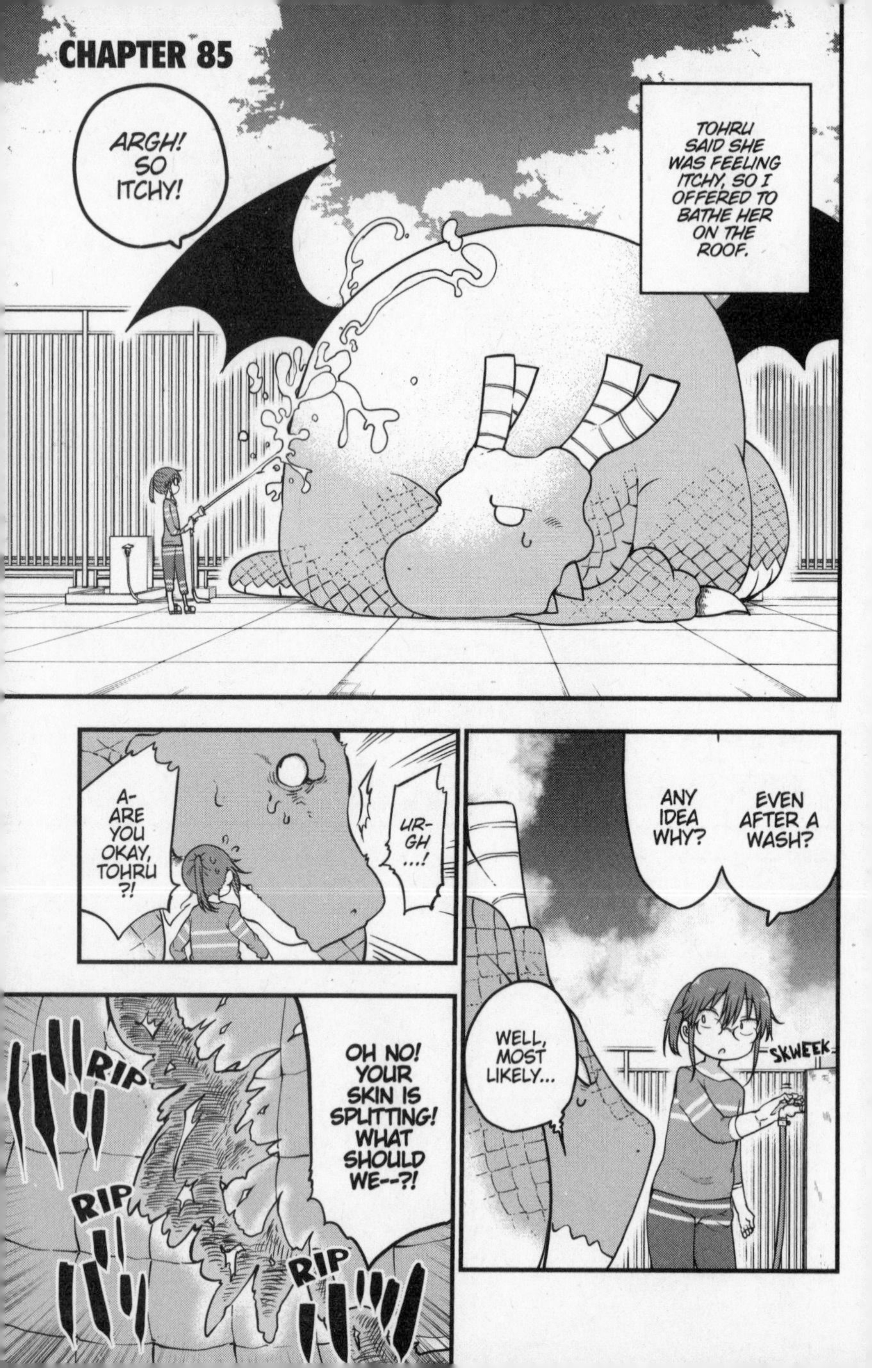
CHAPTER 85
TOHRU SAID SHE WAS FEELING ITCHY, SO I OFFERED TO BATHE HER ON THE ROOF.
ARGH! SO ITCHY!
EVEN AFTER A WASH?
ANY IDEA WHY?
WELL, MOST LIKELY...
SKWEEK
URGH...!
A-ARE YOU OKAY, TOHRU?!
OH NO! YOUR SKIN IS SPLITTING! WHAT SHOULD WE--?!
RIP
RIP
RIP

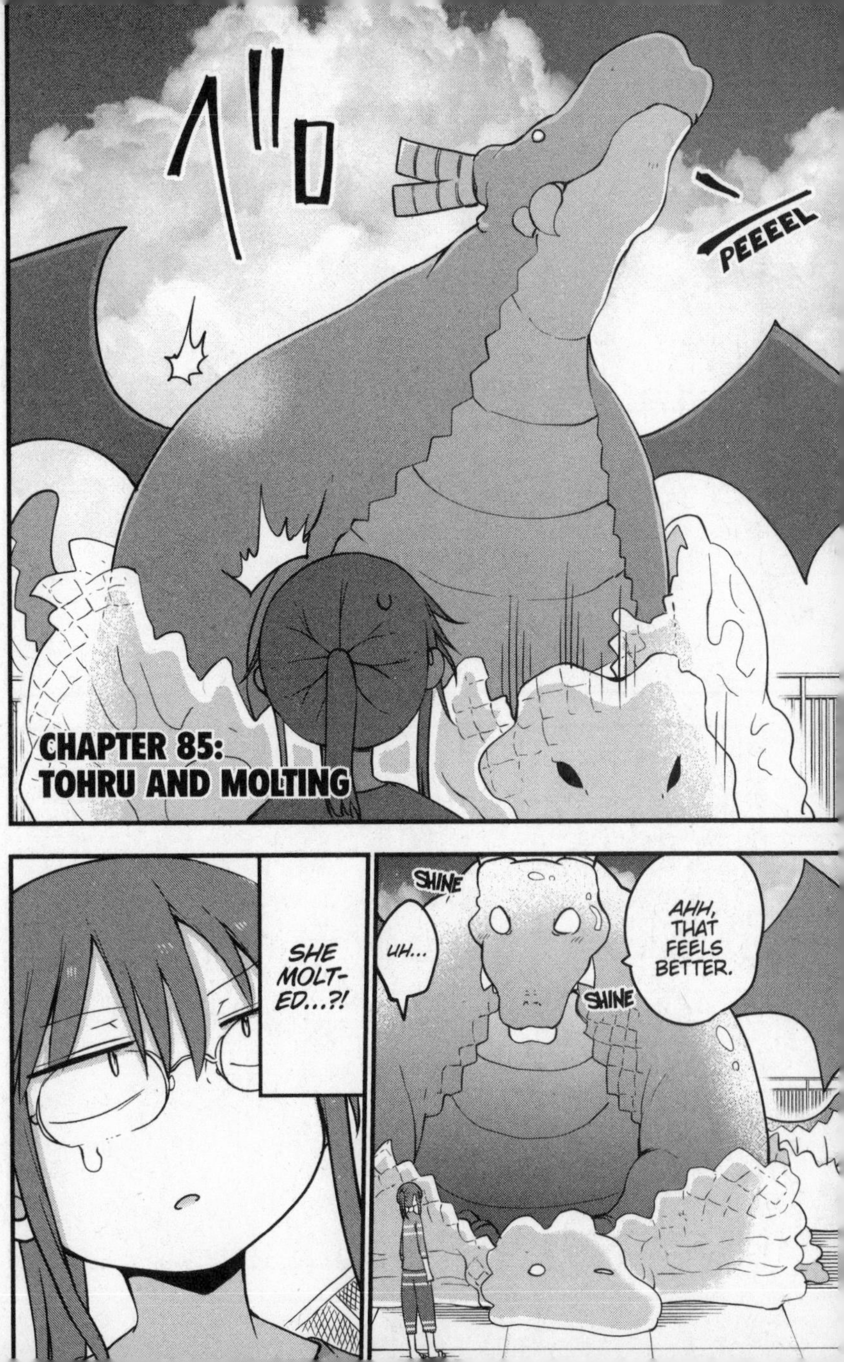
PEEEEL
CHAPTER 85:
TOHRU AND MOLTING
SHINE
AHH, THAT FEELS BETTER.
UH...
SHINE
SHE MOLT-ED...?!

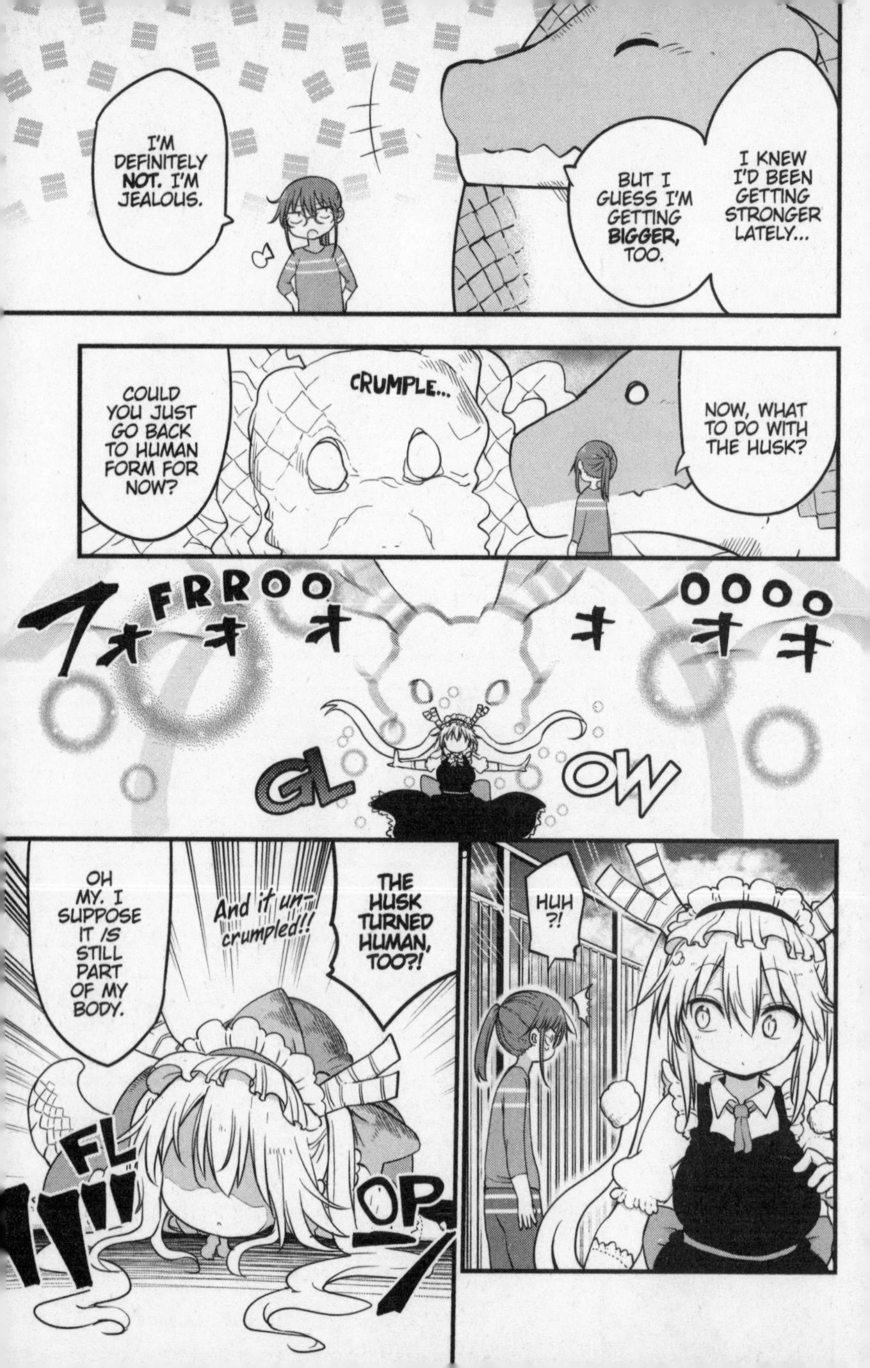
I KNEW I'D BEEN GETTING STRONGER LATELY...
BUT I GUESS I'M GETTING BIGGER, TOO.
I'M DEFINITELY NOT. I'M JEALOUS.
NOW, WHAT TO DO WITH THE HUSK?
CRUMPLE...
COULD YOU JUST GO BACK TO HUMAN FORM FOR NOW?
FRROO OOOO
GL OW
HUH?!
THE HUSK TURNED HUMAN, TOO?!
And it un-crumpled!!
OH MY. I SUPPOSE IT IS STILL PART OF MY BODY.
FL OP

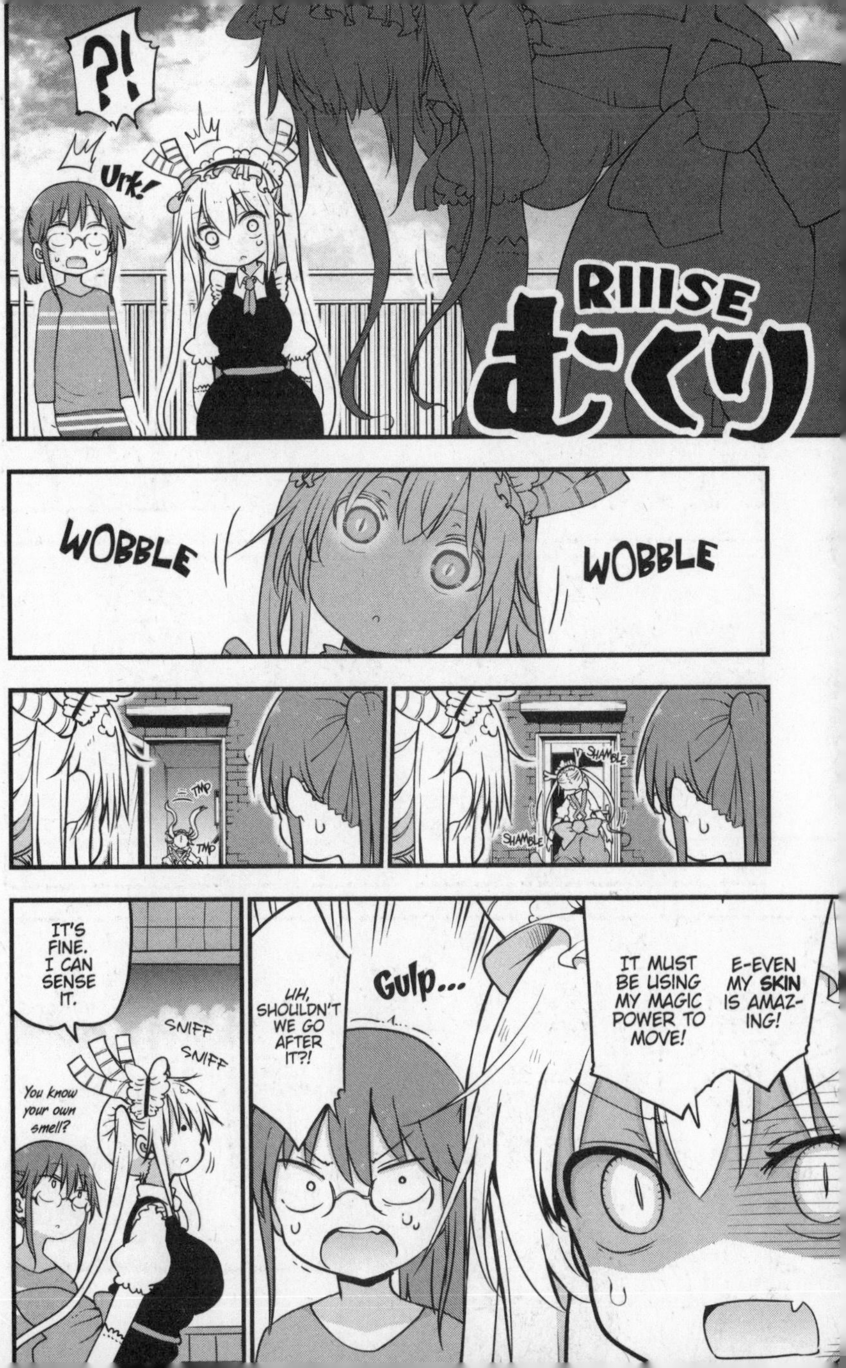
?!
Urk!
RIIISE
めくり
WOBBLE
WOBBLE
SHAMBLE
SHAMBLE
TMP
TMP
E-EVEN MY SKIN IS AMAZ-ING!
IT MUST BE USING MY MAGIC POWER TO MOVE!
Gulp...
UH, SHOULDN'T WE GO AFTER IT?!
IT'S FINE. I CAN SENSE IT.
SNIFF
SNIFF
You know your own smell?

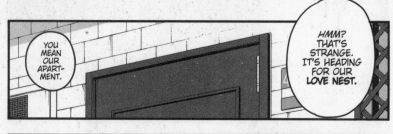

HMM? THAT'S STRANGE. IT'S HEADING FOR OUR LOVE NEST.
YOU MEAN OUR APART-MENT.
Oh!
SWISH
SWISH
PAT PAT
SHUFF...
SHUFF...
UM, IS IT DOING CHORES?
MAYBE IT'S JUST RE-ENACTING FAMILIAR MOVE-MENTS?
TWO LADY TOH-RUS?!
Oh my gosh!
THIS MUST BE THE EVIL TWIN!!
EXCUSE ME?! I'M THE REAL THING!!
Whaaaa?!

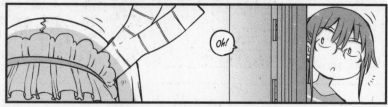

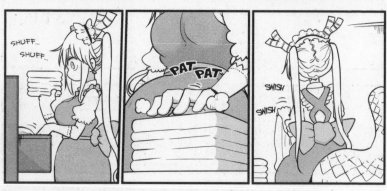

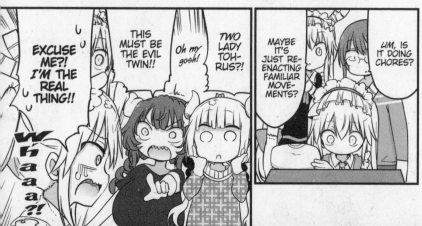

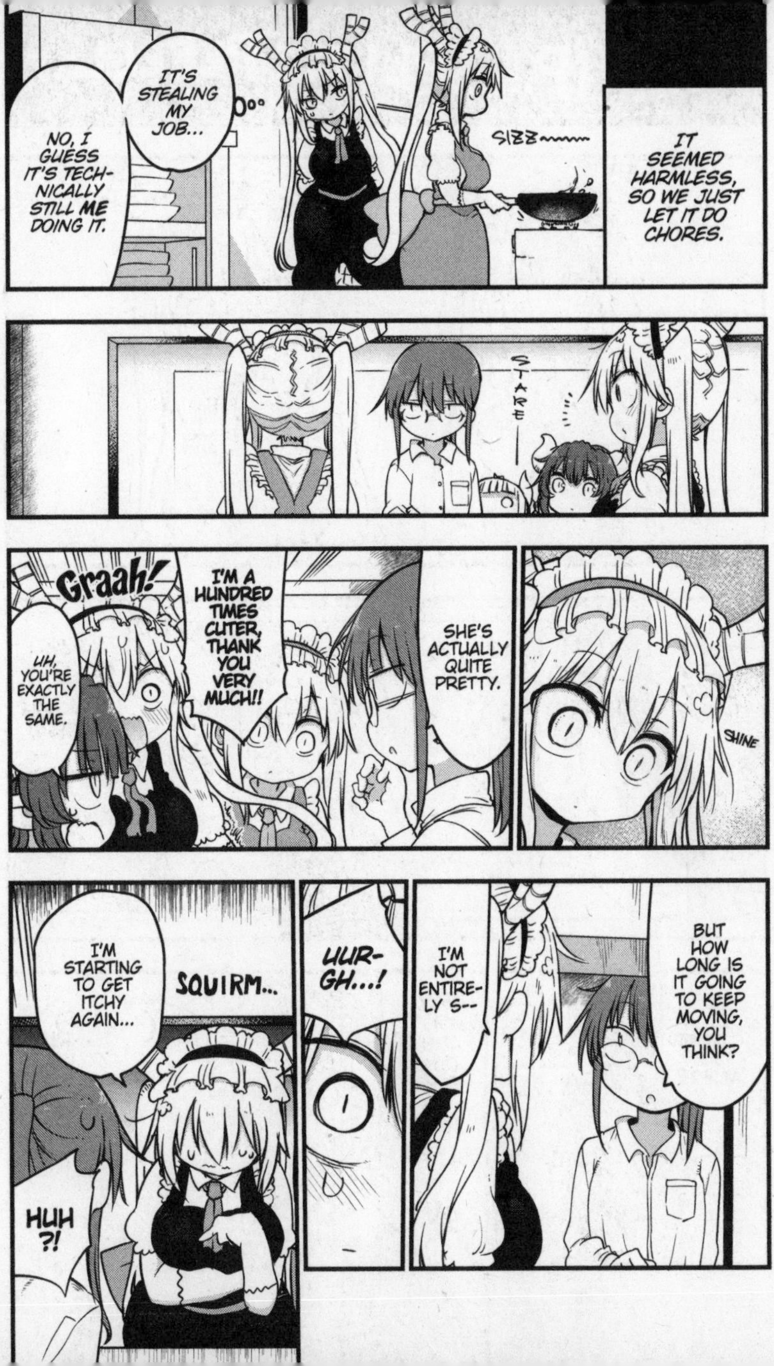
IT SEEMED HARMLESS, SO WE JUST LET IT DO CHORES.
SIZZ
IT'S STEALING MY JOB...
NO, I GUESS IT'S TECHNICALLY STILL ME DOING IT.
STARE
SHINE
SHE'S ACTUALLY QUITE PRETTY.
I'M A HUNDRED TIMES CUTER, THANK YOU VERY MUCH!!
Graah!
UH, YOU'RE EXACTLY THE SAME.
BUT HOW LONG IS IT GOING TO KEEP MOVING, YOU THINK?
I'M NOT ENTIRELY S--
UURGH...!
SQUIRM...
I'M STARTING TO GET ITCHY AGAIN...
HUH?!

RRRIP... SPLIT... PEEEEL...

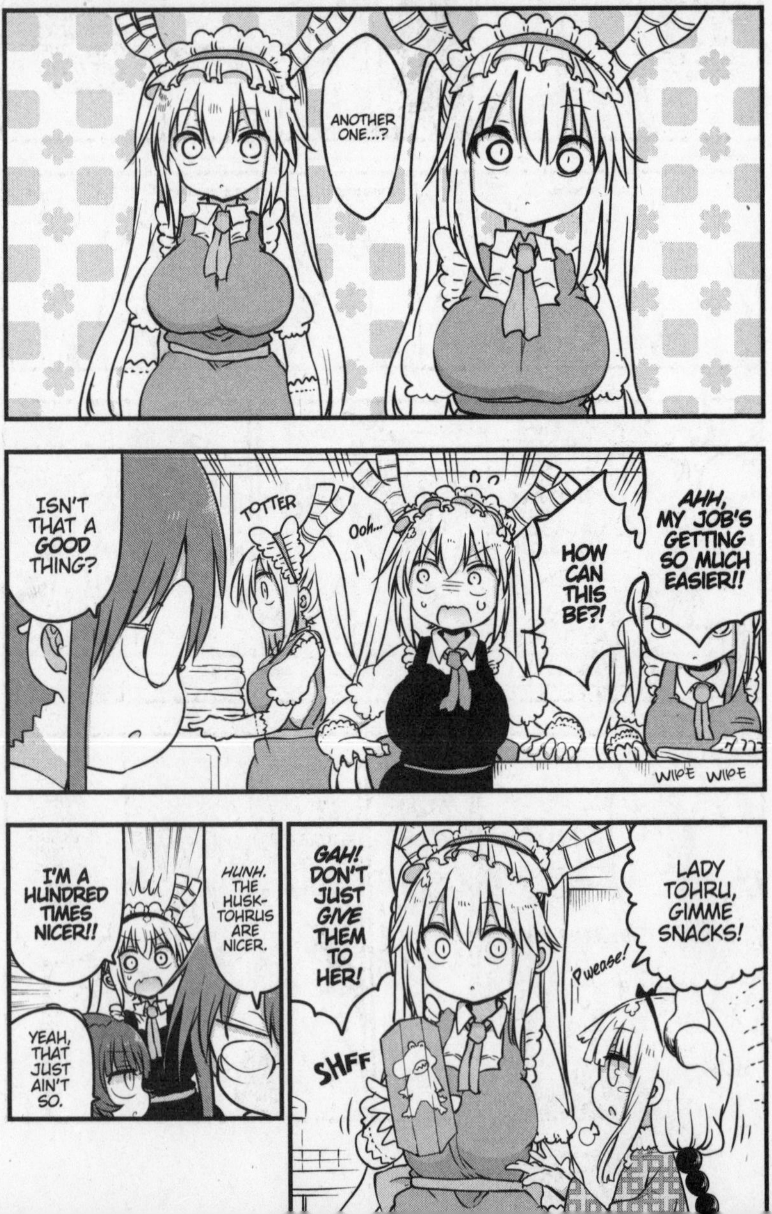
ANOTHER ONE...?
AHH, MY JOB'S GETTING SO MUCH EASIER!!
HOW CAN THIS BE?!
Ooh...
TOTTER
ISN'T THAT A GOOD THING?
WIPE WIPE
LADY TOHRU, GIMME SNACKS!
Pwease!
GAH! DON'T JUST GIVE THEM TO HER!
SHFF
HUNH. THE HUSK-TOHRUS ARE NICER.
I'M A HUNDRED TIMES NICER!!
YEAH, THAT JUST AIN'T SO.

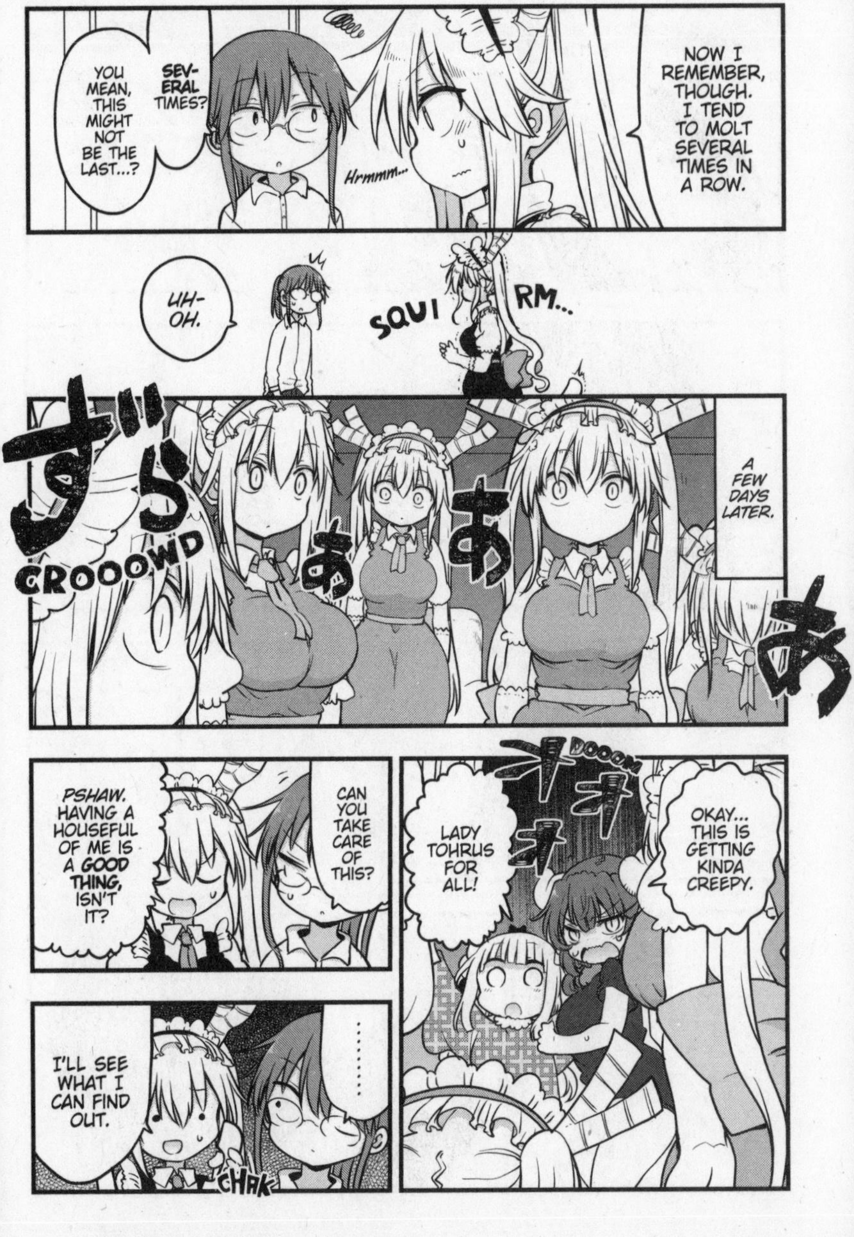
NOW I REMEMBER, THOUGH. I TEND TO MOLT SEVERAL TIMES IN A ROW.
SEV-ERAL TIMES?
YOU MEAN, THIS MIGHT NOT BE THE LAST...?
Hrmmm...
SQUI RM...
UH-OH.
A FEW DAYS LATER.
あ
あ
あ
ずら
CROOOWD
OKAY... THIS IS GETTING KINDA CREEPY.
DOOOM
オオオ
LADY TOHRUS FOR ALL!
CAN YOU TAKE CARE OF THIS?
PSHAW. HAVING A HOUSEFUL OF ME IS A **GOOD THING,** ISN'T IT?
......
I'LL SEE WHAT I CAN FIND OUT.
CHAK

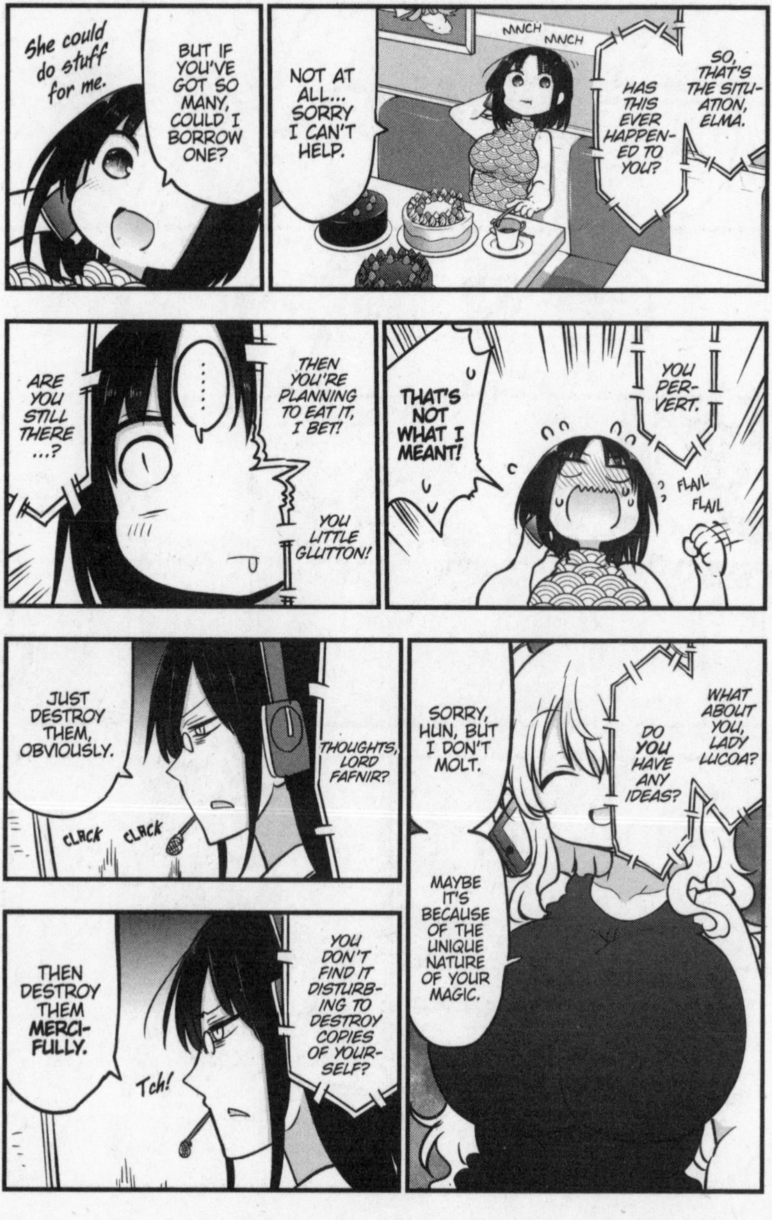
SO, THAT'S THE SITUATION, ELMA.
HAS THIS EVER HAPPENED TO YOU?
MNCH MNCH
NOT AT ALL... SORRY I CAN'T HELP.
BUT IF YOU'VE GOT SO MANY, COULD I BORROW ONE?
She could do stuff for me.
YOU PERVERT.
THAT'S NOT WHAT I MEANT!
FLAIL FLAIL
THEN YOU'RE PLANNING TO EAT IT, I BET!
......
ARE YOU STILL THERE ...?
YOU LITTLE GLUTTON!
WHAT ABOUT YOU, LADY LUCOA?
DO YOU HAVE ANY IDEAS?
SORRY, HUN, BUT I DON'T MOLT.
MAYBE IT'S BECAUSE OF THE UNIQUE NATURE OF YOUR MAGIC.
THOUGHTS, LORD FAFNIR?
JUST DESTROY THEM, OBVIOUSLY.
CLACK CLACK
YOU DON'T FIND IT DISTURBING TO DESTROY COPIES OF YOURSELF?
THEN DESTROY THEM MERCIFULLY.
Tch!

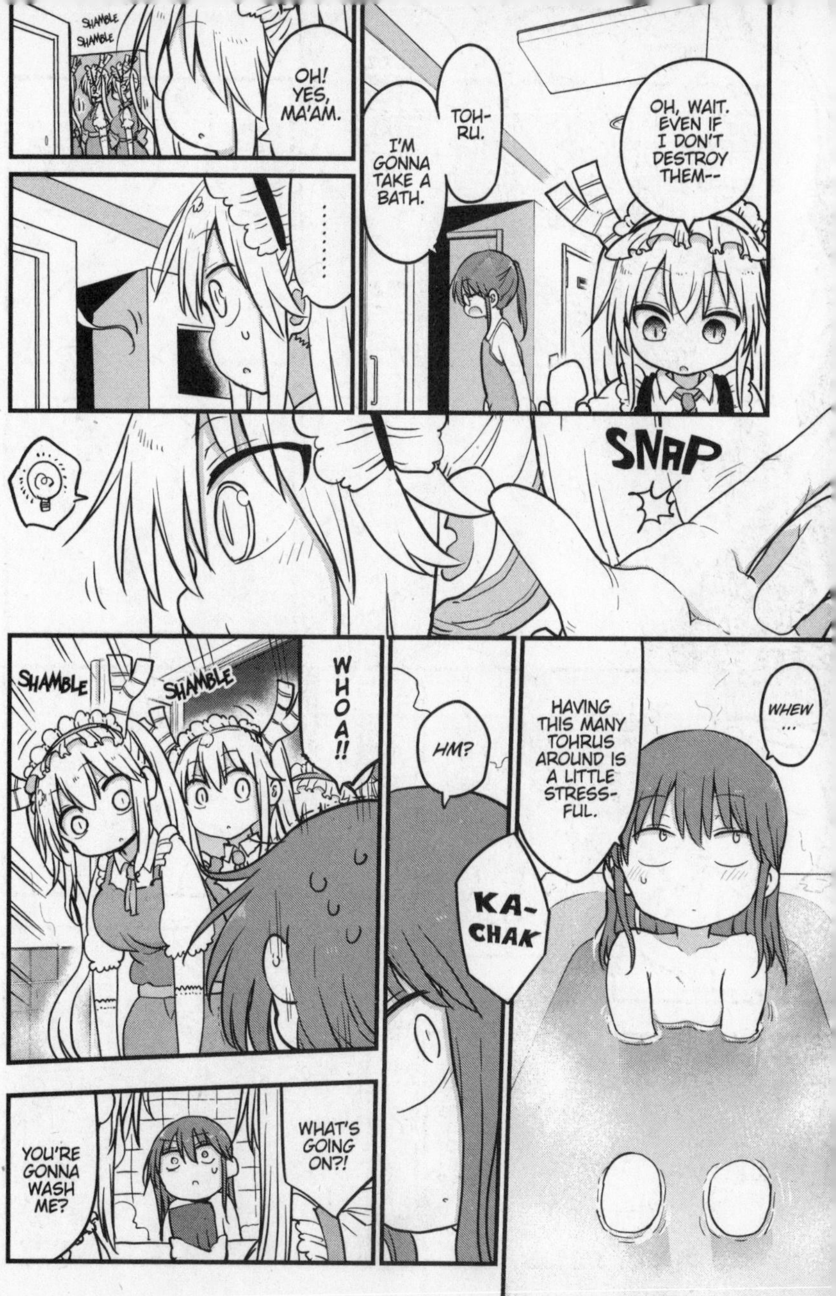
OH, WAIT. EVEN IF I DON'T DESTROY THEM--
TOH-RU.
I'M GONNA TAKE A BATH.
SHAMBLE
SHAMBLE
OH! YES, MA'AM.
......
SNAP
WHEW...
HAVING THIS MANY TOHRUS AROUND IS A LITTLE STRESS-FUL.
KA-CHAK
HM?
WHOA!!
SHAMBLE
SHAMBLE
WHAT'S GOING ON?!
YOU'RE GONNA WASH ME?

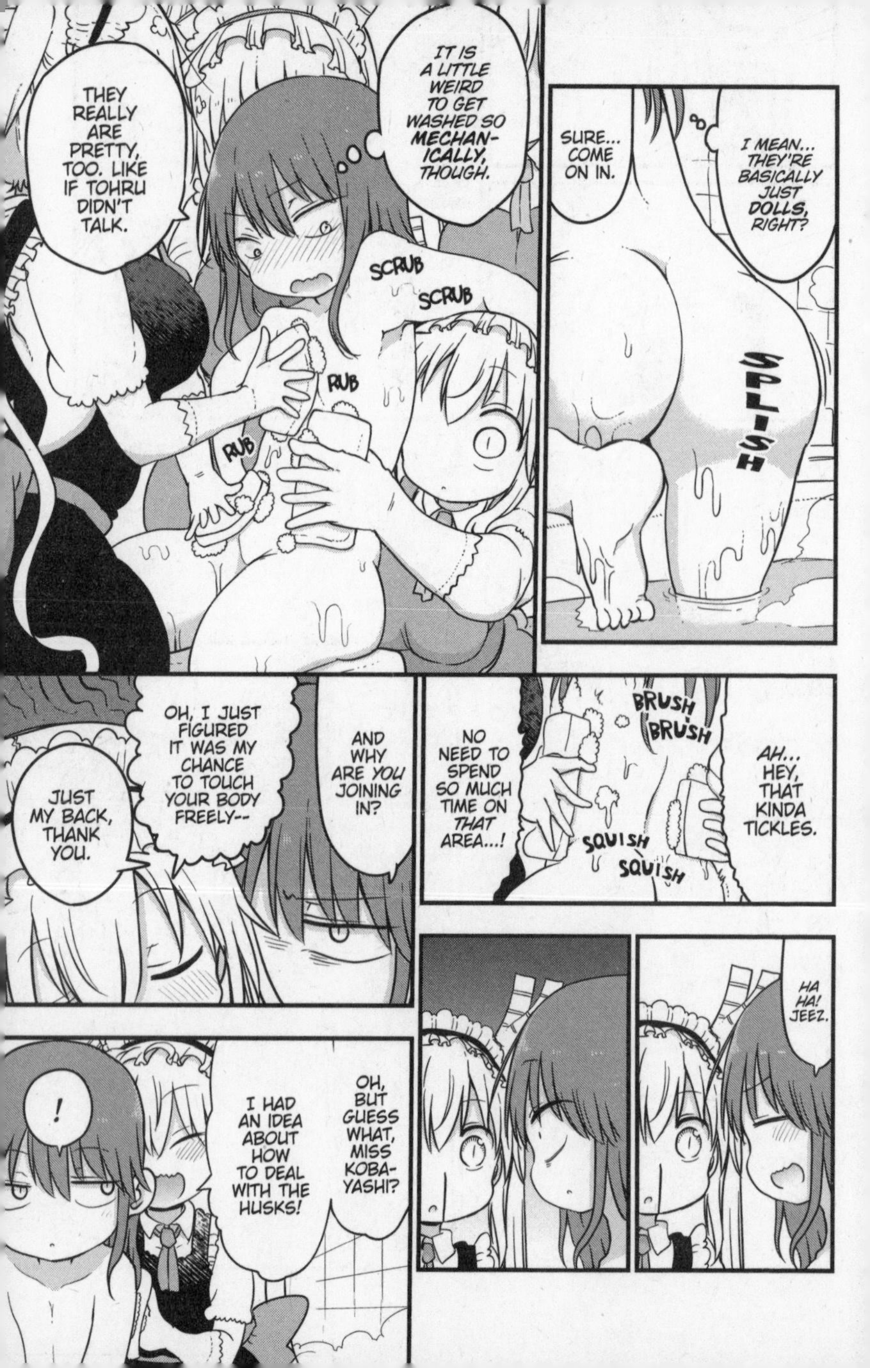
I MEAN... THEY'RE BASICALLY JUST DOLLS, RIGHT?
SURE... COME ON IN.
SPLISH
IT IS A LITTLE WEIRD TO GET WASHED SO MECHANICALLY, THOUGH.
THEY REALLY ARE PRETTY, TOO. LIKE IF TOHRU DIDN'T TALK.
SCRUB
SCRUB
RUB
RUB
AH... HEY, THAT KINDA TICKLES.
BRUSH
BRUSH
NO NEED TO SPEND SO MUCH TIME ON THAT AREA...!
SQUISH
SQUISH
AND WHY ARE YOU JOINING IN?
OH, I JUST FIGURED IT WAS MY CHANCE TO TOUCH YOUR BODY FREELY--
JUST MY BACK, THANK YOU.
HA HA! JEEZ.
OH, BUT GUESS WHAT, MISS KOBAYASHI?
I HAD AN IDEA ABOUT HOW TO DEAL WITH THE HUSKS!
!

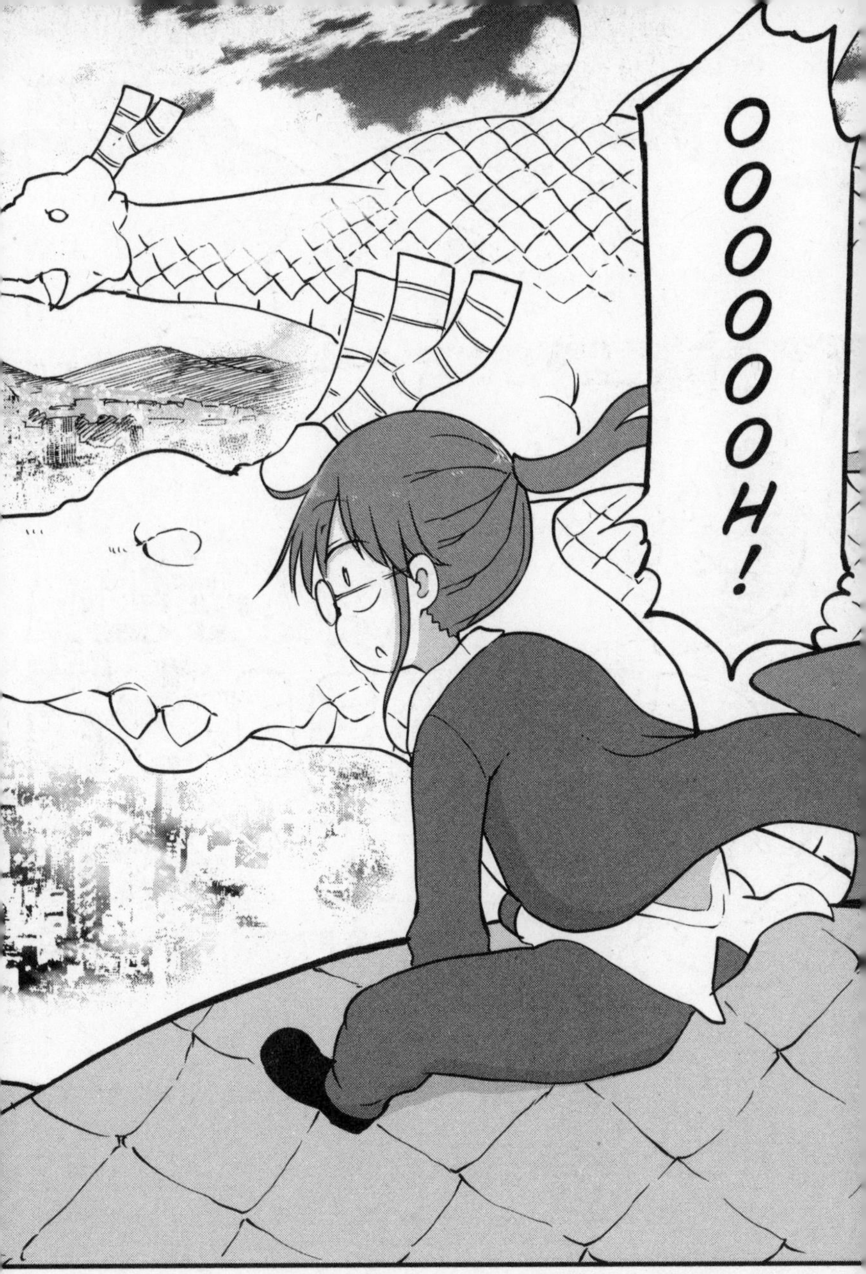
OOOOOOOH!

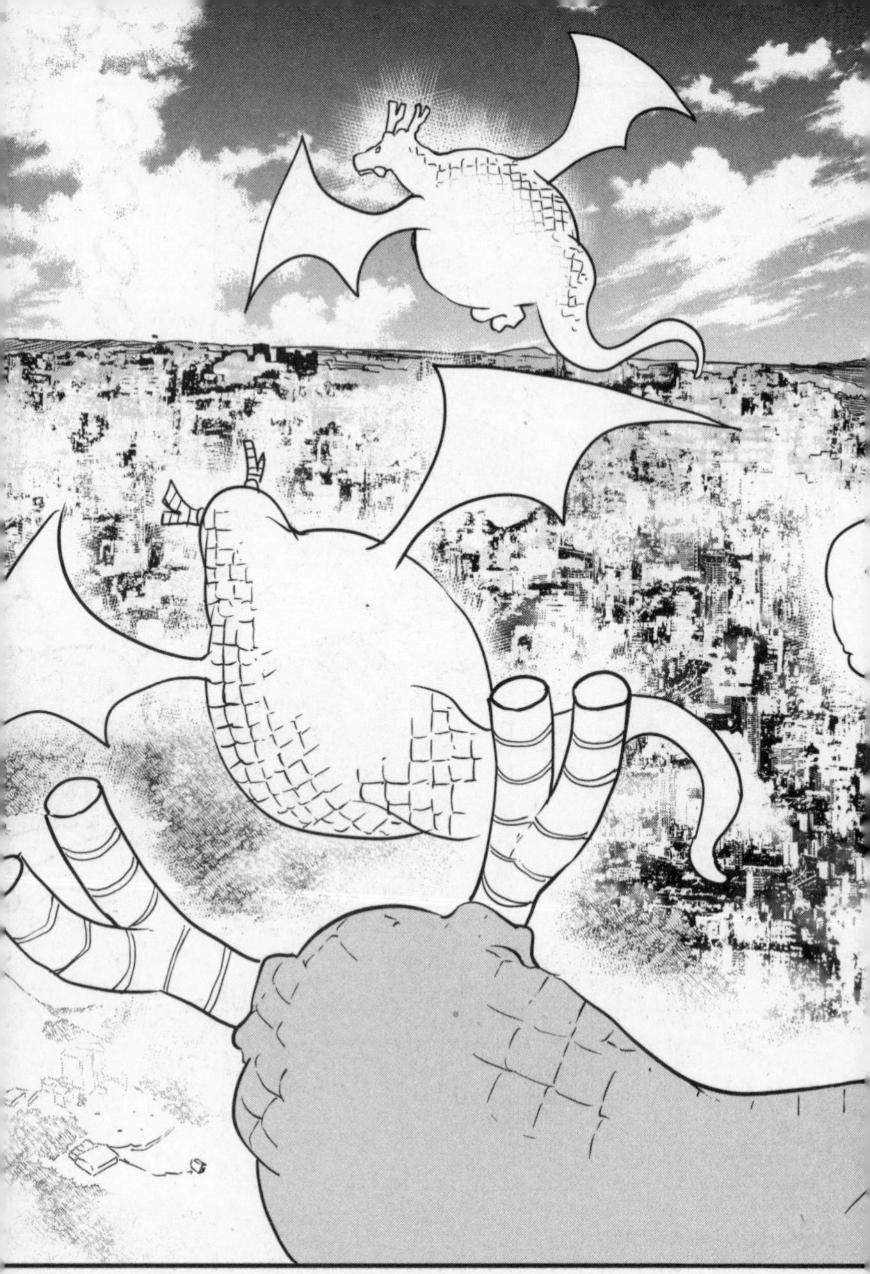

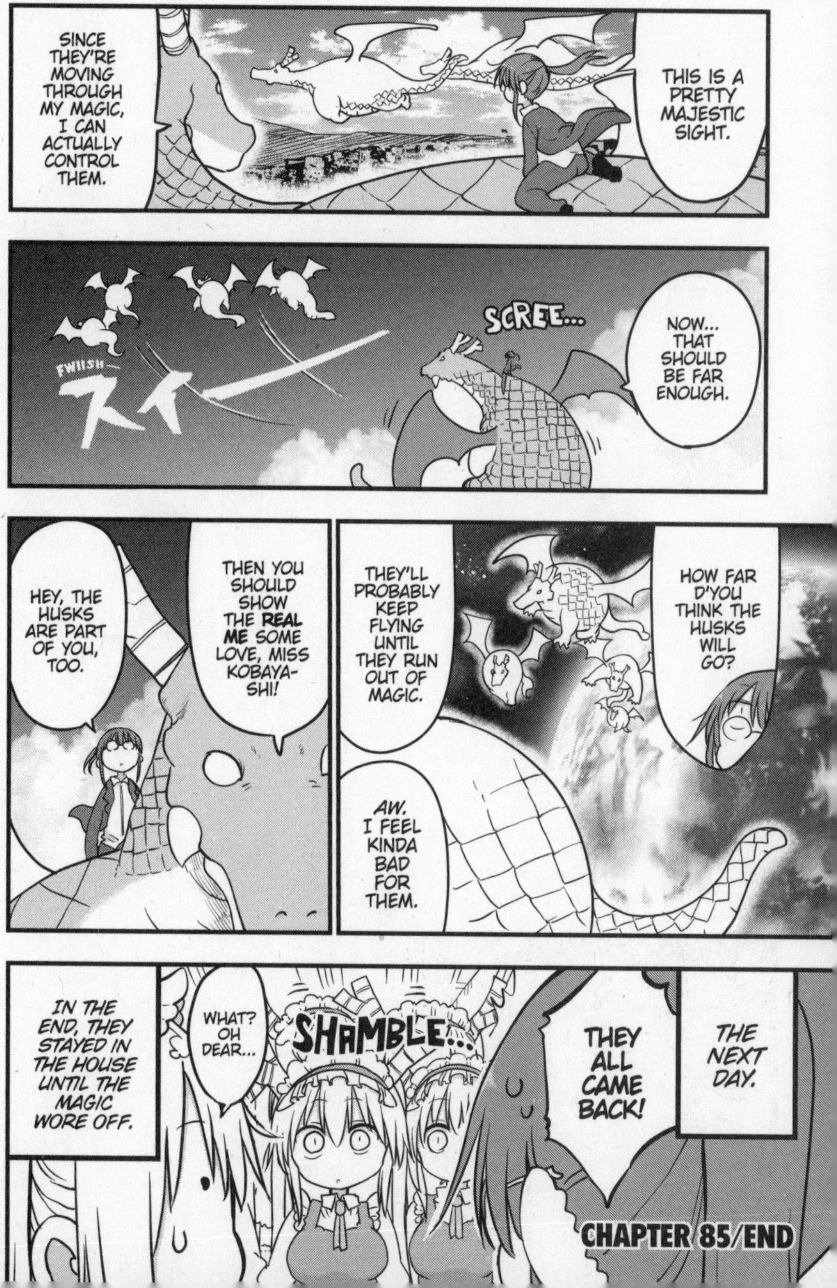
THIS IS A PRETTY MAJESTIC SIGHT.
SINCE THEY'RE MOVING THROUGH MY MAGIC, I CAN ACTUALLY CONTROL THEM.
NOW... THAT SHOULD BE FAR ENOUGH.
SCREE...
FWIISH—
スイ
HOW FAR D'YOU THINK THE HUSKS WILL GO?
THEY'LL PROBABLY KEEP FLYING UNTIL THEY RUN OUT OF MAGIC.
AW. I FEEL KINDA BAD FOR THEM.
THEN YOU SHOULD SHOW THE REAL ME SOME LOVE, MISS KOBAYASHI!
HEY, THE HUSKS ARE PART OF YOU, TOO.
THE NEXT DAY.
THEY ALL CAME BACK!
SHAMBLE...
WHAT? OH DEAR...
IN THE END, THEY STAYED IN THE HOUSE UNTIL THE MAGIC WORE OFF.
CHAPTER 85/END

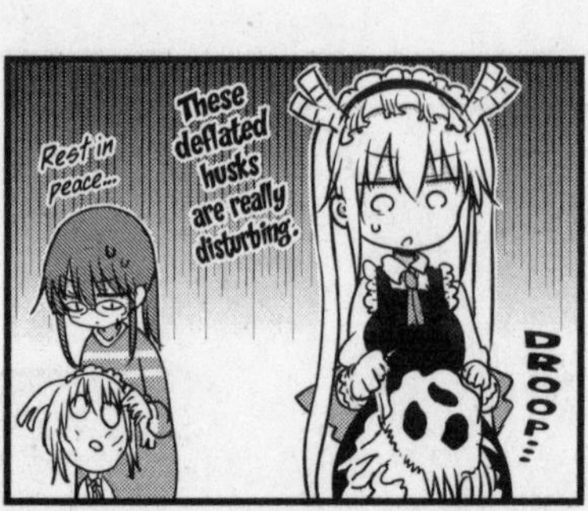
These deflated husks are really disturbing.
Rest in peace...
DROOP...

Miss Kobayashi's Dragon Maid

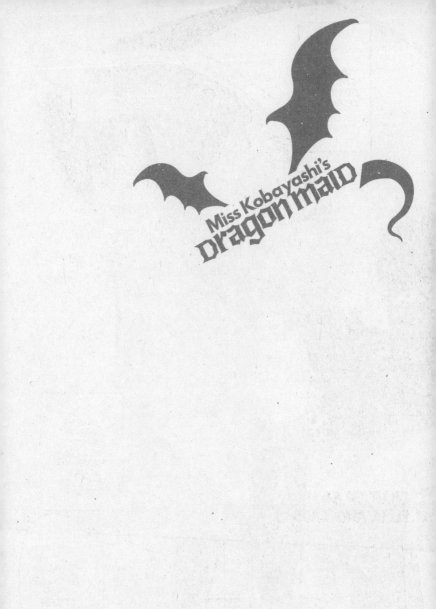

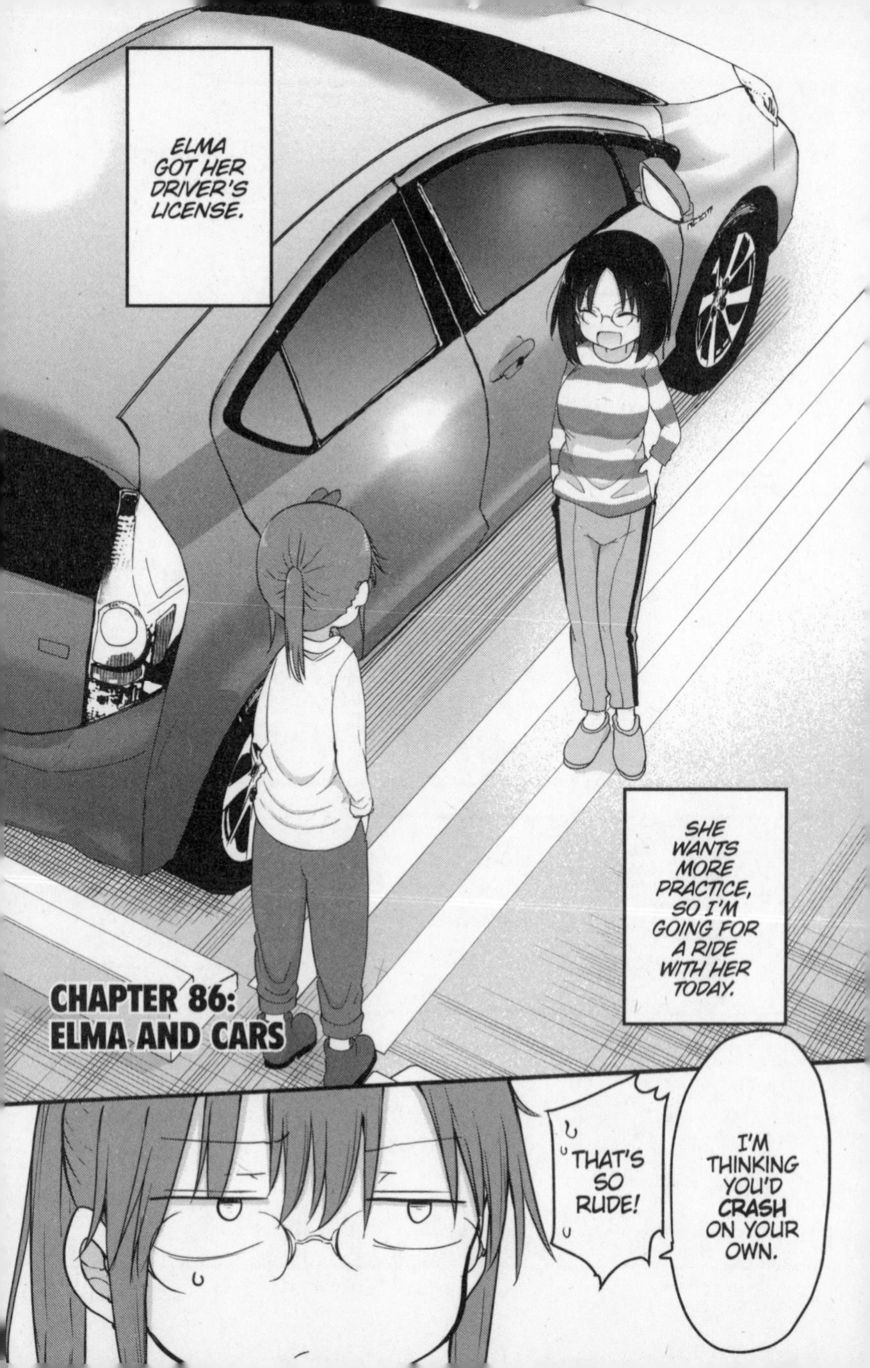
ELMA GOT HER DRIVER'S LICENSE.
SHE WANTS MORE PRACTICE, SO I'M GOING FOR A RIDE WITH HER TODAY.
CHAPTER 86: ELMA AND CARS
I'M THINKING YOU'D CRASH ON YOUR OWN.
THAT'S SO RUDE!

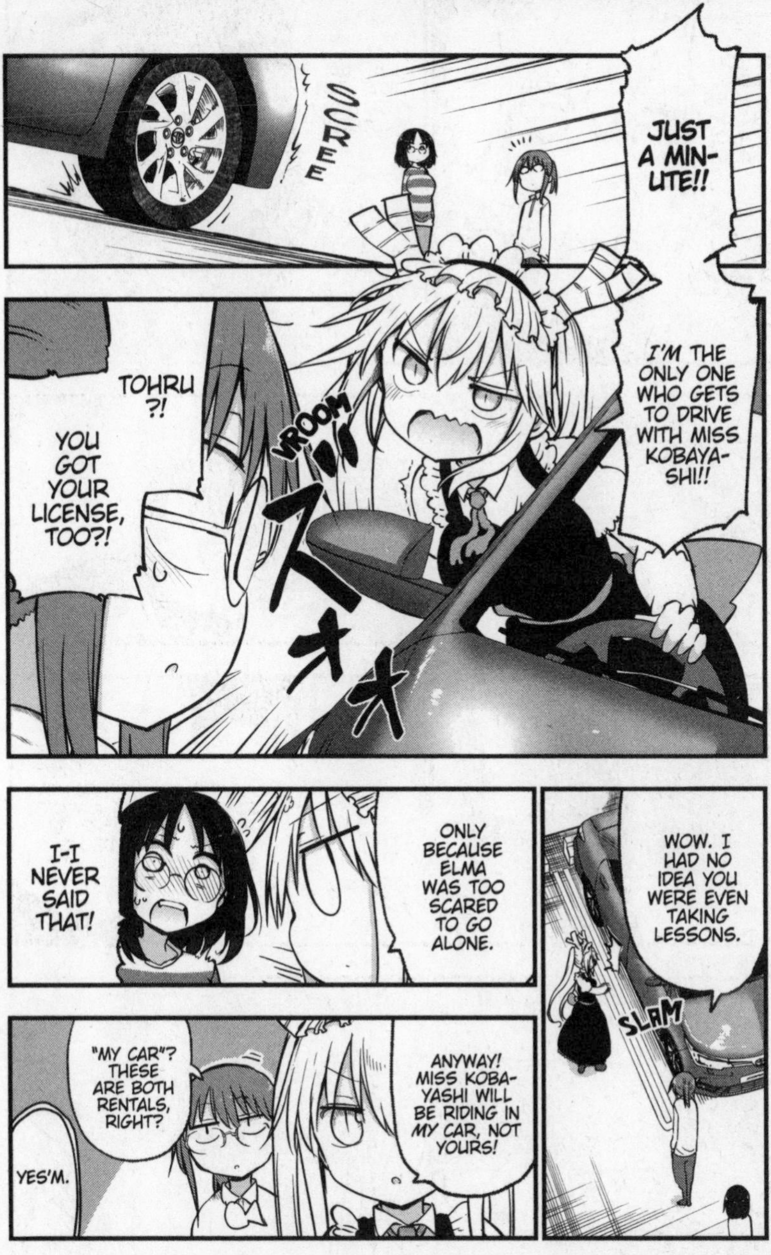
JUST A MIN-UTE!!
SCREE
I'M THE ONLY ONE WHO GETS TO DRIVE WITH MISS KOBAYA-SHI!!
VROOM
TOHRU?!
YOU GOT YOUR LICENSE, TOO?!
WOW. I HAD NO IDEA YOU WERE EVEN TAKING LESSONS.
SLAM
ONLY BECAUSE ELMA WAS TOO SCARED TO GO ALONE.
I-I NEVER SAID THAT!
ANYWAY! MISS KOBA-YASHI WILL BE RIDING IN MY CAR, NOT YOURS!
"MY CAR"? THESE ARE BOTH RENTALS, RIGHT?
YES'M.

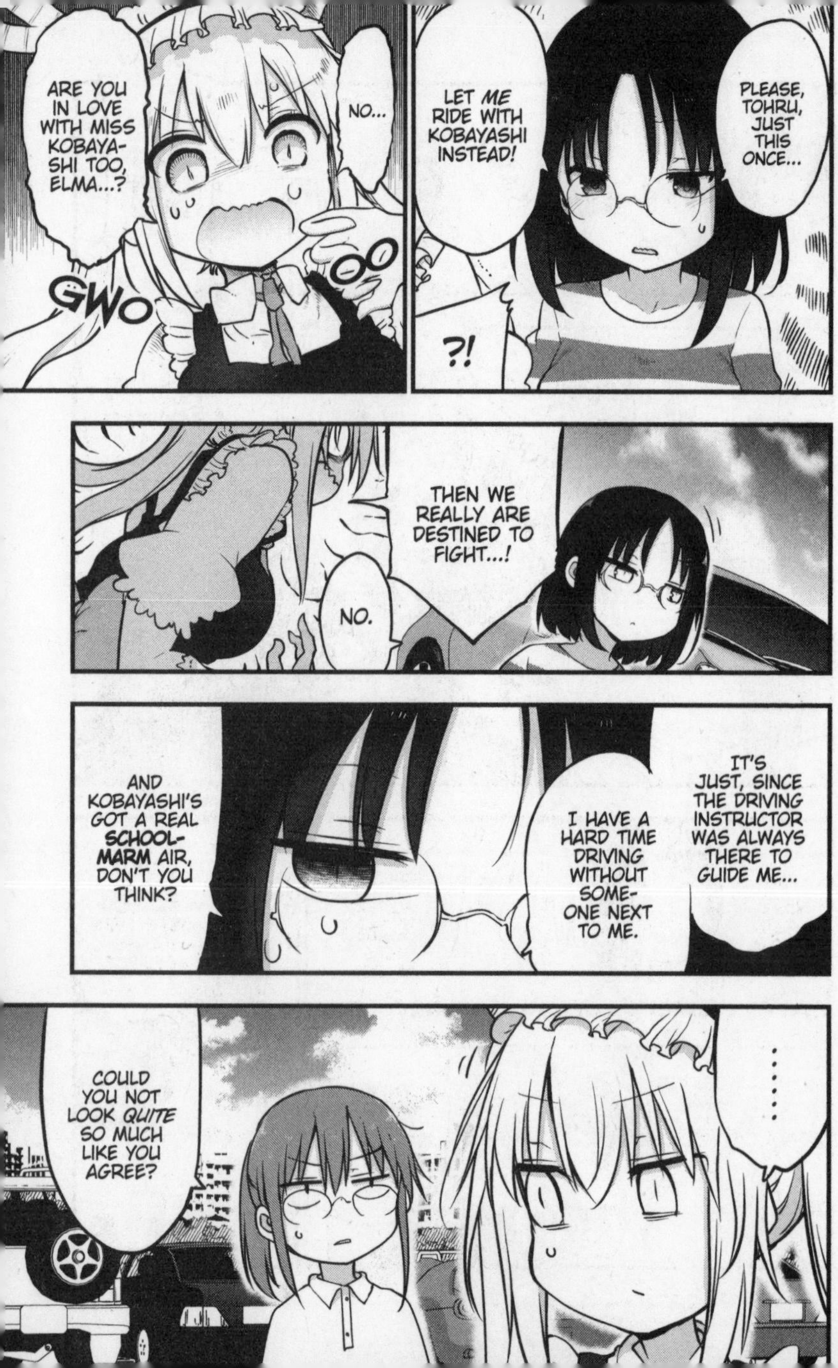
PLEASE, TOHRU, JUST THIS ONCE...
LET *ME* RIDE WITH KOBAYASHI INSTEAD!
?!
NO...
ARE YOU IN LOVE WITH MISS KOBAYASHI TOO, ELMA...?
GWO
THEN WE REALLY ARE DESTINED TO FIGHT...!
NO.
IT'S JUST, SINCE THE DRIVING INSTRUCTOR WAS ALWAYS THERE TO GUIDE ME...
I HAVE A HARD TIME DRIVING WITHOUT SOMEONE NEXT TO ME.
AND KOBAYASHI'S GOT A REAL **SCHOOLMARM** AIR, DON'T YOU THINK?
......
COULD YOU NOT LOOK *QUITE* SO MUCH LIKE YOU AGREE?

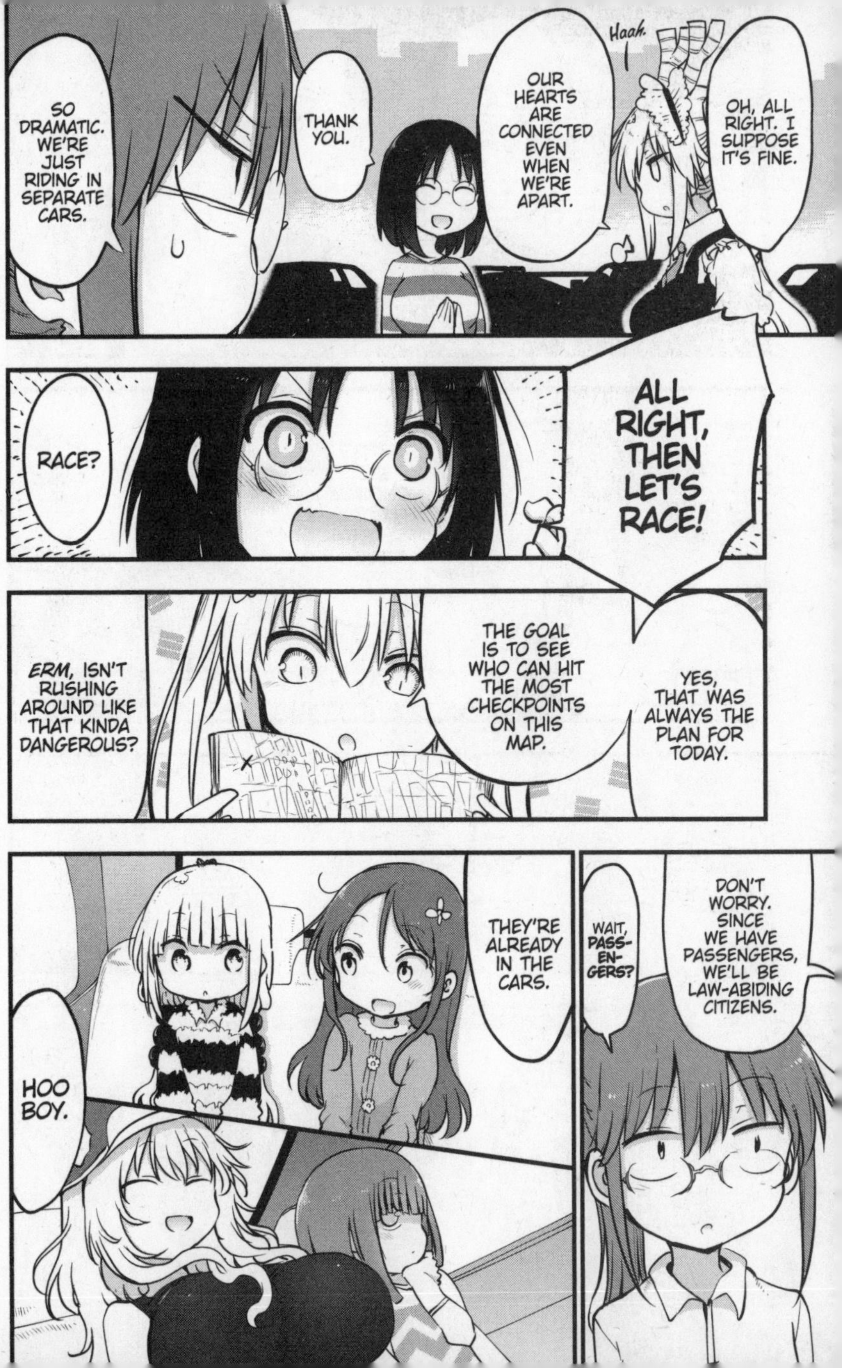
Haah.
OH, ALL RIGHT. I SUPPOSE IT'S FINE.
OUR HEARTS ARE CONNECTED EVEN WHEN WE'RE APART.
THANK YOU.
SO DRAMATIC. WE'RE JUST RIDING IN SEPARATE CARS.
ALL RIGHT, THEN LET'S RACE!
RACE?
YES, THAT WAS ALWAYS THE PLAN FOR TODAY.
THE GOAL IS TO SEE WHO CAN HIT THE MOST CHECKPOINTS ON THIS MAP.
ERM, ISN'T RUSHING AROUND LIKE THAT KINDA DANGEROUS?
DON'T WORRY. SINCE WE HAVE PASSENGERS, WE'LL BE LAW-ABIDING CITIZENS.
WAIT, PASSENGERS?
THEY'RE ALREADY IN THE CARS.
HOO BOY.

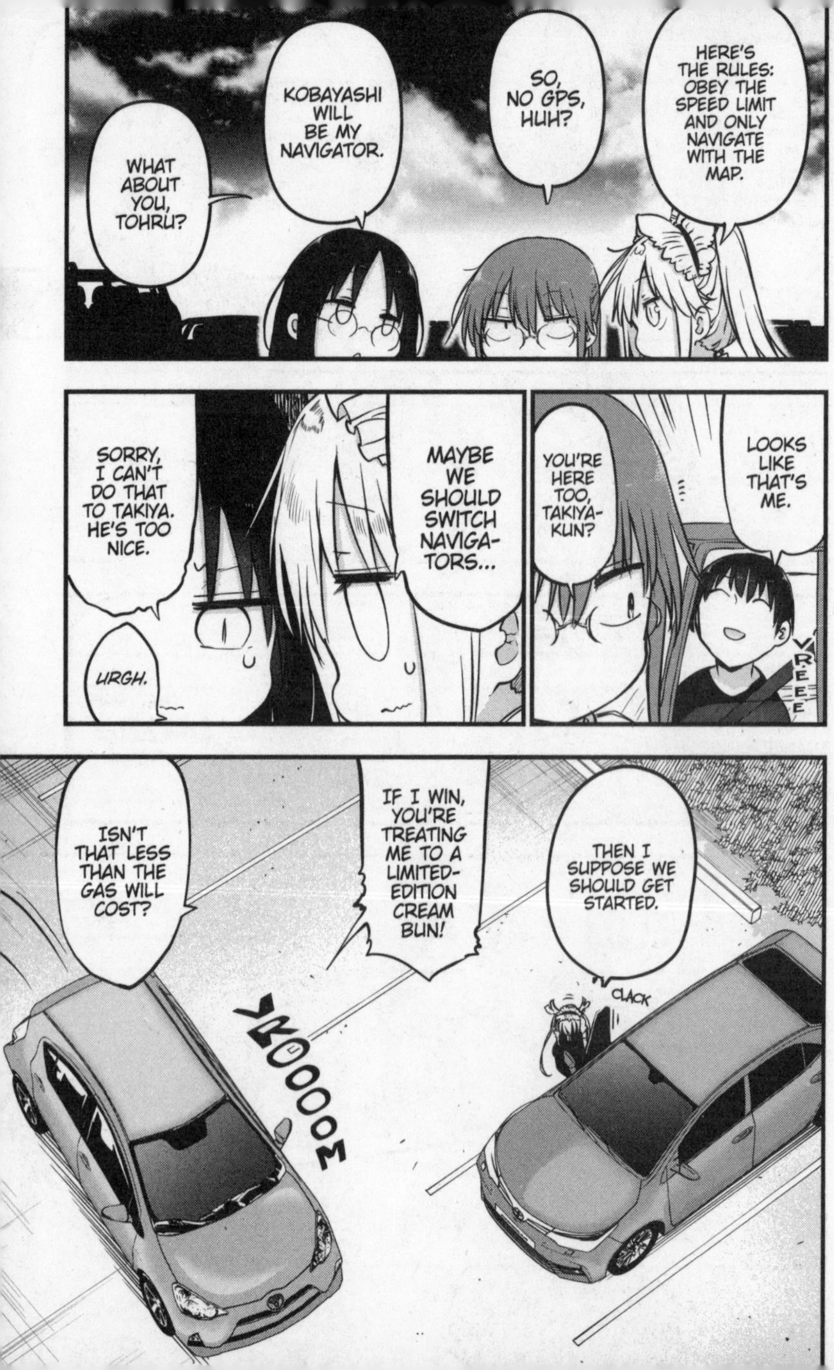
HERE'S THE RULES: OBEY THE SPEED LIMIT AND ONLY NAVIGATE WITH THE MAP.
SO, NO GPS, HUH?
KOBAYASHI WILL BE MY NAVIGATOR.
WHAT ABOUT YOU, TOHRU?
LOOKS LIKE THAT'S ME.
YOU'RE HERE TOO, TAKIYA-KUN?
VREEE
MAYBE WE SHOULD SWITCH NAVIGA-TORS...
SORRY, I CAN'T DO THAT TO TAKIYA. HE'S TOO NICE.
URGH.
THEN I SUPPOSE WE SHOULD GET STARTED.
CLACK
IF I WIN, YOU'RE TREATING ME TO A LIMITED-EDITION CREAM BUN!
ISN'T THAT LESS THAN THE GAS WILL COST?
VROOOOOM

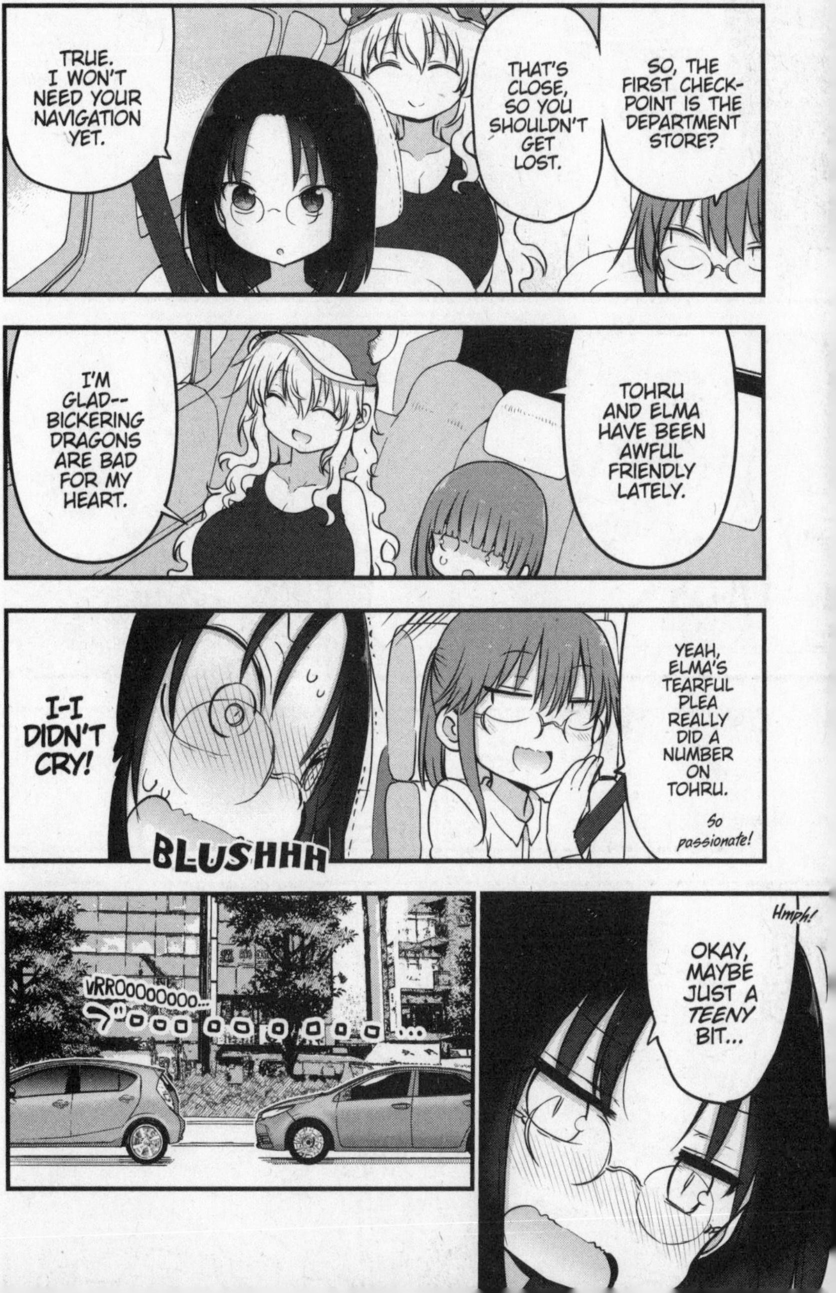
SO, THE FIRST CHECK-POINT IS THE DEPARTMENT STORE?
THAT'S CLOSE, SO YOU SHOULDN'T GET LOST.
TRUE. I WON'T NEED YOUR NAVIGATION YET.
TOHRU AND ELMA HAVE BEEN AWFUL FRIENDLY LATELY.
I'M GLAD-- BICKERING DRAGONS ARE BAD FOR MY HEART.
YEAH, ELMA'S TEARFUL PLEA REALLY DID A NUMBER ON TOHRU.
So passionate!
I-I DIDN'T CRY!
BLUSHHH
Hmph!
OKAY, MAYBE JUST A TEENY BIT...
VRROOOOOOOOO...

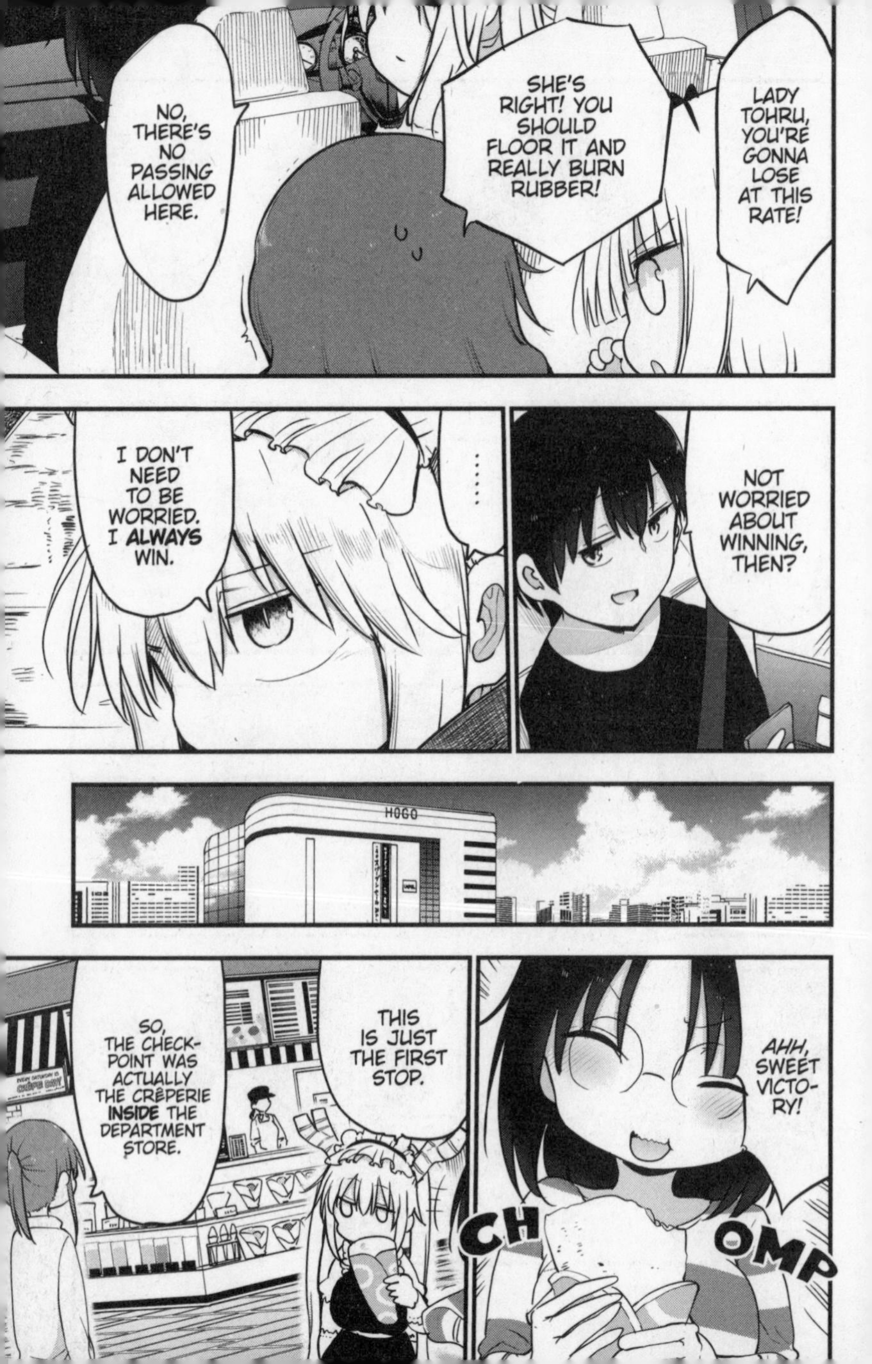
LADY TOHRU, YOU'RE GONNA LOSE AT THIS RATE!
SHE'S RIGHT! YOU SHOULD FLOOR IT AND REALLY BURN RUBBER!
NO, THERE'S NO PASSING ALLOWED HERE.
NOT WORRIED ABOUT WINNING, THEN?
......
I DON'T NEED TO BE WORRIED. I **ALWAYS** WIN.
HOGO
AHH, SWEET VICTORY!
CH
OMP
THIS IS JUST THE FIRST STOP.
SO, THE CHECK-POINT WAS ACTUALLY THE CRÊPERIE **INSIDE** THE DEPARTMENT STORE.

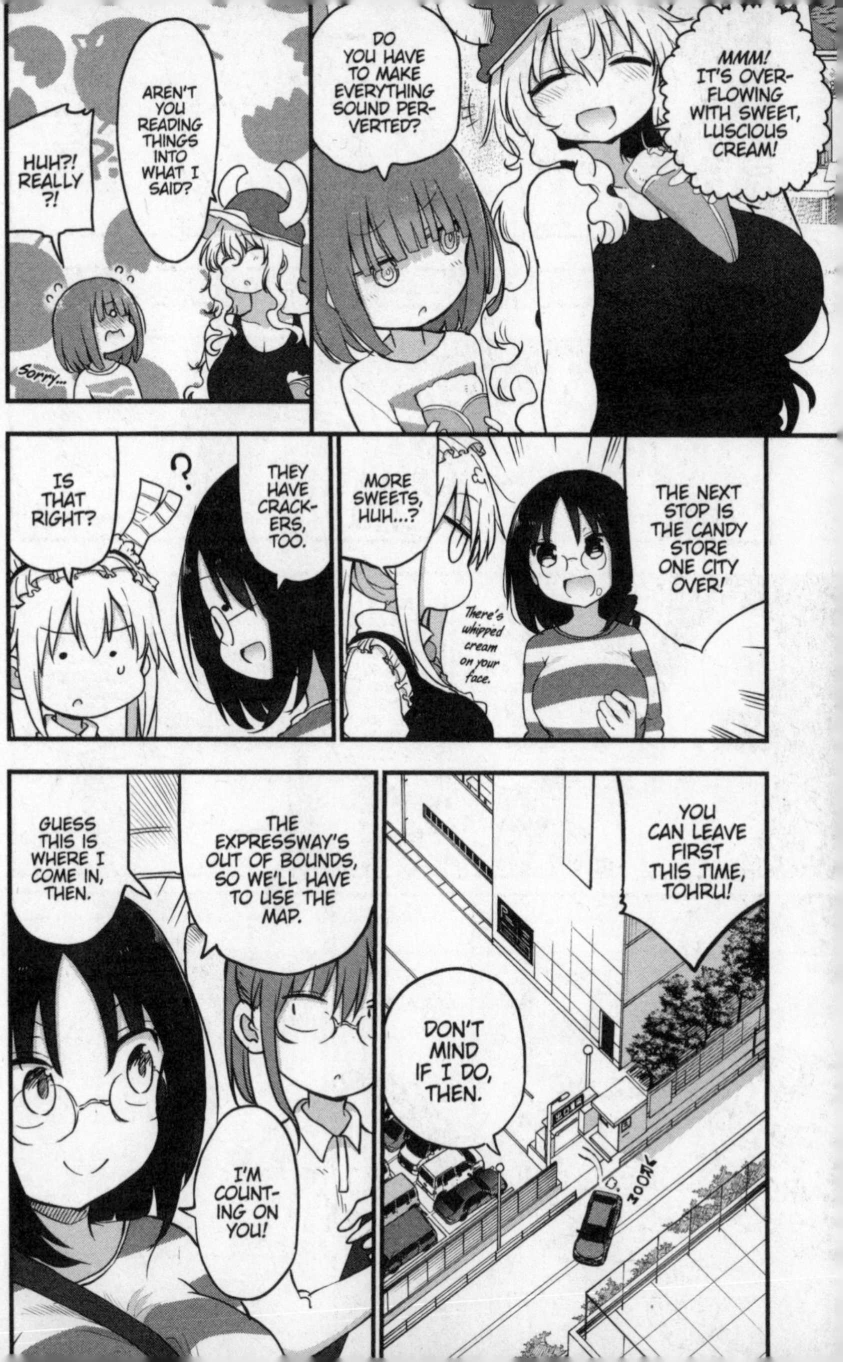
MMM! IT'S OVERFLOWING WITH SWEET, LUSCIOUS CREAM!
DO YOU HAVE TO MAKE EVERYTHING SOUND PERVERTED?
AREN'T YOU READING THINGS INTO WHAT I SAID?
HUH?! REALLY ?!
Sorry...
THE NEXT STOP IS THE CANDY STORE ONE CITY OVER!
MORE SWEETS, HUH...?
There's whipped cream on your face.
THEY HAVE CRACKERS, TOO.
IS THAT RIGHT?
YOU CAN LEAVE FIRST THIS TIME, TOHRU!
DON'T MIND IF I DO, THEN.
THE EXPRESSWAY'S OUT OF BOUNDS, SO WE'LL HAVE TO USE THE MAP.
GUESS THIS IS WHERE I COME IN, THEN.
I'M COUNTING ON YOU!

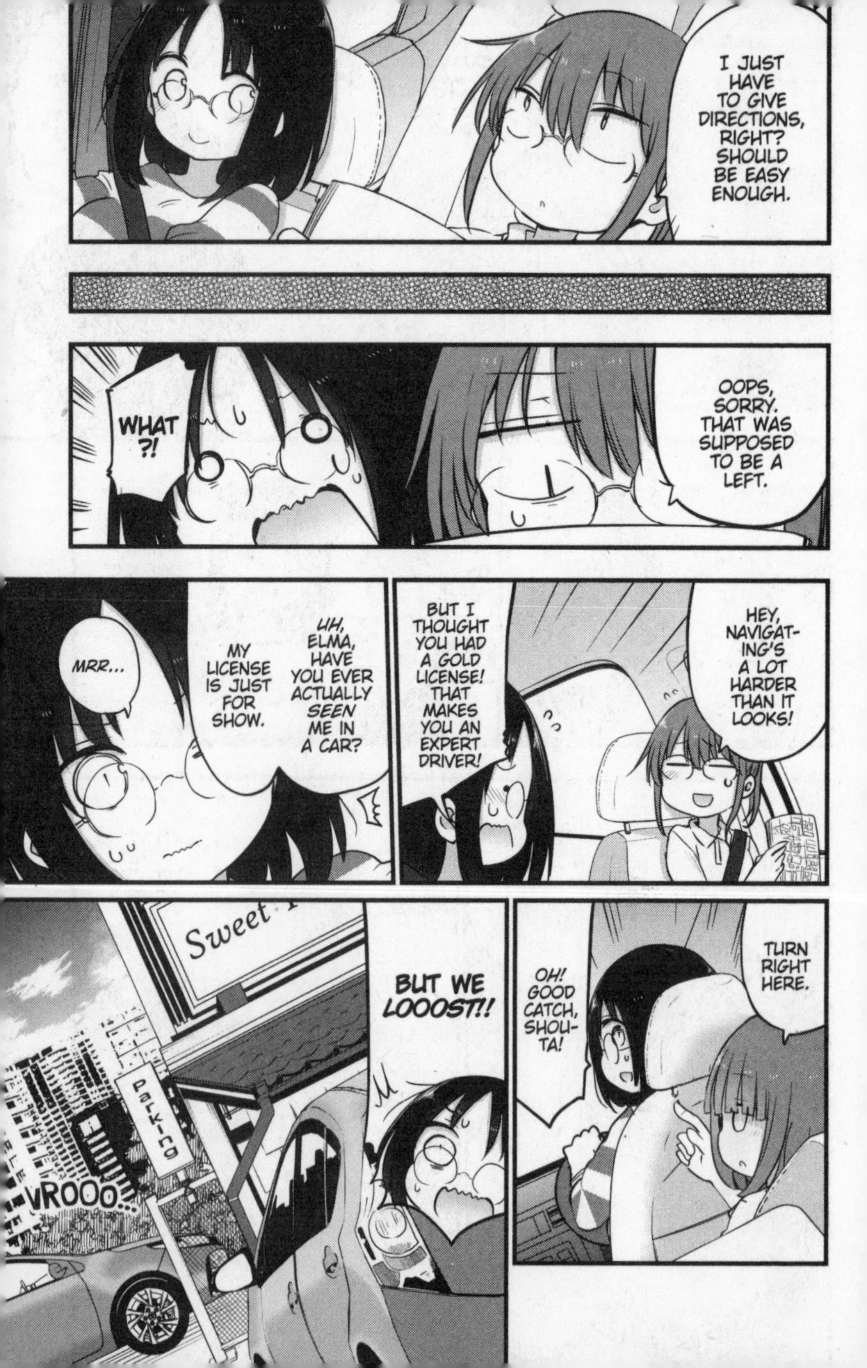
I JUST HAVE TO GIVE DIRECTIONS, RIGHT? SHOULD BE EASY ENOUGH.
OOPS, SORRY. THAT WAS SUPPOSED TO BE A LEFT.
WHAT ?!
HEY, NAVIGAT-ING'S A LOT HARDER THAN IT LOOKS!
BUT I THOUGHT YOU HAD A GOLD LICENSE! THAT MAKES YOU AN EXPERT DRIVER!
UH, ELMA, HAVE YOU EVER ACTUALLY *SEEN* ME IN A CAR?
MY LICENSE IS JUST FOR SHOW.
MRR...
TURN RIGHT HERE.
OH! GOOD CATCH, SHOU-TA!
BUT WE *LOOOST!!*
Sweet
Parking
VROOO...

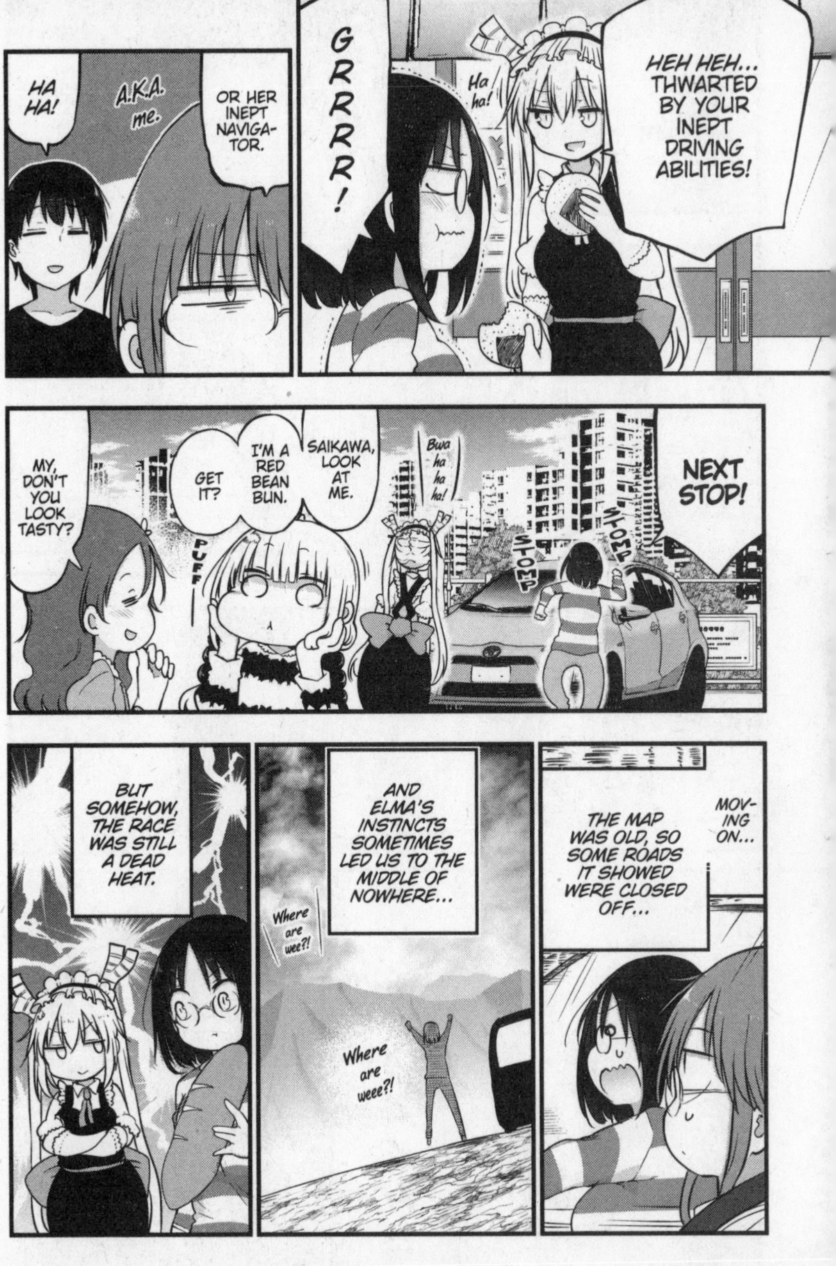
HEH HEH... THWARTED BY YOUR INEPT DRIVING ABILITIES!
Ha ha!
GRRRR!
OR HER INEPT NAVIGATOR.
A.K.A. me.
HA HA!
NEXT STOP!
STOMP
STOMP
Bwa ha ha ha!
SAIKAWA, LOOK AT ME.
I'M A RED BEAN BUN.
GET IT?
PUFF
MY, DON'T YOU LOOK TASTY?
MOV-ING ON...
THE MAP WAS OLD, SO SOME ROADS IT SHOWED WERE CLOSED OFF...
AND ELMA'S INSTINCTS SOMETIMES LED US TO THE MIDDLE OF NOWHERE...
Where are weee?!
Where are weee?!
BUT SOMEHOW, THE RACE WAS STILL A DEAD HEAT.

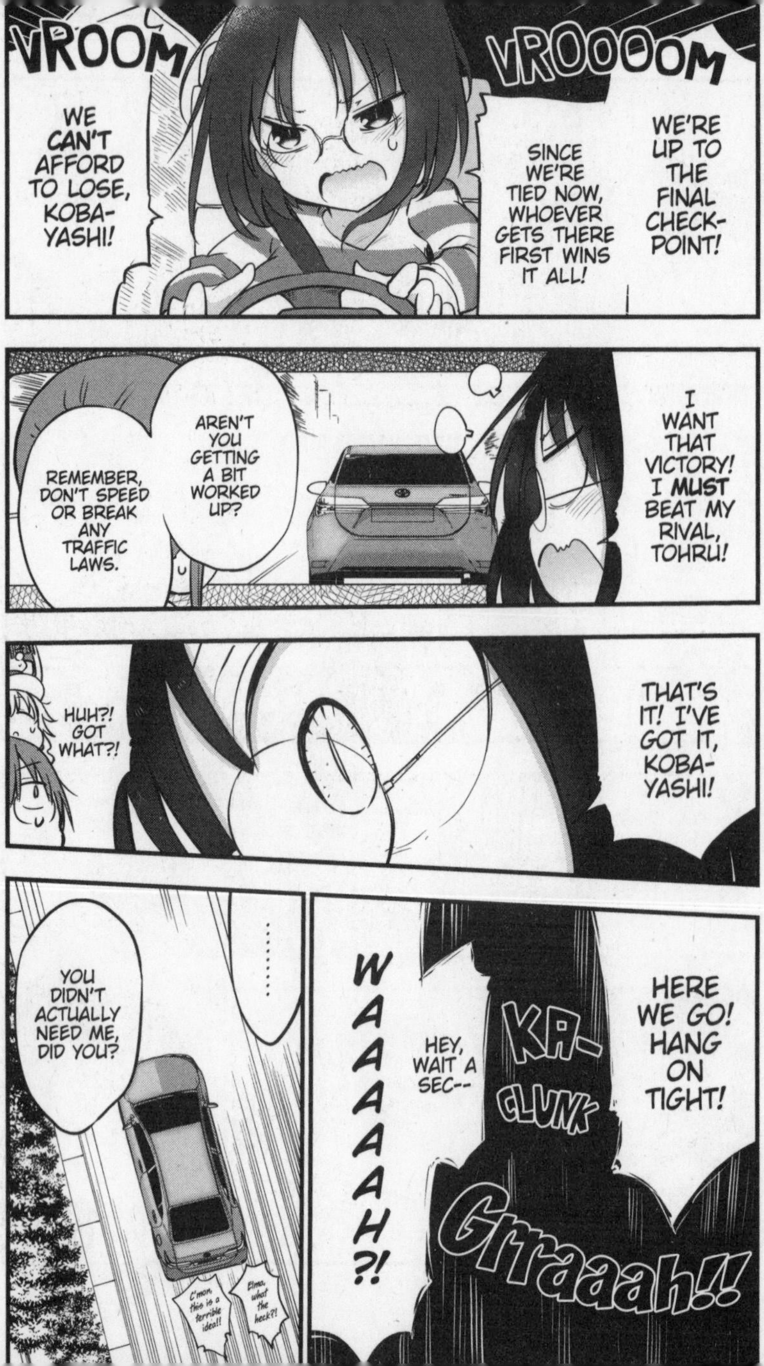
VROOOOM
WE'RE UP TO THE FINAL CHECKPOINT!
SINCE WE'RE TIED NOW, WHOEVER GETS THERE FIRST WINS IT ALL!
VROOM
WE CAN'T AFFORD TO LOSE, KOBAYASHI!
I WANT THAT VICTORY! I MUST BEAT MY RIVAL, TOHRU!
AREN'T YOU GETTING A BIT WORKED UP?
REMEMBER, DON'T SPEED OR BREAK ANY TRAFFIC LAWS.
THAT'S IT! I'VE GOT IT, KOBAYASHI!
HUH?! GOT WHAT?!
HERE WE GO! HANG ON TIGHT!
KA-CLUNK
HEY, WAIT A SEC--
Grraaah!!
WAAAAAAH?!
......
YOU DIDN'T ACTUALLY NEED ME, DID YOU?
Elma, what the heck?!
C'mon, this is a terrible idea!!

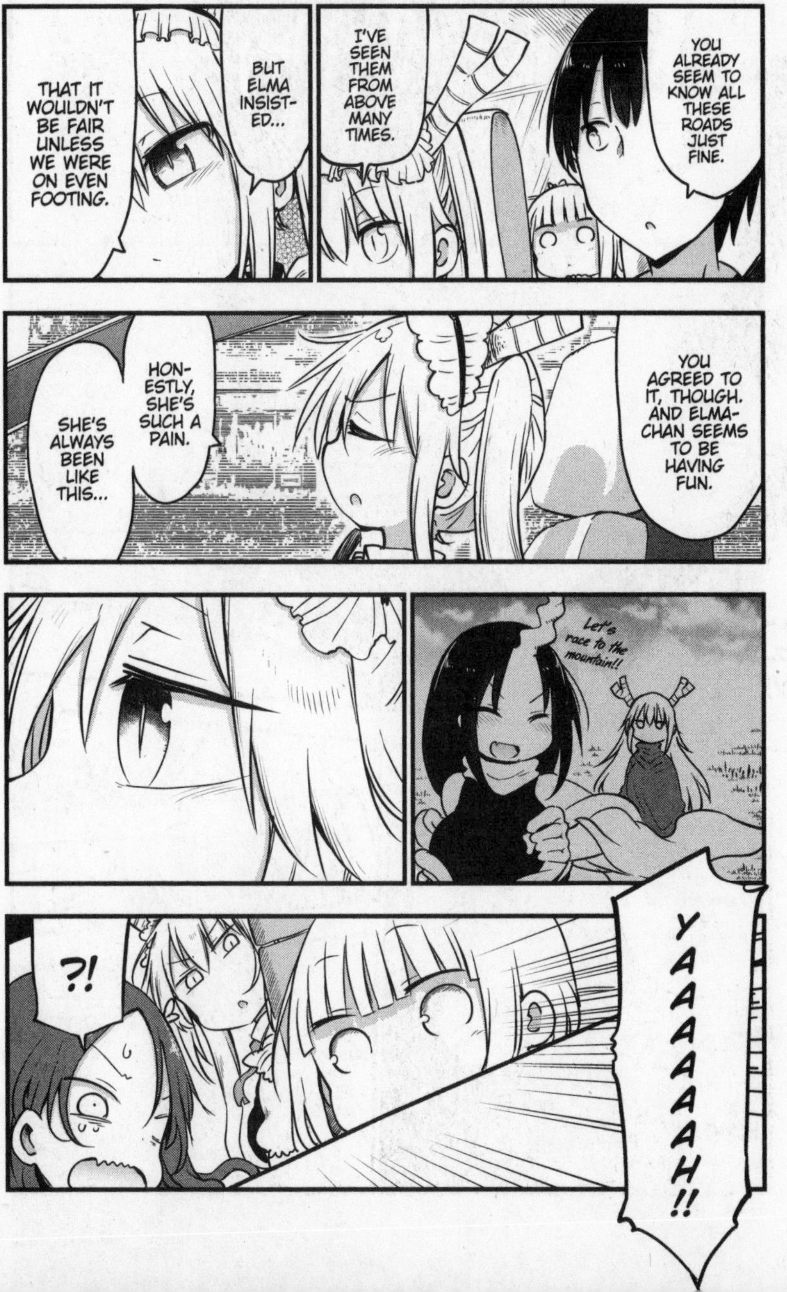
YOU ALREADY SEEM TO KNOW ALL THESE ROADS JUST FINE.
I'VE SEEN THEM FROM ABOVE MANY TIMES.
BUT ELMA INSIST-ED...
THAT IT WOULDN'T BE FAIR UNLESS WE WERE ON EVEN FOOTING.
YOU AGREED TO IT, THOUGH. AND ELMA-CHAN SEEMS TO BE HAVING FUN.
HON-ESTLY, SHE'S SUCH A PAIN.
SHE'S ALWAYS BEEN LIKE THIS...
Let's race to the mountain!!
YAAAAAAH!!
?!

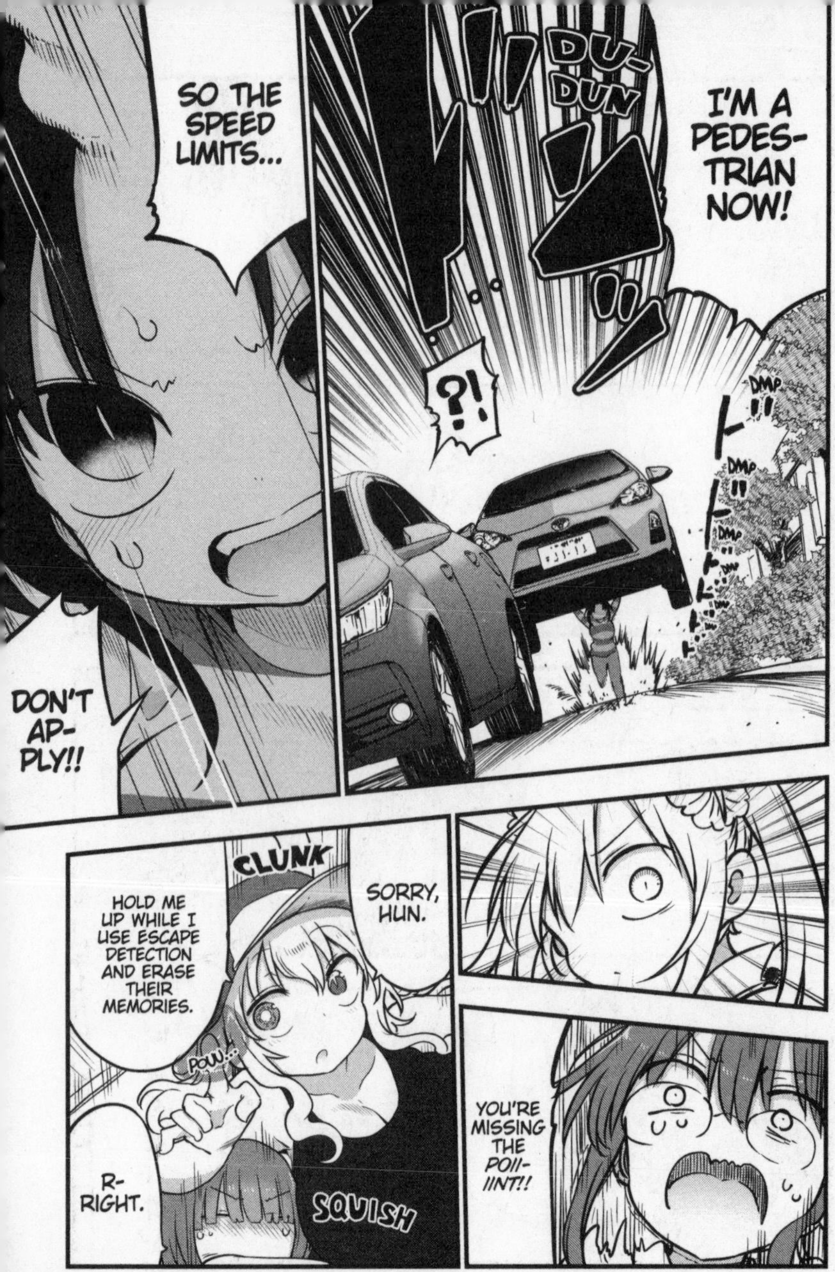
I'M A PEDES-TRIAN NOW!
DU-DUN
?!
DMP
DMP
DMP
DMP
SO THE SPEED LIMITS...
DON'T AP-PLY!!
YOU'RE MISSING THE POII-IINT!!
CLUNK
SORRY, HUN.
HOLD ME UP WHILE I USE ESCAPE DETECTION AND ERASE THEIR MEMORIES.
POW...
R-RIGHT.
SQUISH

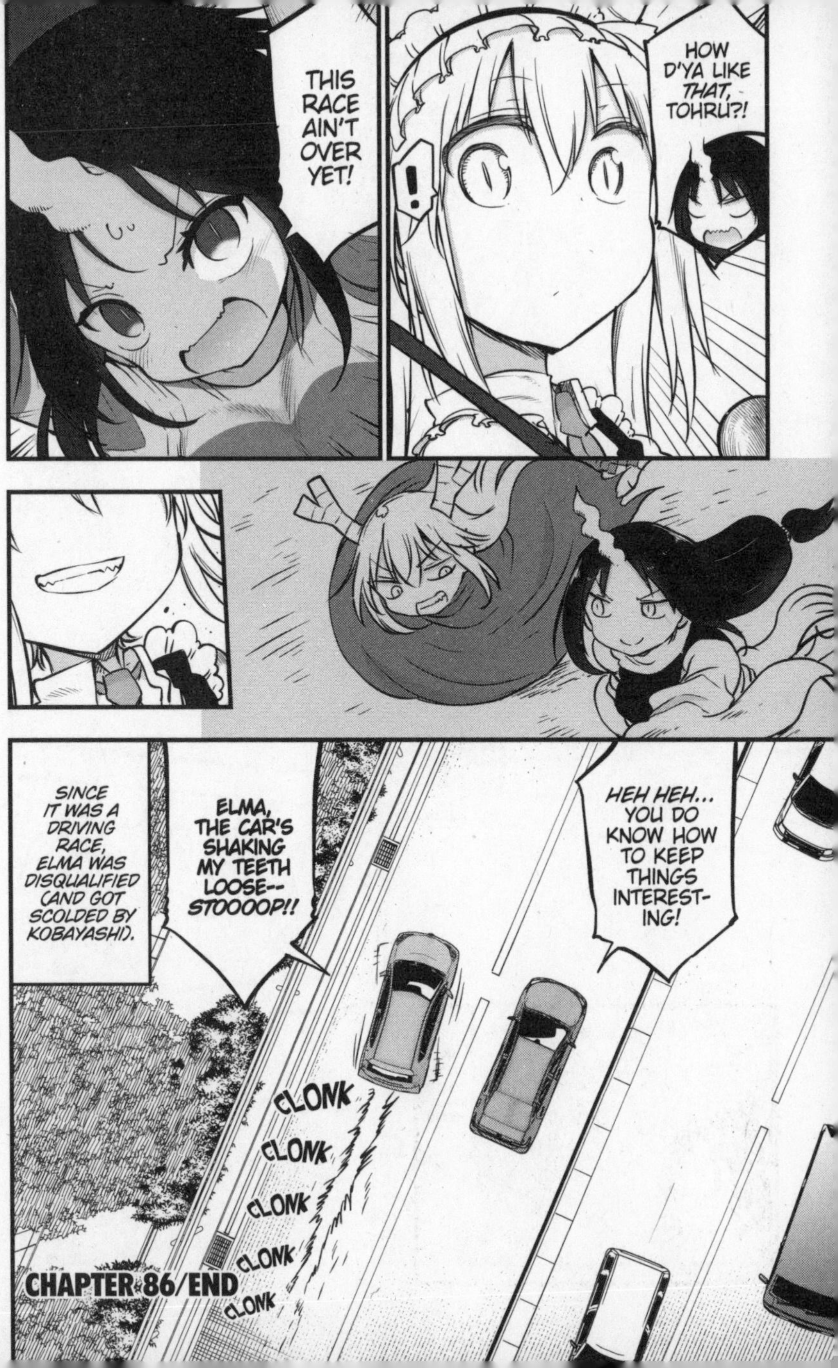
HOW D'YA LIKE THAT, TOHRU?!
!
THIS RACE AIN'T OVER YET!
HEH HEH... YOU DO KNOW HOW TO KEEP THINGS INTEREST-ING!
ELMA, THE CAR'S SHAKING MY TEETH LOOSE--STOOOOP!!
SINCE IT WAS A DRIVING RACE, ELMA WAS DISQUALIFIED (AND GOT SCOLDED BY KOBAYASHI).
CLONK
CLONK
CLONK
CLONK
CLONK
CHAPTER 86/END

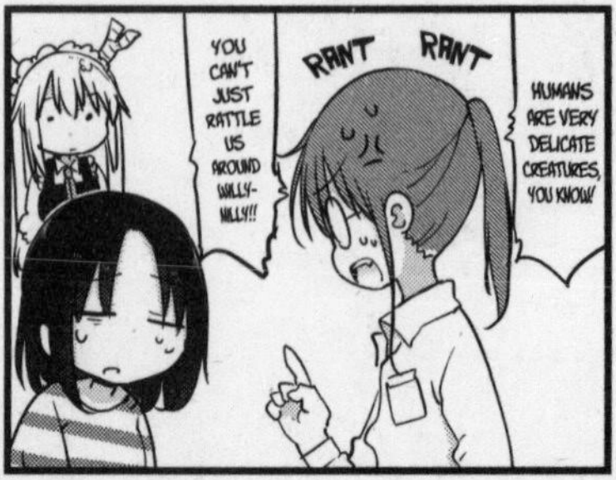
HUMANS ARE VERY DELICATE CREATURES, YOU KNOW!
RANT RANT
YOU CAN'T JUST RATTLE US AROUND WILLY-NILLY!!

Miss Kobayashi's
DRAGON MAID

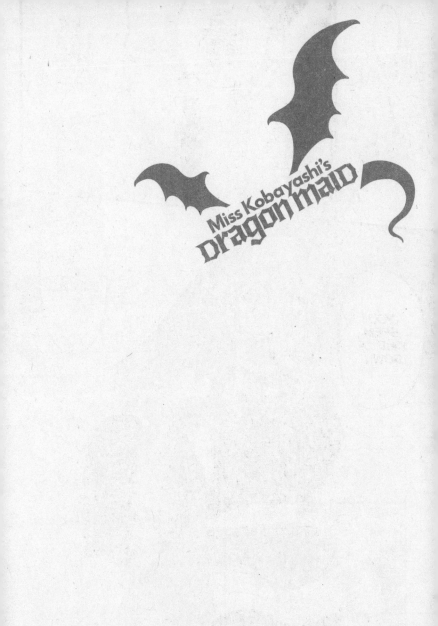

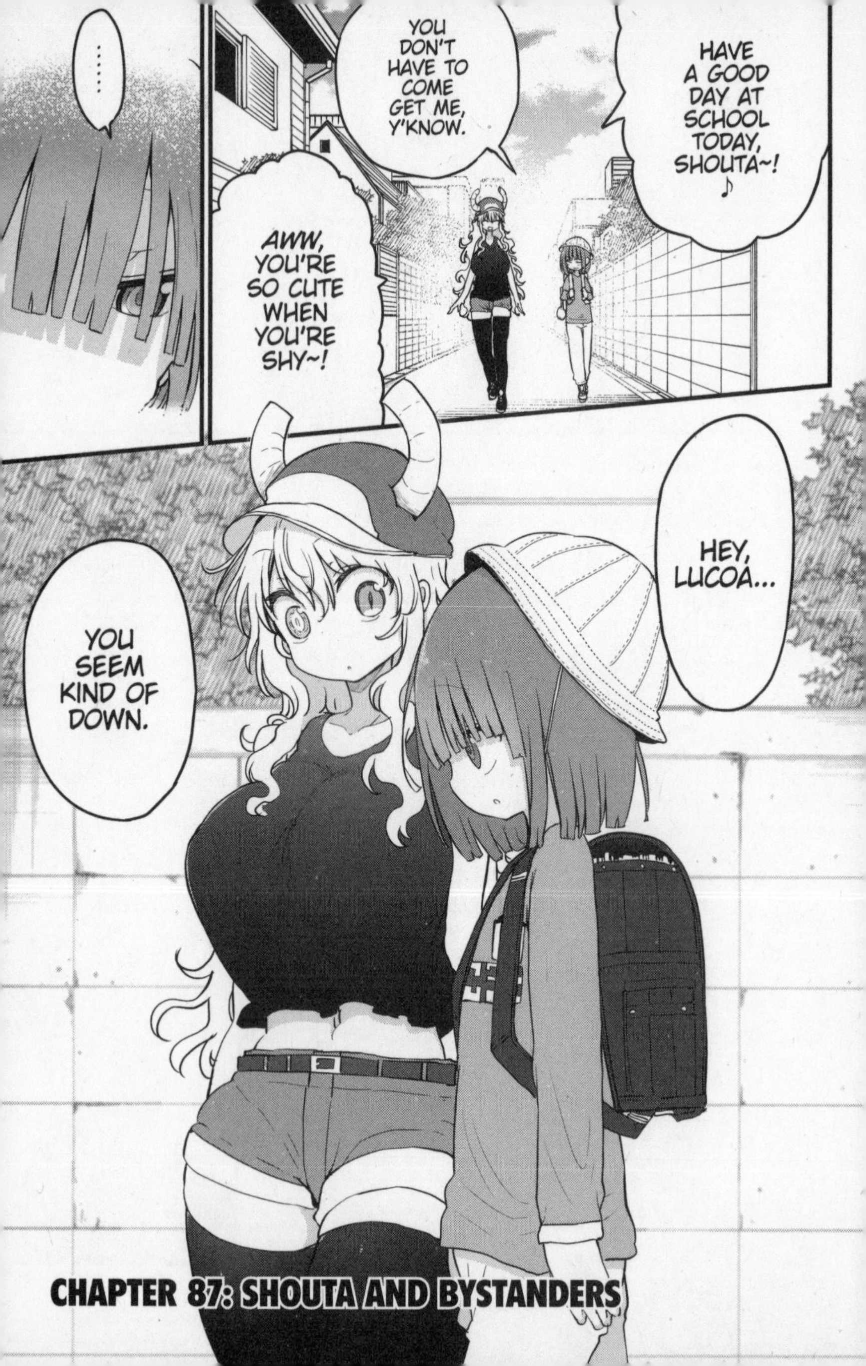
HAVE A GOOD DAY AT SCHOOL TODAY, SHOUTA~! ♪
YOU DON'T HAVE TO COME GET ME, Y'KNOW.
AWW, YOU'RE SO CUTE WHEN YOU'RE SHY~!
......
HEY, LUCOA...
YOU SEEM KIND OF DOWN.
CHAPTER 87: SHOUTA AND BYSTANDERS

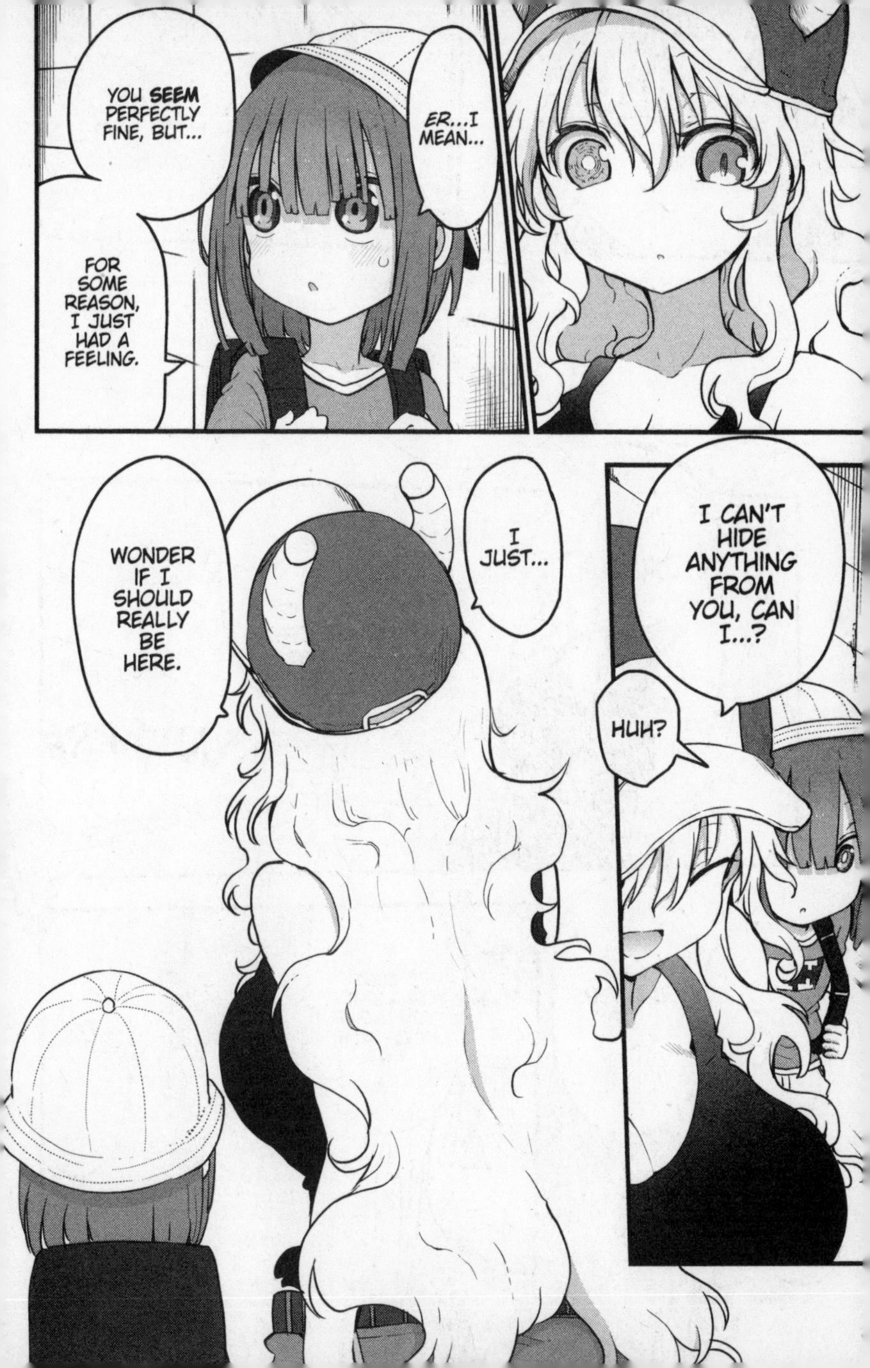
ER...I MEAN...
YOU SEEM PERFECTLY FINE, BUT...
FOR SOME REASON, I JUST HAD A FEELING.
I CAN'T HIDE ANYTHING FROM YOU, CAN I...?
HUH?
I JUST...
WONDER IF I SHOULD REALLY BE HERE.

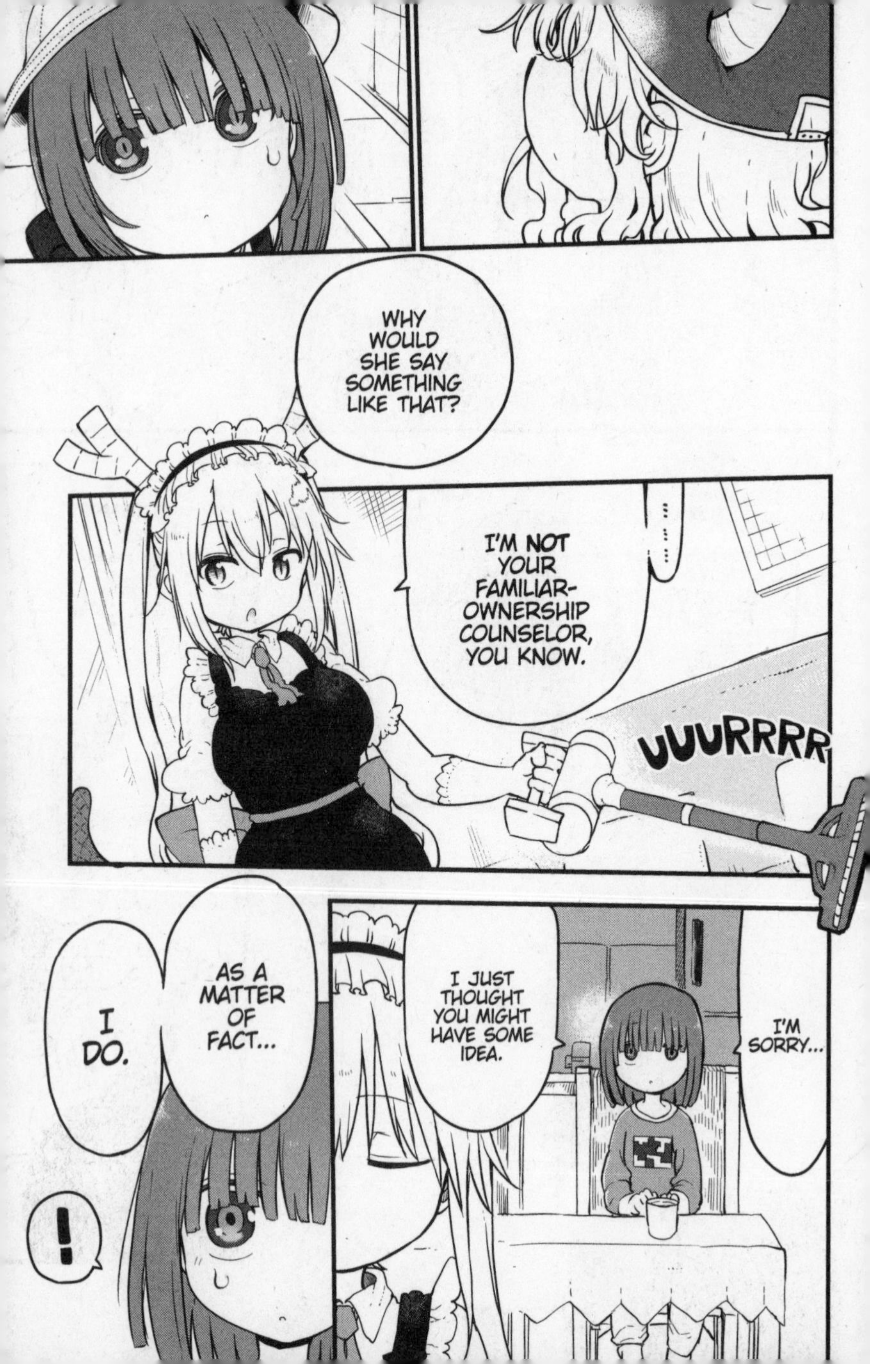
WHY WOULD SHE SAY SOMETHING LIKE THAT?
...
I'M NOT YOUR FAMILIAR-OWNERSHIP COUNSELOR, YOU KNOW.
UUURRRR
I'M SORRY...
I JUST THOUGHT YOU MIGHT HAVE SOME IDEA.
AS A MATTER OF FACT...
I DO.
!

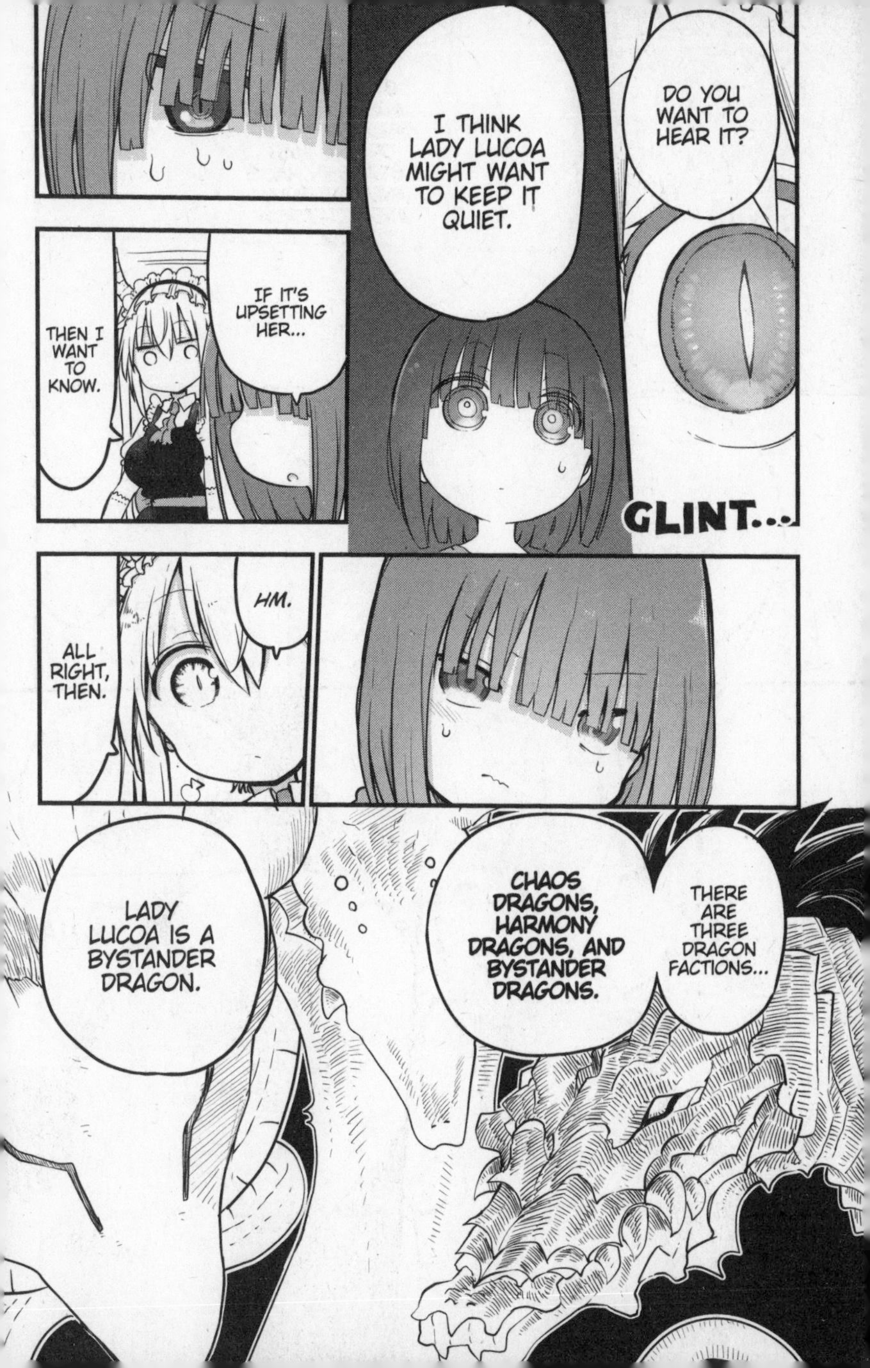
DO YOU WANT TO HEAR IT?
GLINT...
I THINK LADY LUCOA MIGHT WANT TO KEEP IT QUIET.
IF IT'S UPSETTING HER...
THEN I WANT TO KNOW.
HM.
ALL RIGHT, THEN.
THERE ARE THREE DRAGON FACTIONS...
CHAOS DRAGONS, HARMONY DRAGONS, AND BYSTANDER DRAGONS.
LADY LUCOA IS A BYSTANDER DRAGON.

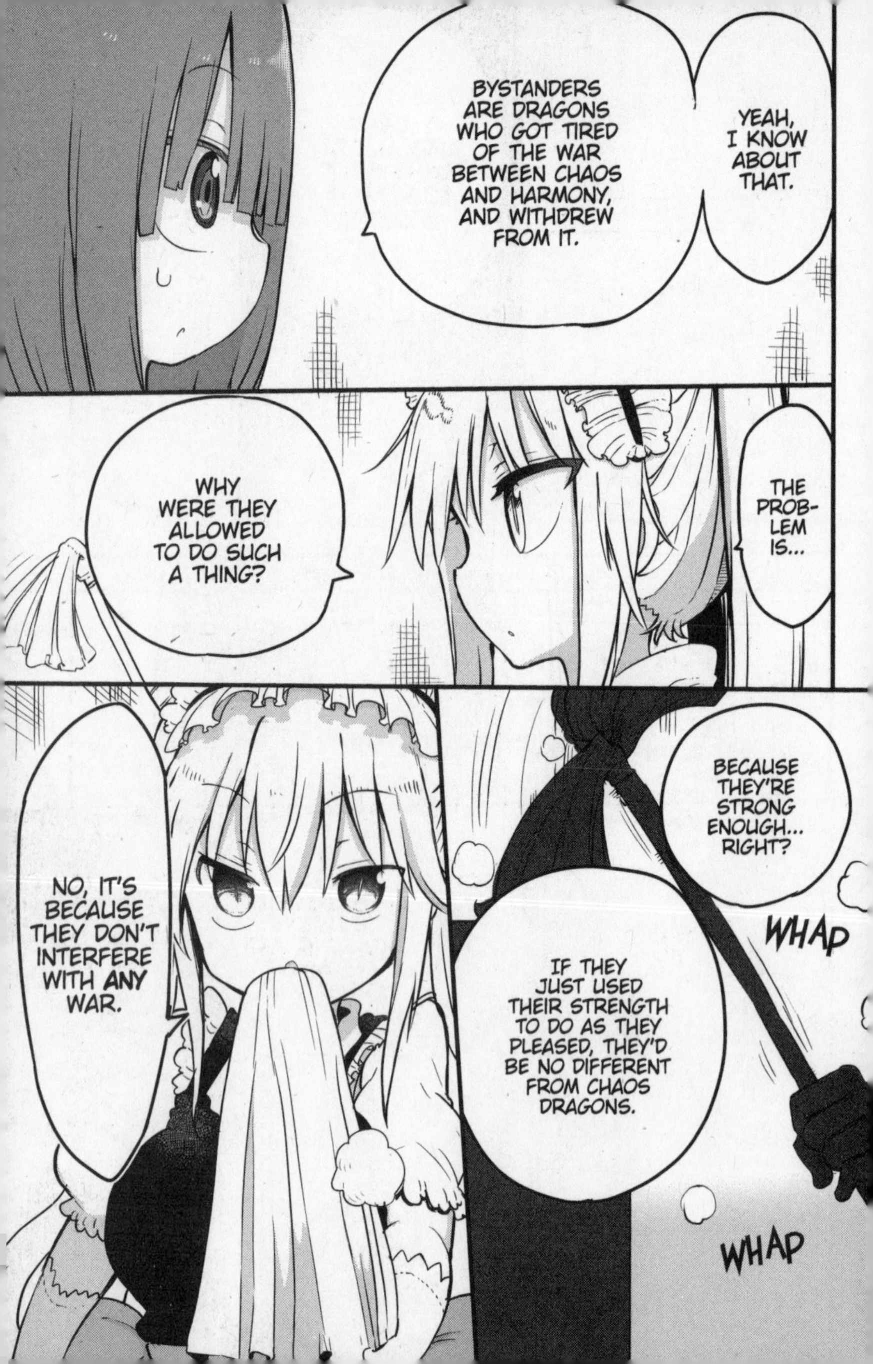
YEAH, I KNOW ABOUT THAT.
BYSTANDERS ARE DRAGONS WHO GOT TIRED OF THE WAR BETWEEN CHAOS AND HARMONY, AND WITHDREW FROM IT.
THE PROB-LEM IS...
WHY WERE THEY ALLOWED TO DO SUCH A THING?
BECAUSE THEY'RE STRONG ENOUGH... RIGHT?
WHAP
NO, IT'S BECAUSE THEY DON'T INTERFERE WITH ANY WAR.
IF THEY JUST USED THEIR STRENGTH TO DO AS THEY PLEASED, THEY'D BE NO DIFFERENT FROM CHAOS DRAGONS.
WHAP

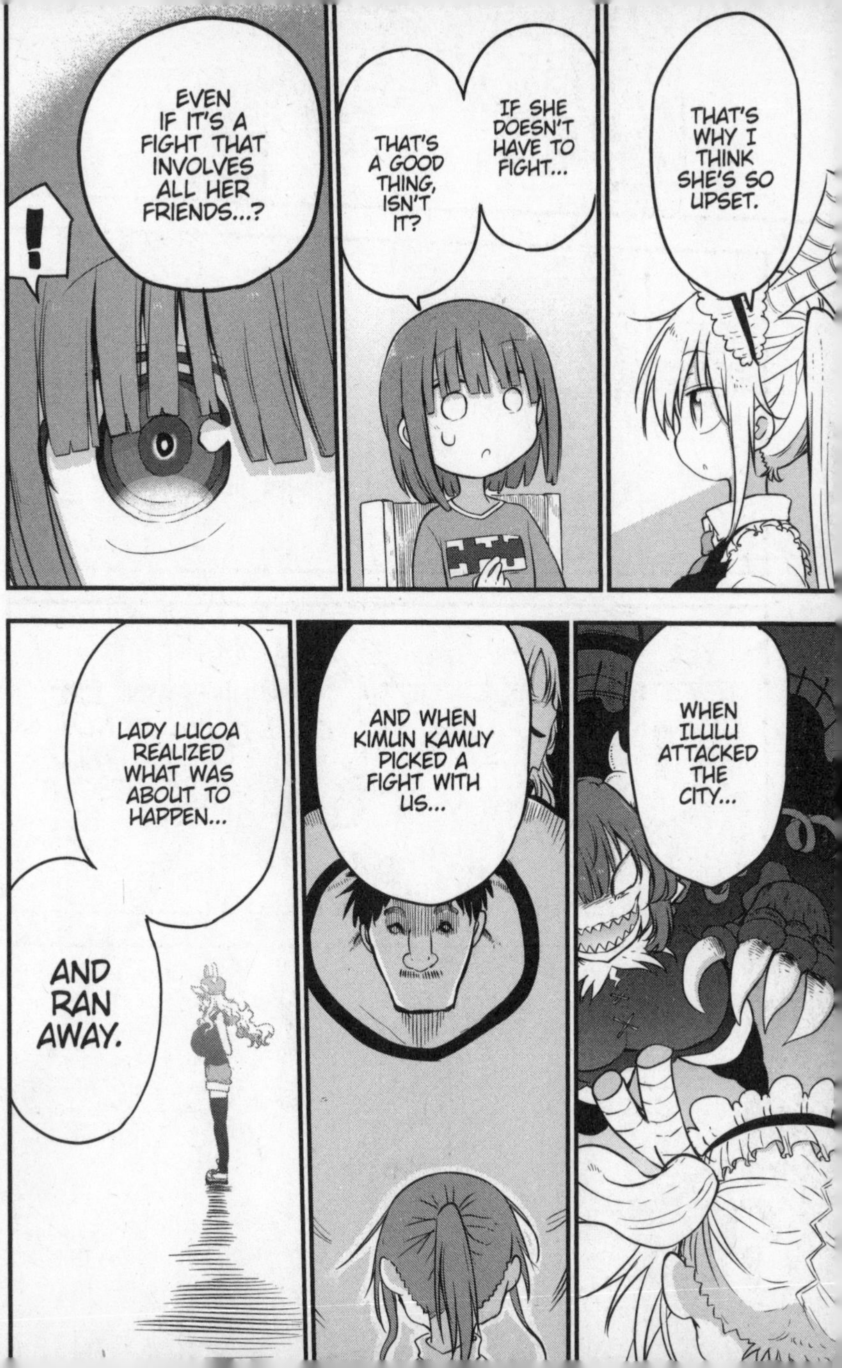
THAT'S WHY I THINK SHE'S SO UPSET.
IF SHE DOESN'T HAVE TO FIGHT...
THAT'S A GOOD THING, ISN'T IT?
EVEN IF IT'S A FIGHT THAT INVOLVES ALL HER FRIENDS...?
!
WHEN ILULU ATTACKED THE CITY...
AND WHEN KIMUN KAMUY PICKED A FIGHT WITH US...
LADY LUCOA REALIZED WHAT WAS ABOUT TO HAPPEN...
AND RAN AWAY.

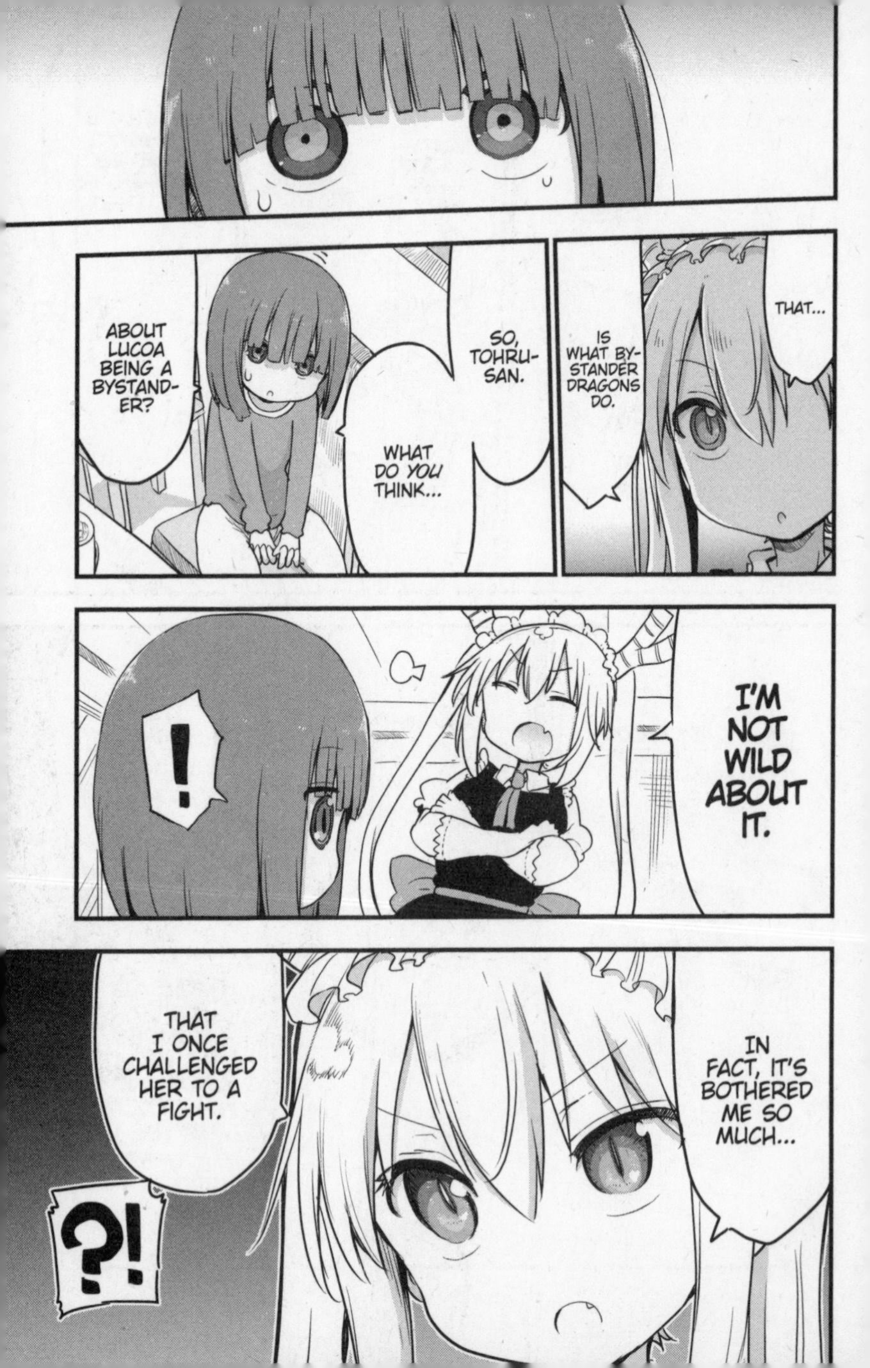
THAT...
IS WHAT BYSTANDER DRAGONS DO.
SO, TOHRU-SAN.
WHAT DO *YOU* THINK...
ABOUT LUCOA BEING A BYSTANDER?
I'M NOT WILD ABOUT IT.
!
IN FACT, IT'S BOTHERED ME SO MUCH...
THAT I ONCE CHALLENGED HER TO A FIGHT.
?!

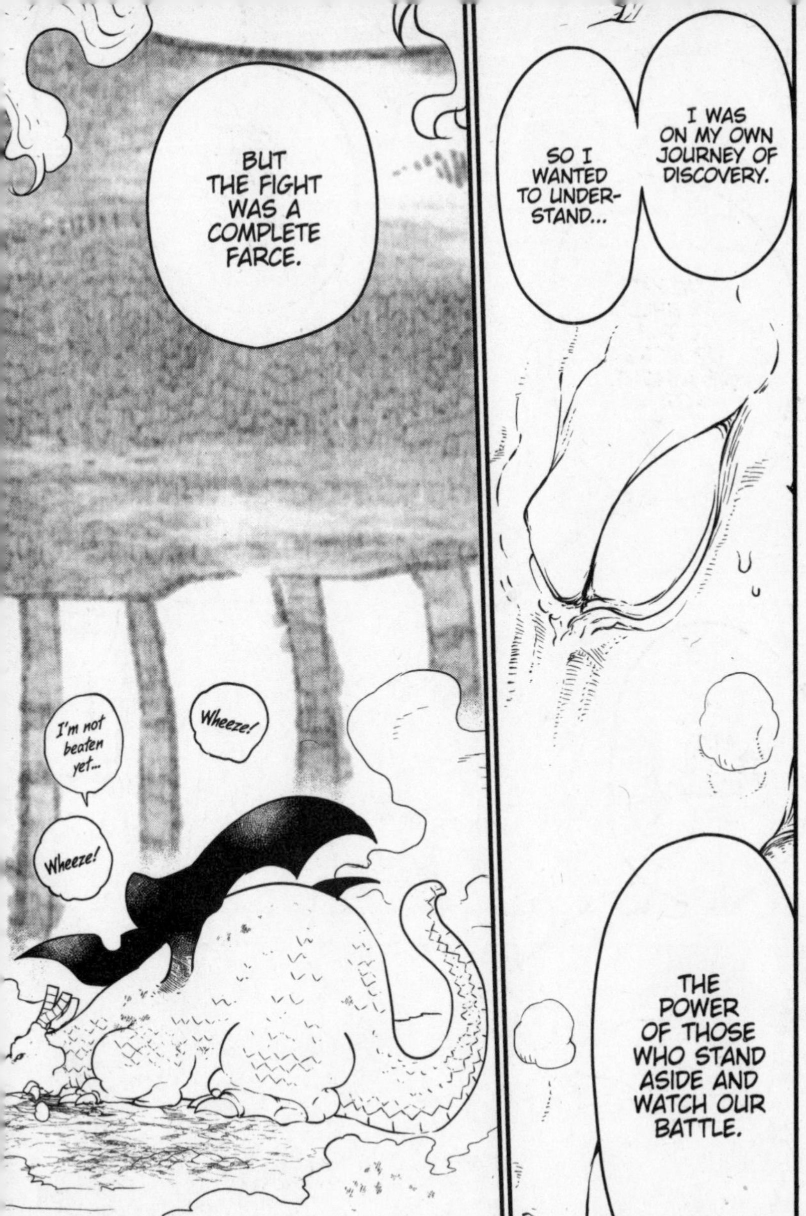
I WAS ON MY OWN JOURNEY OF DISCOVERY.
SO I WANTED TO UNDER-STAND...
THE POWER OF THOSE WHO STAND ASIDE AND WATCH OUR BATTLE.
BUT THE FIGHT WAS A COMPLETE FARCE.
Wheeze!
I'm not beaten yet...
Wheeze!

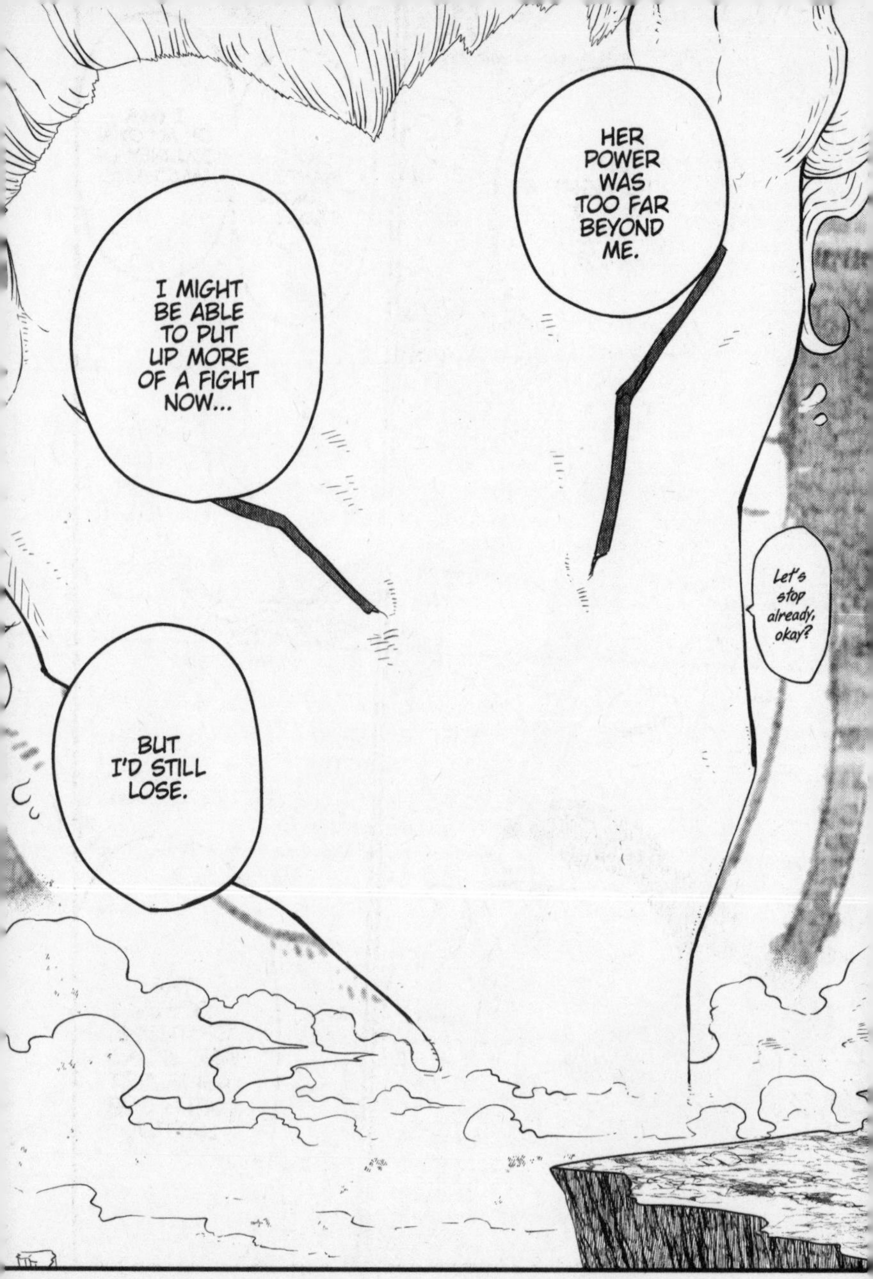
HER POWER WAS TOO FAR BEYOND ME.
I MIGHT BE ABLE TO PUT UP MORE OF A FIGHT NOW...
Let's stop already, okay?
BUT I'D STILL LOSE.

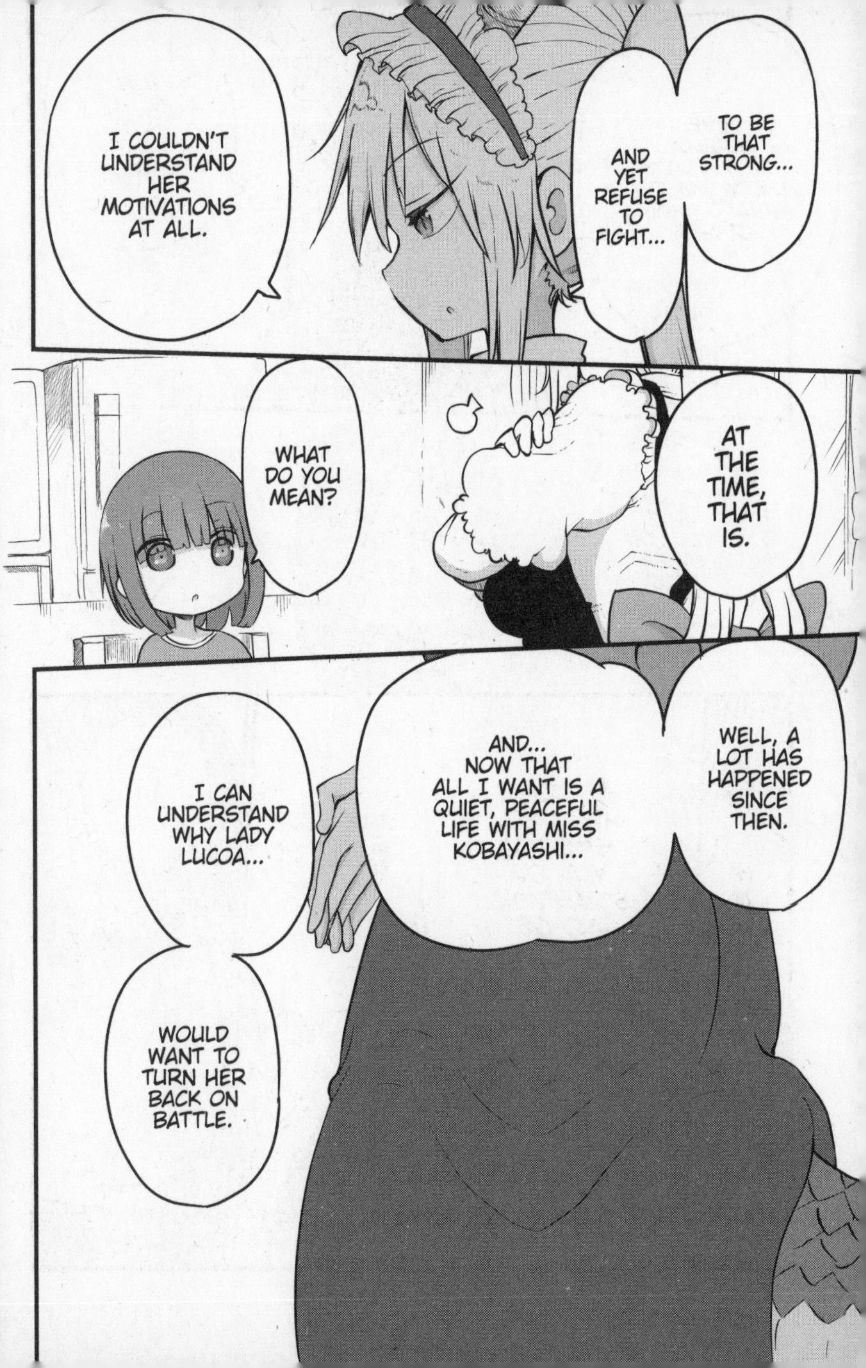
TO BE THAT STRONG...
AND YET REFUSE TO FIGHT...
I COULDN'T UNDERSTAND HER MOTIVATIONS AT ALL.
AT THE TIME, THAT IS.
WHAT DO YOU MEAN?
WELL, A LOT HAS HAPPENED SINCE THEN.
AND... NOW THAT ALL I WANT IS A QUIET, PEACEFUL LIFE WITH MISS KOBAYASHI...
I CAN UNDERSTAND WHY LADY LUCOA...
WOULD WANT TO TURN HER BACK ON BATTLE.

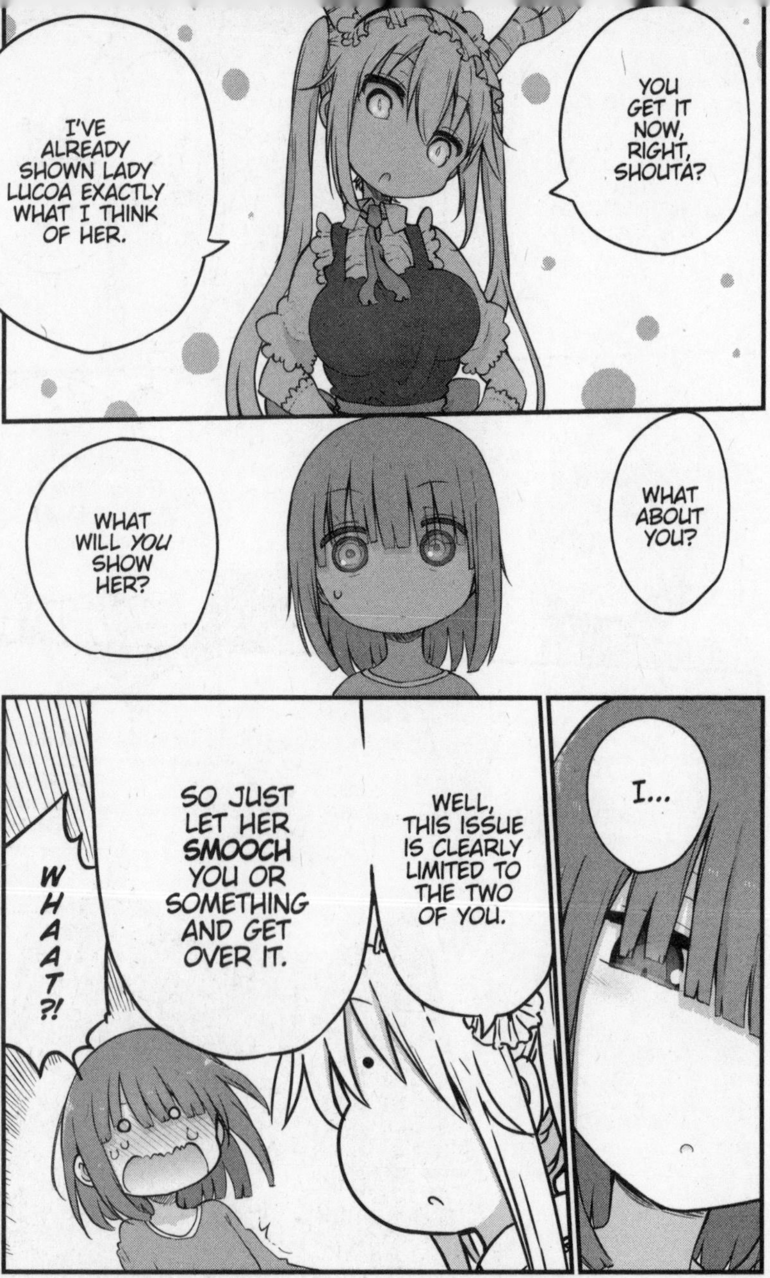
YOU GET IT NOW, RIGHT, SHOUTA?
I'VE ALREADY SHOWN LADY LUCOA EXACTLY WHAT I THINK OF HER.
WHAT ABOUT YOU?
WHAT WILL YOU SHOW HER?
I...
WELL, THIS ISSUE IS CLEARLY LIMITED TO THE TWO OF YOU.
SO JUST LET HER SMOOCH YOU OR SOMETHING AND GET OVER IT.
WHAAT?!

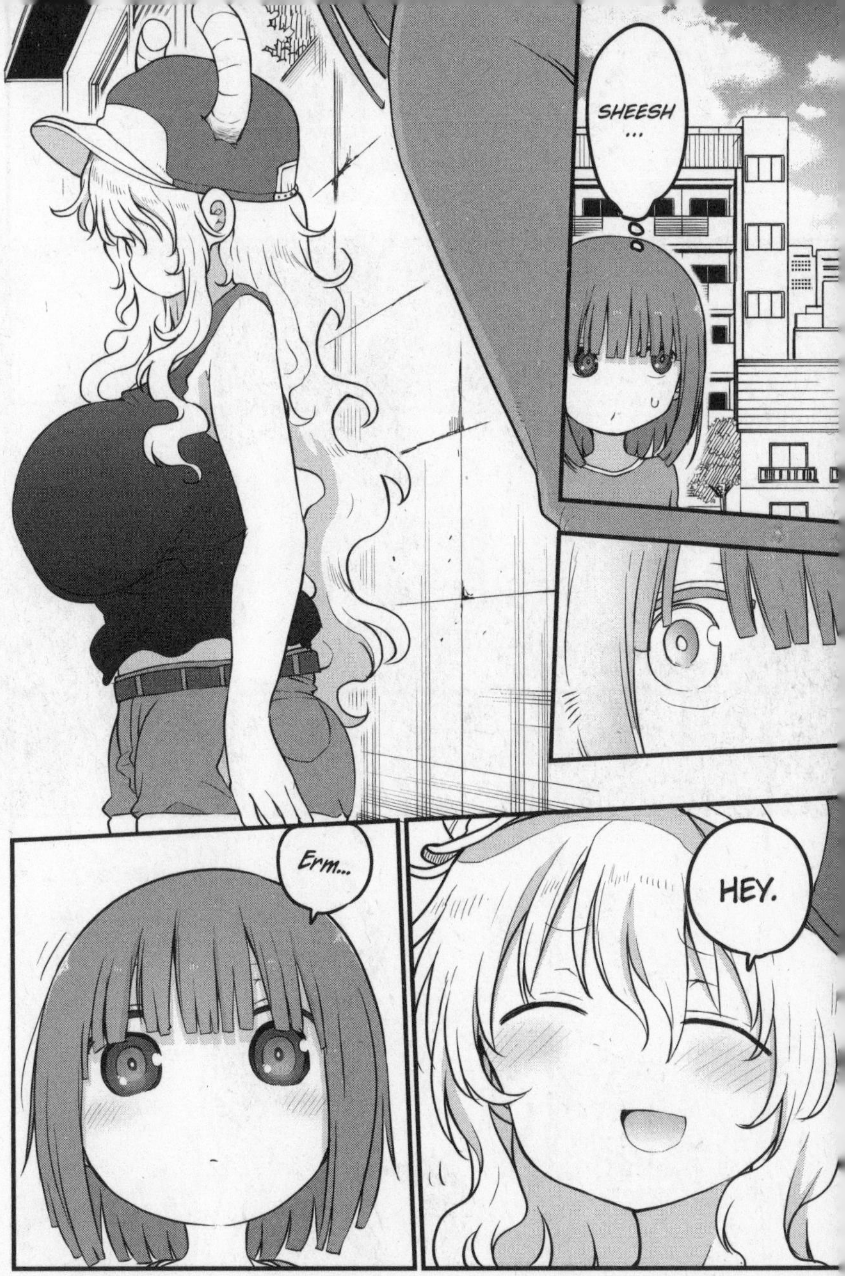
SHEESH ...
HEY.
Erm...

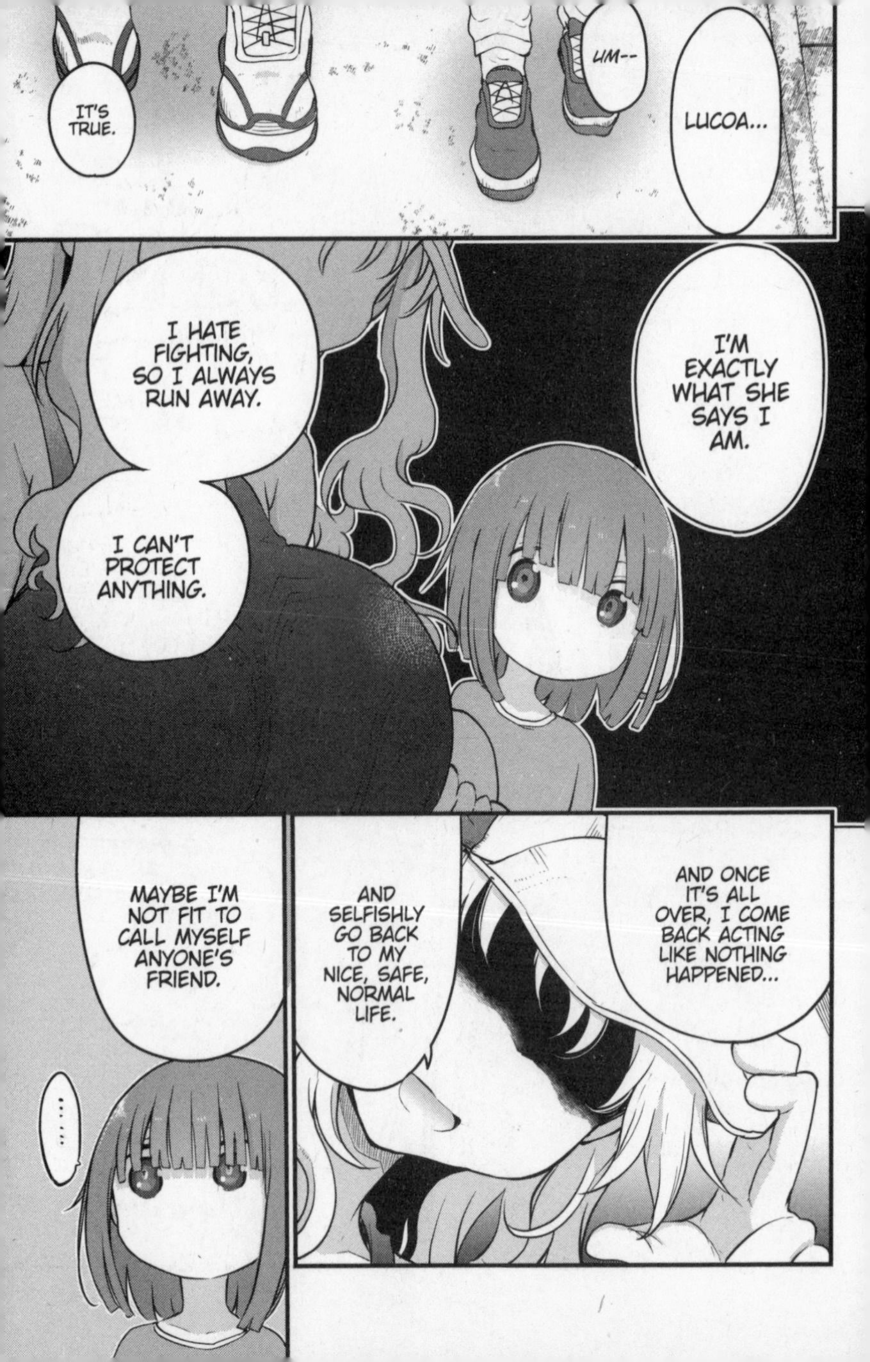
LUCOA...
UM--
IT'S TRUE.
I'M EXACTLY WHAT SHE SAYS I AM.
I HATE FIGHTING, SO I ALWAYS RUN AWAY.
I CAN'T PROTECT ANYTHING.
AND ONCE IT'S ALL OVER, I COME BACK ACTING LIKE NOTHING HAPPENED...
AND SELFISHLY GO BACK TO MY NICE, SAFE, NORMAL LIFE.
MAYBE I'M NOT FIT TO CALL MYSELF ANYONE'S FRIEND.
......

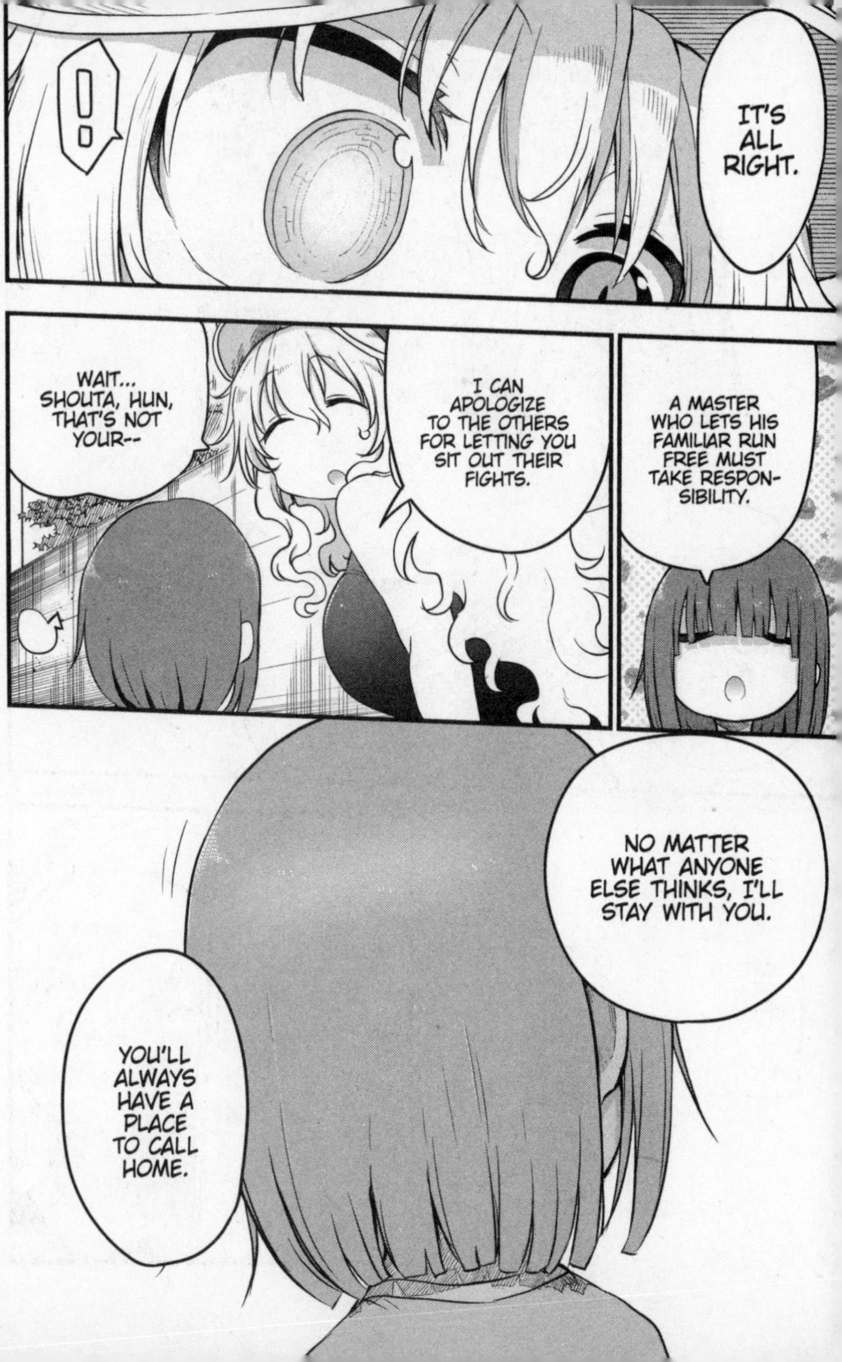
IT'S ALL RIGHT.
!
A MASTER WHO LETS HIS FAMILIAR RUN FREE MUST TAKE RESPON-SIBILITY.
I CAN APOLOGIZE TO THE OTHERS FOR LETTING YOU SIT OUT THEIR FIGHTS.
WAIT... SHOUTA, HUN, THAT'S NOT YOUR--
NO MATTER WHAT ANYONE ELSE THINKS, I'LL STAY WITH YOU.
YOU'LL ALWAYS HAVE A PLACE TO CALL HOME.

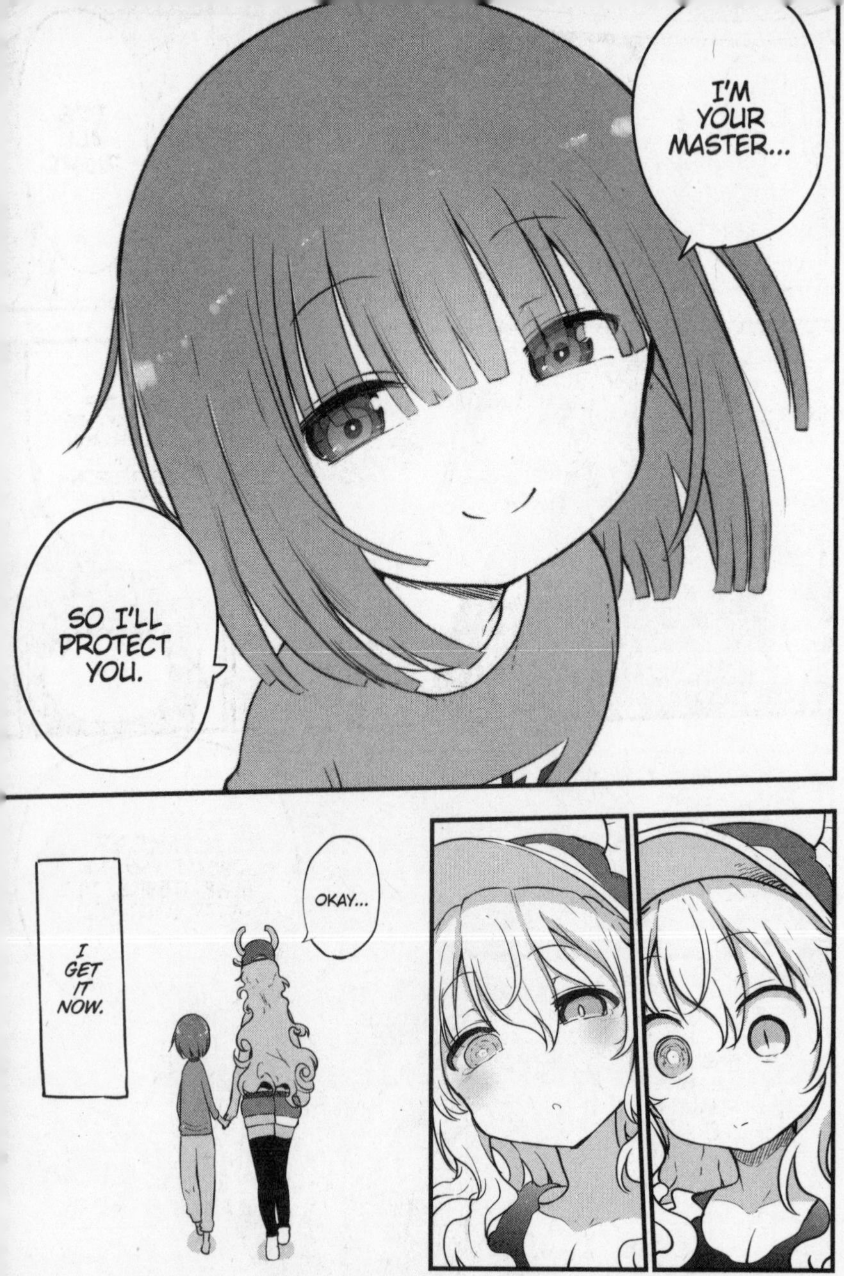
I'M YOUR MASTER...
SO I'LL PROTECT YOU.
OKAY...
I GET IT NOW.

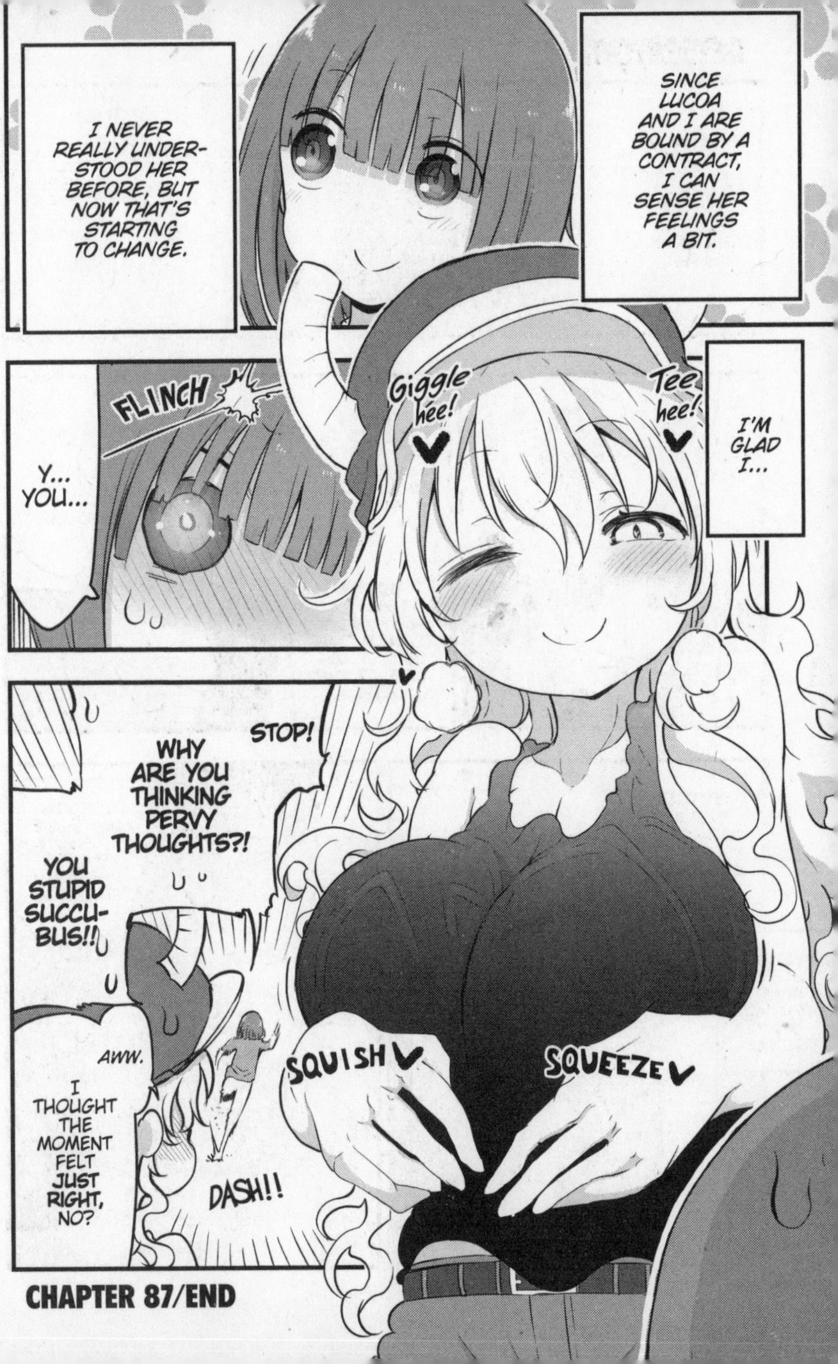
SINCE LUCOA AND I ARE BOUND BY A CONTRACT, I CAN SENSE HER FEELINGS A BIT.
I NEVER REALLY UNDER-STOOD HER BEFORE, BUT NOW THAT'S STARTING TO CHANGE.
I'M GLAD I...
Tee hee!
Giggle hee!
SQUEEZE
SQUISH
FLINCH
Y... YOU...
STOP!
WHY ARE YOU THINKING PERVY THOUGHTS?!
YOU STUPID SUCCU-BUS!!
AWW.
I THOUGHT THE MOMENT FELT JUST RIGHT, NO?
DASH!!

CHAPTER 87/END

AFTERWORD

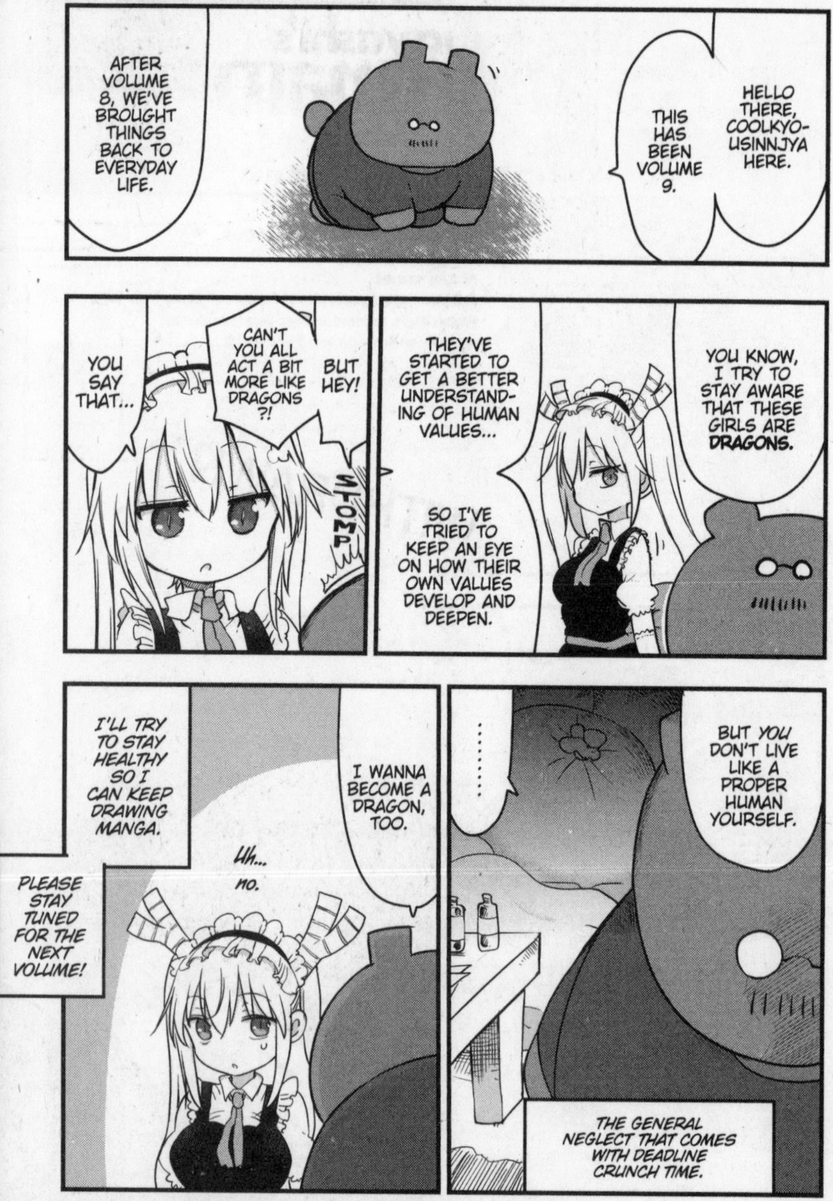
HELLO THERE, COOLKYO-USINNJYA HERE.
THIS HAS BEEN VOLUME 9.
AFTER VOLUME 8, WE'VE BROUGHT THINGS BACK TO EVERYDAY LIFE.
YOU KNOW, I TRY TO STAY AWARE THAT THESE GIRLS ARE **DRAGONS.**
THEY'VE STARTED TO GET A BETTER UNDERSTANDING OF HUMAN VALUES...
SO I'VE TRIED TO KEEP AN EYE ON HOW THEIR OWN VALUES DEVELOP AND DEEPEN.
BUT HEY!
CAN'T YOU ALL ACT A BIT MORE LIKE DRAGONS?!
STOMP
YOU SAY THAT...
BUT *YOU* DON'T LIVE LIKE A PROPER HUMAN YOURSELF.
......
THE GENERAL NEGLECT THAT COMES WITH DEADLINE CRUNCH TIME.
I WANNA BECOME A DRAGON, TOO.
Uh... no.
I'LL TRY TO STAY HEALTHY SO I CAN KEEP DRAWING MANGA.
PLEASE STAY TUNED FOR THE NEXT VOLUME!

Assistants: Namazenmai-sama, Giovanni Works-sama

SEVEN SEAS ENTERTAIN

Miss Kob
Drag

story and a

TRANSLATION
Jenny McKeon

ADAPTATION
Shanti Whitesides

LETTERING
Jennifer Skarupa

LOGO DESIGN
KC Fabellon

COVER DESIGN
Nicky Lim

PROOFREADING
Stephanie Cohen

PREPRESS TECHNICIAN
Rhiannon Rasmussen-Silverstein

PRODUCTION MANAGER
Lissa Pattillo

MANAGING EDITOR
Julie Davis

ASSOCIATE PUBLISHER
Adam Arnold

PUBLISHER
Jason DeAngelis

Under license from Futabasha Publishers Ltd.

Seven Seas press and purchase enquiries can be sent to Marketing Manager Lianne Sentar at press@gomanga.com. Information regarding the distribution and purchase of digital editions is available from Digital Manager CK Russell at digital@gomanga.com.

ISBN: 978-1-64275-118-5

Printed in Canada

First Printing: May 2020

10 9 8 7 6 5 4 3 2 1

FOLLOW US ONLINE: ***www.sevenseasentertainment.com***

READING DIRECTIONS

This book reads from ***right to left***, Japanese style. If this is your first time reading manga, you start reading from the top right panel on each page and take it from there. If you get lost, just follow the numbered diagram here. It may seem backwards at first, but you'll get the hang of it! Have fun!!

1
2
3
4
5
6
7
8
9

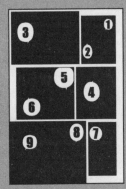